New York Times Best

Jordan Rubin

THE

RAW TRUTH

Transform your health
with the power of
living nutrients

The RAW TRUTH

by Jordan Rubin

Copyright © 2010 by Jordan Rubin

First Edition

Cover design by Dave Johnson

Interior book design by Angela Wilkeson

Garden of Life, LLC.

5500 Village Blvd.

West Palm Beach, FL 33407

(561) 748-2477

Printed in the United States of America

ISBN: 978-0-692-01238-3

100% Recycled

We Buy

Certified Renewable Energy
Green-e org

We Buy 100% Certified Renewable Energy

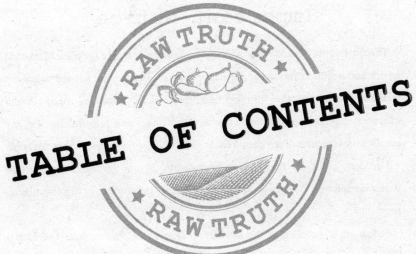

TABLE OF CONTENTS

Important Notice

This book is not intended to provide medical advice or to take the place of medical advice and treatment from your personal physician. Readers are advised to consult their own doctors or other qualified health professionals regarding specific health questions. Neither the publisher nor the author takes any responsibility for any possible consequences of any person reading or following the information in this book. All readers, especially those taking prescription or over-the-counter medications should consult with their physicians before beginning any nutrition or supplementation program.

Below are a sampling of the disclaimers required by various state and federal agencies regarding raw dairy, raw eggs, raw fish, and raw juice, which are mentioned in the body of the book:

- Raw milk products may contain disease-causing microorganisms. Persons at highest risk for of disease from these organisms include newborns and infants, the elderly, pregnant women, those taking corticosteroids, antibiotics and antacids, and those having chronic illnesses and other conditions that weaken their immunity.

- Consuming raw or undercooked eggs may increase your risk of food-borne illness.

- Consuming raw or undercooked seafood may increase your risk of food-borne illness.

- Juice that has not been pasteurized may contain bacteria that can increase the risk of food-borne illness. People most at risk are children, the elderly, and persons with a weakened immune system.

Related to the dietary supplements discussed in this book:

[†] **These statements have not been evaluated by the Food and Drug Administration. This product is not intended to diagnose, treat, cure or prevent any disease.**

Introduction:

From Tragedy

to Triumph

If you've ever driven around California's beach towns, then you know how hard it can be to find a place to park.

It's even tougher when you're driving in a motor home.

So you can imagine how my blood pressure was rising when I was on a mission to find a parking place in Pacific Beach, a half-dozen miles north of downtown San Diego. I was twenty years old, living in a 1968 Dodge bunkhouse RV, and seeking answers and solutions for the dozen-plus illnesses and ailments ravaging my body.

I wanted to park close to a natural grocery market called Boney's (since renamed Henry's), which sold raw, unpasteurized dairy products as well as fresh raw juices. Boney's was one of the few markets in San Diego County—this was back in the mid-1990s—that sold cultured raw dairy foods such as raw milk kefir, raw cream, and raw cottage cheese as well as raw carrot juice and fresh-pressed raw green juices.

I needed to be first in line when the store opened Tuesday mornings so I could ensure my supply of the foods I needed for my health program. I also liked Boney's selection of raw nuts (such as raw almonds) and raw dried fruits (such as mango and pineapple). While my diet

wasn't totally raw, I knew that eating foods that were uncooked, untreated, and unadulterated was critical to the health I was hoping to regain.

I had been suffering from Crohn's disease. Crohn's plays havoc on the body in many ways and causes various symptoms that require medical intervention. It also causes the unlucky sufferer to experience malabsorption of food, which in turn causes nutritional deficiencies requiring a nutritionally intense diet and supplements. This is why many Crohn's patients tend to be rail thin. I was no exception

After months of wasting away and two lengthy hospital stays, I looked like a skeleton. My weight plummeted to a low of 104 pounds at a height of nearly six feet, one inch. When I left home, which was only to visit doctors, I was confined to a wheelchair. During the course of my illnesses, I visited seventy medical experts and was treated with the best of conventional and alternative medicine approaches, but I saw no improvement.

Desperate to get my health back—as well as my life—I decided to travel to San Diego and learn how to eat like my ancestors. By following health principles dating back to the time of the Bible, I believed that consuming raw nutrients from living foods, along with beneficial probiotics, would put me on the road to health.

I purchased that well-used motor home upon arrival and headed for the San Diego beach

scene, whose epicenter was a strand of sand between Pacific Beach and Mission Beach. When I could find a place, I parked near the beach during the day and then looked for a quiet street at night to sleep where I would crack open the windows and breathe in the ocean air.

To occupy myself, I read plenty of books, including one called *The Milk Book* by William Campbell Douglass, M.D., which opened my eyes to the virtues of consuming cultured raw dairy products. I came to believe that drinking raw milk kefir from grass-fed dairy cows would be greatly beneficial to my digestive tract because pasteurization kills probiotics, zaps most of the enzymes and vitamins, and alters the protein and fats in milk.

Along the coast, Boney's Market in Pacific Beach was the best place in town for purchasing raw dairy, but actually procuring it turned out to be more difficult than I anticipated. In addition to the struggle of finding a parking place on crowded Garnet Avenue, just a few blocks from Crystal Pier and the beach, raw dairy shipments arrived only once a week on Tuesdays—if at all—and often sold out within hours.

*Jordan's results are extraordinary. You should not expect miraculous results.

I solved my dilemma by parking in the Boney's parking lot on Monday night and sleeping in my motor home. That way I was sure to be first in line when the doors opened at 8 a.m., and I wouldn't have to worry about finding a parking spot—which was like killing two birds with one stone.

There was only one producer of raw dairy back in the mid-1990s in California, and that was the Steuve family, a storied and historic group of German dairy farmers who had formed Alta Dena Dairy. One of the offshoots of Alta Dena was Steuve's natural raw-certified dairy products, and my favorite product was raw kefir.

The raw kefir came in quart cardboard containers, and I made sure to consume two or more quarts a day. When raw cream was available, I mixed it with raw carrot juice, a common practice in Europe. I was convinced, thanks to my reading of Dr. Douglass's book, that the powerful enzymes and billions of live probiotics in Steuve's raw kefir colonized my gut with good microbes, enabling my digestive system to function in a healthy state. Since supply of raw dairy could be sketchy, I purchased a pair of coolers and filled them with ice to keep myself in raw kefir, cream, and cottage cheese until the next week.

The diet I followed during this time—heavy in raw dairy, salads made from organic produce, cultured veggies (raw sauerkraut), raw carrot and vegetable juices, and a special probiotic supplement containing beneficial microorganisms from healthy soil and plants—put me back on the road to health.

Living by myself, hanging out in my RV, or sitting on the wall of the Mission Beach boardwalk watching the majestic sunsets that appeared virtually every evening gave me plenty of time to think. I thought about how fortunate I was to have access to raw foods, including raw cultured dairy products, raw cream, and raw veggie juices. California had one of the most liberal laws concerning raw dairy in the country; at the time, only a handful of states had legalized the retail sale of this nearly perfect food.

Something told me fifteen years ago—I don't know why—that access to raw living foods would become even more restrictive in the future. One afternoon, while gazing at the Pacific Ocean from the boardwalk, I made two vows to myself:

1. **One day I would have my own ranch and farm to grow and raise these powerful raw foods for myself, my future family, and my friends and loved ones.**

2. **One day I would create raw whole food nutritional supplements to provide everyone with a convenient way to get the power of raw nutrients into their diet and lives.**

Looking for a Definition

So what *is* raw food?

Raw food is just what you think it would be: any food that has been uncooked, untreated, or unadulterated. Raw food advocates believe that the greater the percentage of raw food in the diet, the greater the health benefits. No matter where you stand on raw food, everyone agrees that consuming more fresh greens, vegetables, fruits, fats, and proteins is an excellent way to reach or maintain your optimal health.

The idea of consuming raw foods isn't exactly a new concept. Adam and Eve subsisted on raw fruits, vegetables, seeds and nuts. Over the next several thousand years, people started cooking and preserving their food. Flash forward a few millennia, and our high-tech world has figured out how to take fresh fruits, farm-grown vegetables, and protein-rich meats and process these gifts from nature into manufactured, microwave-friendly, mass-produced, and often genetically modified Frankenfoods that are anything but healthy for us.

Some of you might be seeking a health turnaround in your life. While some might simply want to learn more about the "raw lifestyle" and follow a diet of foods that are uncooked, untreated, and unadulterated, others may be interested in a simpler, more wholesome diet and way of life.

No matter what drew you to this book, understand that the health principles you'll discover in *The Raw Truth* represent an important first step in your health journey. You need to take

control of your own health, and this book will help you to transform your health from the inside out with the power of living nutrients.

The first topic we need to talk about are the two types of raw food diets. These days, those who follow a raw food diet fall into one of two camps:

- **RAW FOOD VEGANS.** Veganism is a strict vegetarian diet that excludes meat, eggs, dairy products, and other animal-derived ingredients. A vegan diet includes all grains, beans, legumes, vegetables, and fruits and the nearly infinite number of foods made by combining them.

A raw vegan diet is restrictive and consists of unprocessed raw plant foods that have not been heated above 115°F because foods cooked above this temperature lose enzymes and, in the opinions of raw foodists, much of the value. Raw vegans typically eat raw organic fruit, vegetables, nuts, seeds, sprouted grains, and legumes.

The word "vegan" seems like it's been around only a decade or two, but the word was coined in 1944 by Donald Watson, founder of the Vegan Society, who said he took the first three and last two letters of *vegetarian* to form the word "vegan." These days, it's cool to call yourself a vegan, and more than a few celebrities have adopted the raw food lifestyle as their own (see sidebar on page 14).

Raw food vegans point to pioneers like Arnold Ehret and Anne Wigmore for their inspiration. Ehret was a German health educator born in the latter half of the 19th century, long before veganism became a household word. Ehret wrote that "paradise health" was attainable through fasting and eating fresh, uncooked fruits and vegetables, and no meat or animal products. His followers became known as "Ehretists," and Arnold Ehret still has many adherents today.

Ehret came to the United States just before the start of World War I to share his philosophy on ideal eating, and he became a popular lecturer under the billing of "natural healer." A prolific author, Ehret's seminal book was *The Mucusless Diet Healing System*. "If your blood is formed from eating the foods I teach [fruits and green, leafy vegetables], your soul will shout for joy and triumph over all misery of life," he wrote. "For the first time, you will feel a vibration of vitality through your body—like a slight electric current—that shakes you delightfully."

Anne Wigmore, who lived from 1909 to 1994, wasn't as poetic but just as dedicated to educating people about the benefits of raw juices, especially wheatgrass and a diet of raw sprouts, fruits, vegetables, and sprouted nuts, seeds, and grains. Known as the "mother of living foods," Wigmore was the first proponent of consuming wheatgrass juice for detoxifying and nourishing the body, mind, and spirit.

Apple Vs. Applesauce

In 2010, I presented nearly one hundred seminars entitled "Six Keys to Extraordinary Health" throughout the U.S. Many times when I stepped before an audience, I posed this simple question:

If someone offered you an apple from a tree or a small jar of applesauce made from the very same apple, which would you choose?

You should have seen the eyes light up and the hands go in the air. Everyone was eager to tell me, "The apple!"

And they would be correct because a raw apple, picked from a tree as it ripens, will always be more nutritious and more alive than applesauce, which is a purée of cooked or baked apples.

When an apple is peeled and cooked, you lose antioxidants and pectin, which is a powerful fiber compound. When you cook the apple, enzymes and probiotics contained in and on the apple, as well as many of the vitamins, are partially or completely destroyed, including half of the fruit's vitamin C content. Even though the very same apple was used to make the sauce, it doesn't take a rocket scientist to figure out that a fresh raw apple trumps processed applesauce every time.

The author of a dozen books, Anne Wigmore's best-known work was *The Wheatgrass Book: How to Grow and Use Wheatgrass to Maximize Your Health and Vitality*. In 1968, she co-founded the Hippocrates Health Institute, a residential health and wellness program that is still in operation today near my Florida hometown of West Palm Beach. Named after the ancient Greek doctor who said, "Let food be thy medicine," the Hippocrates philosophy is founded on the belief that a vegan, living, enzyme-rich diet is integral to optimum health.

- **RAW FOOD OMNIVORES.** Those who consume a selection of raw fruits, vegetables, nuts, and seeds *plus* eggs, fish, meat, and non-pasteurized and non-homogenized dairy products such as raw milk, raw kefir, raw cheese, and raw milk yogurt, are known as raw food omnivores.

One of the more well-known proponents of a raw food omnivore diet is Aajonus Vonderplanitz, an American with a German-sounding name living in another California coastal town—Malibu. Vonderplanitz has been eating an all-raw diet for the last forty years. His regimen consists of raw meat, raw fish, raw organ meats, raw dairy, raw eggs, honey, vegetable juices, and a small amount of raw fruit.

He is the author of *We Want to Live: The Primal Diet*, which outlines the properties of various raw foods and how they affect cleansing, detoxification, and rebuilding. Vonderplanitz is also president of a campaign group known as "Right to Choose Healthy Food," which has been lobbying California legislators to relax restrictions on the sale of raw dairy and other raw foods.

Another strong advocate of raw food omnivorism is the Weston A. Price Foundation, a respected non-profit organization dedicated to "restoring nutrient-dense foods to the American diet through education, research, and activism." The organization's president, Sally Fallon Morell, believes that animal fats, especially those consumed raw, are vital nutrients necessary for normal growth, proper function of the brain and nervous system, supporting the immune and cardiovascular systems, and maintaining optimal energy levels.

Whatever side you fall on—raw food vegan, raw food omnivore, or a combination of both *with* the addition of cooked foods—I trust that after reading this book you will agree that raw, living nutrients are important to everyone's diet.

Moving Ahead

In my own life, I can look back to my ten months in San Diego as a time when I discovered the benefits of consuming raw, living nutrients. After my health transformation in San Diego, I returned to my hometown of West Palm Beach with a renewed sense of purpose and a mission to empower extraordinary health. I hadn't forgotten the pair of vows I made, but purchasing a ranch or farm to raise my own food wasn't going to happen at the age of twenty-one while working a job that paid $4.25 an hour. But my second vow—creating raw whole food nutritional supplements—would happen sooner than I ever dreamed possible.

After taking a job at a local health food store, a medical journalist wanted to write a story about my health comeback in a natural medicine journal. In the article, I recounted the dietary principles I followed and the special probiotics I consumed in the article, which created quite a buzz. I soon learned that there was great demand for this dietary information as well as the probiotic supplement that made such a difference in my health.

That's when Garden of Life was born. Today, Garden of Life is a health and wellness

company that empowers extraordinary health by creating whole food nutritional supplements, functional foods, and educational resources. During the early days of Garden of Life, I began studying nutrition and gained a deeper understanding of the holistic wellness plan that would later become the framework for my first three books: *Patient Heal Thyself, Restoring Your Digestive Health*, and *The Maker's Diet*.

Over the last two years, Garden of Life has pioneered the raw food supplement movement, creating the very first raw food multivitamins, green foods, protein, meal replacement, cleansing system, probiotics, and enzymes, just to name a few. Each of these formulas contain raw, whole food nutrients and bioactive compounds that are uncooked, untreated, and unadulterated. With the introduction of raw food nutritional supplements, Garden of Life makes it possible for everyone to experience the power of raw, living nutrients.

My first vow of creating a "beyond organic" farm and ranch would prove to be challenging but unbelievably rewarding. At the writing of this book, our journey is just beginning. I have been married eleven years to Nicki, and we have three children six years of age and under, so following through on this promise to myself is very real to me. Nicki and I talked through my vision, and when she was on board, we started looking around the country at various ranching and farming operations that would meet the vision that I had in mind. Finally, after a five-year search, we found just the right situation—seven different pieces of property totaling thousands of acres in southern Missouri's Ozark mountains and Georgia's Blue Ridge mountains.

In the next few years, we hope to be producing high quality "beyond organic" spring water, vegetables, fruits, and animal foods as well as teaching the next generation of world-changing, future-minded agriculturalists that we can transform the health of this nation by getting back to our roots, capturing the power of the sun, and fully utilizing the God-given resources we have to create extraordinary health.

Whether you're a vegan, vegetarian, or omnivore, I believe it's imperative that you do everything within your power to consume more raw living nutrients with each passing day. I believe there are health revelations in the following pages of this book that can benefit anybody and everybody. The Raw Truth is this: the way nutrients were intended to be consumed is in their uncooked, untreated, and unadulterated form.

Where We Go from Here

In the 1990s movie, *The Princess Bride*, Count Rugen said, "If you don't have your health, you haven't got nothing."

Isn't that the raw truth?

Beginning each chapter of *The Raw Truth*, I'll be sharing the stories of some of the "legends" of natural health to shed light on topics such as raw vitamins, raw probiotics, raw enzymes, raw fiber, and raw greens. Often viewed as wacky health nuts, these men and women devoted their lives to teaching people how to take control of their health by harnessing the power of raw, living nutrients. These pioneers are the fathers and mothers of the modern natural health movement, and it is on their broad shoulders that I stand to bring you this important message.

The first person I want to tell you about is Dr. Bernard Jensen, a pioneer of digestive cleansing. Dr. Jensen was a nutritional hero of mine, and I had the great privilege to be with him at his bedside weeks before he died. Even with his life waning, he was still passionate about nutrition and asked me to get out a pen and paper as he shared some of the health principles he had taught to millions during his illustrious career as a health practitioner, author, and teacher. His book, *Tissue Cleansing Through Bowel Movement*, made a huge impact on me in the late 1990s.

Whether you're thinking about becoming a raw food vegan, a raw food omnivore, or committing to eating raw foods in greater quantities, it's always an excellent idea to embark on a cleanse—a top-to-bottom scrubbing of the gastrointestinal tract—before you get started. I'll be sharing Dr. Jensen's principles for cleansing in our first chapter.

A Match Made in Hollywood: Celebrities and Raw Food

You know raw food is getting big with the Hollywood set when the paparazzi stake out raw food restaurants in West L.A., waiting for Hollywood celebrities and their entourages to show up.

Eating raw is the chic thing to do among the A-listers and assorted hangers—on who populate the pages of *People*, *US Weekly*, and the supermarket tabloids. While only a handful of movie stars claim to have gone 100 percent raw—Demi Moore, Woody Harrelson, Laura Dern, and Angela Bassett are the most notable—a groundswell of interest in eating raw has swept through the ranks of Hollywood celebrities in the last couple of years. Tobey Maguire of Spiderman and singer Thom Yorke of Radiohead have let the world know that they are vegans.

Captains of industry have also jumped on the vegan bandwagon. Las Vegas casino mogul Steve Wynn, Ford chairman Bill Ford, Twitter co-founder Biz Stone, Whole Foods Market CEO John Mackey, and even former heavyweight boxing champion Mike Tyson have gone vegan.

Back in Hollywood, the in crowd often gathers at Juliano's Raw, purportedly the most popular raw food restaurant in Southern California. Robin Williams and Danny Glover have been regulars at this raw vegan restaurant located on Broadway in Santa Monica, where Juliano—a dude with no use for a surname—bounds around a kitchen strewn with coconuts, kiwis, avocados, and dried seaweed. "Food gets ticked if you put fire to it," he told one interviewer.

Juliano's creations include French fries made from crumbled bread and zucchini, noodles made from mango, and "decadent" desserts produced from carob, vanilla beans, dates, and honey. His fruit-topped pizza "crust" comes from a mulch of activated buckwheat groats that is solidified in the sun for ten to twelve hours. Juliano's inventive entrees and treats, besides being ultra-healthy, also have to taste good, which is why Hollywood celebrities are beating a path to his door. You might see film stars like Natalie Portman or Joaquin Phoenix supping on uncooked veggie-loaded lasagna, burritos, and "meatloaf"—all vegan and all raw.

Juliano's isn't the only raw food restaurant in Tinseltown. Pamela Anderson of *Baywatch* fame says her favorite places to eat in L.A. are Flore Vegan Cuisine, Madeline Bistro, Pure Luck Restaurant, and Astro Burger, the latter located on Melrose near Paramount Studios. That's where she satisfies her jones for veggie chili dogs and soy chicken fajitas.

There's plenty of room on the vegan bandwagon, and it's great to see the idea of consuming a raw food diet catching on with celebrities of every stripe.

CHAPTER 1

RAW Cleansing

Health Legend:

Bernard Jensen,

Ph.D., and D.C.

THE RAW TRUTH

One time early in his speaking career—this was probably more than fifty years ago—Bernard Jensen was asked to talk to a church group about principles of good health. A firm believer in the importance of digestive wellness, Dr. Jensen quickly dived into the topic of enemas and colon cleansing.

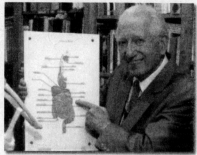

Dr. Bernard Jensen*

You can imagine how these bathroom topics went over with a prim-and-proper churchgoing audience back in the day. The story goes that Dr. Jensen had to duck a few ripe tomatoes thrown in his direction, but he kept on spreading his message about the virtues relieving the body of built-up toxins through an aggressive enema regimen.

Irrepressible, resolute, and positive that the key to good health lay in periodically "detoxifying" the body through proper bowel management, Bernard Jensen was a pioneer in colon cleansing. Born in the Central California farming community of Stockton in 1908, young Bernard followed his father into the field of chiropractic health and studied the science of chiropractic at a college in Oakland, California.

Much like me, at the age of twenty, Bernard faced health challenges. A Seventh Day Adventist physician took an interest in Bernard's plight and taught him the principles of eating right and living a healthy, productive life. He experienced a remarkable turnaround, which fueled a lifelong interest into understanding the inherent wisdom in the body's ability to heal itself.

Bernard graduated from chiropractic college, and during his early years of practice and throughout his life, he traveled to far-away lands—fifty five countries in all—to study the oldest, healthiest people on the planet. What he found was that a diet of whole, natural and mostly raw foods, a peaceful disposition, daily exercise, and sufficient sleep were the foundation of living a long and healthy life, but nutrition was the most important piece of the puzzle. "I am firmly convinced that nutrition is the greatest single therapy to be applied in the holistic healing arts and that we must treat the whole patient, not the disease," he said.

Dr. Jensen believed that people needed to get away from their day-to-day routine and concentrate on getting better through eating the right foods and having their colons cleansed of the heavy mucus coating thick with toxins and "noxious debris" that had built-up over the years—if not decades. He opened an eighty-five bed sanitarium called the Hidden Valley Health Ranch back in 1955 on 100 acres of lush, rolling foothills east of the Southern California city of Escondido.

* His results were extraordinary. You should not expect miraculous results.

With Dr. Jensen on site, guests attended lectures and seminars; ate healthy, unprocessed foods; communed with nature; and practiced regular colon cleansing. Word of mouth spread about the remarkable results that people were experiencing, and by the late 1950s, Hidden Valley Health Ranch had gained quite a reputation. Heads of state, sports figures, Hollywood celebrities, and ordinary folks came from around the world to hear from Dr. Jensen on how to eat right and adopt a healthier lifestyle. One of the celebrities was the famous actress Mae West, who in her later life became a good friend of Dr. Jensen and followed his colon cleansing therapy as a way, she claimed, to preserve her great beauty.

Dr. Jensen saw more than 350,000 patients in his lifetime and was a prolific author of more than fifty books and booklets, but the book that he'll be most remembered for is *Tissue Cleansing Through Bowel Management*, which was released in 1981. Conceding in his Foreword that writing the book was "somewhat difficult due to the nature of the subject matter," Dr. Jensen made the case that there was nothing to be ashamed of in discussing the bowel, which is merely a natural part of the body. Cleansing, detoxification, and elimination should be a routine part of a total health program and part of everyone's health care strategy, he said. To properly cleanse the body tissues, organs, and skin, the place to start is with a thorough cleansing of the bowel.

As I mentioned in the Introduction, I was with Dr. Jensen in 2001 three weeks before his death, when he was ninety-two years old. I told him that his work had a huge impact on me in the late 1990s. I'm pleased to say that this health legend's message still lives on, and there's even a "Tissue Cleansing Through Bowel Management Appreciation Society" on Facebook.

Turning a Corner—Literally

So what is cleansing? Why is it important?

A cleanse is a health regimen designed to remove toxins from the body. Most cleanses target the entire body, although there are cleanses that focus on specific organs such as the liver, kidneys, and skin.

Cleansing is important because one of the body's natural ways of staying healthy is its ability to detoxify itself. We need a mechanism to expel the harmful substances we absorb, inhale, or ingest, and cleansing is a natural way of removing the impurities that build up in the body.

A cleanse can be accomplished in various ways. The most common is a temporary change of diet by fasting or eating certain foods such as raw fruit high in fiber, or drinking lots of liquids to flush toxins from the body. A cleanse can also be accomplished by colonic irrigation, also known as colon hydrotherapy. When the colon is flushed with warm filtered water, this loosens the waste material on the walls of the bowels and prompts the body to "unload" any buildup of fecal waste. Natural physicians like Dr. Jensen believe that certain foods such as cooked and processed meats and refined sugars clog the digestive system, and colonic irrigation is a good way to deal with the removal of these built-up toxins.

Most people do not feel very good during the early stages of cleansing because the release of toxins that are held in the organs of the body now enter the bloodstream. That's why it's important to drink large amounts of water and raw juices to help flush the toxins out through the urine. Taking a sauna is another way to release toxins by opening the skin's pores and sweating them out. After getting over the initial hump, however, most people feel noticeably better, lighter, and happier during and after a cleanse, though it's not uncommon to also experience "detox symptoms" or even an "emotional cleanse" of anger, sadness, or other emotions.

Cleansing should be part of any comprehensive health regimen. I believe if the digestive system is not given a chance to restore itself through cleansing, then we put ourselves at risk.

Let's face it: our bodies must contend with numerous environmental toxins in our foods, in the air we breathe, and from the water we drink. There are residual pesticides and preservatives in our diets, especially if you're not eating raw, organic foods, and there are chemicals in our municipal water. All tend to leave residues in our bodies. Excess toxins can make you feel lethargic and impact your health in many ways.

Our bodies are constantly working to eliminate toxins through the lungs, kidneys, digestive system and, particularly, the liver. Opening every channel for detoxification can definitely aid our livers in the all-important detoxification process. Every minute of every day, a properly functioning liver processes toxins, heavy metals, bacteria, and other impurities from the blood, making them less toxic before returning it into circulation. A healthy liver utilizes complex enzymatic processes to metabolize toxins so they can be easily excreted from the body.

Normally the liver secretes about a quart of bile a day to carry processed non-nutrient environmental chemicals and their metabolites, as well as compounds our bodies normally make, such as cholesterol, to the intestinal tract. The toxins are then carried out of the body by the digestive tract.

The digestive tract, when stretched end to end, measures between twenty-five and thirty-five feet in length and is expertly designed to help the body break down foods and absorb its nutrients and distribute them throughout the body via the bloodstream. Anything that's left over is expelled from the body either through urine or fecal elimination, although wastes and toxins

can be eliminated through exhalation and sweating.

Many people don't realize how much food the gastrointestinal tract must contend with in a lifetime. The figure I've seen is sixty tons of food, but for many of us, our eat-around-the-clock lifestyle never allows the body any "free" time to cleanse itself properly.

If you've been eating a diet heavy in processed foods, then your body is not likely receiving the appropriate nutrients it needs to build and repair muscles, grow strong bones, or keep things moving where it counts. Meals of greasy fried chicken and sticky sweets for dessert are like filling your car's fuel tank with sawdust rather than 93 octane fuel. Processed foods strain the gut, causing the digestive system to work harder to extract nutrients.

If you're feeling "down in the dumps" after you eat, or stuffed, bloated, and constipated, that's a good indication that you should go on a cleanse. When an overloaded gastrointestinal system gets backed up, fecal matter can putrefy in the colon and cause bowel overload. The colon wall absorbs the remaining water in the feces, turning the stool hard as stone pebbles. The harder the feces, the more difficult it is to eliminate.

Oftentimes when I speak, people come up to me afterward and tell me more about their bowel habits than I would ever want to know, including the fact that they rarely go to the bathroom more than once every three days or so. That's not a good sign. Think about it: if you're eating three times a day and not even eliminating once, we're talking about a major backlog. As Dr. Jensen told me, "What goes in doesn't always come out."

But it should. Under ideal conditions, twelve to twenty-four hours should pass between the moment your meal is finished until the moment waste is eliminated at the other end. The amount of time that foods stay in the digestive tract before you have to go to the bathroom is called "bowel transit time." Too long a time, and you have constipation. Too short, and you're dealing with loose bowels. Food that leaves the body in less than twelve hours becomes diarrhea and means that the body cannot adequately absorb or extract the nutrients it needs in such a short time, which is one reason why you feel weak and uneasy after a bout of diarrhea.

Too many carbs can strain the gut as well. Those who munch on glazed doughnuts, French fries, and snack cakes present the body with *too many* carbohydrates to digest. Leftover undigested carbs camp in the gut longer than twenty-four hours and impair digestion. Instead of everything being eliminated on time, the substances putrefy inside the intestines, causing an overgrowth of harmful bacteria and yeasts, which can lead to abdominal discomfort. If the digestive system is not given a chance to restore itself through cleansing, then digestive-related challenges may occur.

THE RAW TRUTH

Instead of eating the Standard American Diet (SAD)—the chips and sodas and bacon cheeseburgers and deep-dish pizzas—I recommend these Top 10 Cleansing Foods be added to your diet. Even if you don't undertake a complete cleanse, eating these raw, healthy foods will go a long way toward giving your gastrointestinal tract a top-to-bottom scrubbing.

My Top 10 Cleansing Foods:

1. **Avocados** are high in fiber, potassium, vitamin E, and healthy monounsaturated fats, and they are a must eat in any eating plan.

2. **Raw coconut cream** is loaded with medium-chain fatty acids that help promote a positive intestinal environment and compounds that help remove toxins from the body.

3. **Flaxseeds and chia seeds** are wonderful sources of fiber, essential fatty acids, and powerful phytochemicals, which lubricate the bowel and promote healthy cellular structure.

4. **Raw cultured veggies such as sauerkraut** have billions of live probiotics and active sulfur compounds, which provide detoxification to the liver and GI tract.

5. **Fresh vegetable juice** made from carrots, celery, parsley, cilantro, cucumber, beets and dozens of other veggies is a key component of any raw cleansing regimen, providing vitamins, minerals, enzymes, and antioxidants the body needs to gently remove toxins.

6. **Blueberries** are low sugar and high fiber, plus the benefits of powerful antioxidants make blueberries a true "superfood."

7. **Cucumbers** are high in fiber and minerals and have excellent hydrating ability.

8. **Tomatoes** are a gentle form of fiber and are high in vitamin C and the antioxidant lycopene.

9. **Raw milk kefir and yogurt** have billions of friendly microbes and support healthy digestion.

10. **Coconut kefir** is loaded with probiotics, enzymes, organic acids and electrolytes such as potassium, which promote cellular cleansing and healthy elimination.

In addition to eating these superior raw foods, I strongly recommend that you embark on a detoxification and cleansing program four times a year—once for each season. And in the last two years, Garden of Life has created a raw cleansing system just for you.

The Raw Cleanse

There are hundreds of websites that tout cleansing through raw diets and recipes, but until recently, no raw cleanse system was available. I always found that a bit of an anomaly because the idea of cleansing the body with raw, living foods has been around for over a century, thanks to pioneers like Dr. Bernard Jensen and his mentor, Dr. Victor Rocine, a Norwegian immigrant and homeopath who lived from 1859 to 1943. For them, raw always represented the standard. Raw foods and juices were foundational elements to cleansing.

So you'd think there would be a raw cleanse system for those embarking on a raw food-cleansing diet. The fact of the matter, however, is that for many nutritional companies, sourcing all of the raw ingredients necessary to create a raw cleanse product is costly and time-consuming. Great effort must go into the research and development of such a cleanse, and many companies prefer not to go through the expense and the perceived hassle of formulating an entirely raw cleanse. Otherwise, there would probably have been a raw cleanse available years ago.

The way I saw things, though, is that if there were two words that should go together, they would be *raw* and *cleanse.* Since raw is such an important purity standard, it made sense to me that there should be a raw cleansing formula available to consumers. Because I understand from personal experience what cleansing can do for you, several years ago I asked my team at Garden of Life to design a gentle digestive cleanse with ingredients that were uncooked, untreated, and unadulterated. The goal was a cleanse that worked in sync with the detoxification process and supported the body's natural digestive and detoxification systems.[†]

At Garden of Life, the raw standard means:

- **HIGHLY ACTIVE, ULTRA-PREMIUM INGREDIENTS THAT CONTAIN LIVE PROBIOTICS AND ENZYMES**

- **NO GLUTEN, SOY ALLERGENS, OR DAIRY**

- **NO BINDERS OR FILLERS**

- **NUTRIENTS THAT ARE DELIVERED IN THEIR UN-DENATURED, WHOLE FOOD FORM WITH ALL THE INHERENT COFACTORS INTACT**

Sounds great on paper, but finding the most pure raw food ingredients was no easy task. We had to use clinically studied ingredients with a long historical background of safety. These ingredients had to accomplish several goals, starting with the removal of unwanted toxins from the body. A top-notch cleanse should also aid the body's natural defense mechanisms and help the body repel toxins.

After a lot of effort and careful study, the result was a seven-day, three-step cleansing supplement system aimed at purifying, capturing, and removing toxins from the body. We call it the Garden of Life RAW Cleanse.

A Crucial Starting Point

It will surprise you to learn that most of the hundreds of cleanses on the market miss the crucial starting point of cleansing, which is a shame since the point of cleansing is to remove toxins from the body to support digestion and overall health. Well, where does digestion begin? Answer: the mouth, where food—and many toxins—first enter the body.

Toxin Defense, the first step in RAW Cleanse, contains a unique oral probiotic known as *Streptococcus salivarius*. Much like the skirmishes being fought in the gut, there's a war going on for space in your mouth between various microorganisms. *S. salivarius* has the ability to promote healthy microorganisms in the mouth.[†] Other microorganisms produce toxins that interfere with the normal function of the body. Toxin Defense also includes the digestive probiotic *Bacillus coagulans*. This powerful probiotic provides support for the gastrointestinal tract, another breeding ground for toxic microorganisms.[†] Much like *S. salivarius*, *Bacillus coagulans* works by inhibiting potentially toxic microorganisms, with their toxins, from traveling further in the body and allowing your digestive system to function at its optimal best.[†]

Toxin Defense is the first component of the RAW Cleanse equation. While minimizing the exposure to toxic invaders is an important first step, neutralizing and removing the toxins already present in your body is of equal importance.[†]

[†] These statements have not been evaluated by the Food and Drug Administration. This product is not intended to diagnose, treat, cure or prevent any disease.

Moving on to Organo Detox

The liver is the largest internal organ in the human body. All blood passes through the liver, and one of the many jobs the liver performs is removing toxins from the blood, as I mentioned earlier. Most cleanses work to remove toxins on the "macro" level, which means they're concerned with removing the major toxins in the liver, kidney, and other organs.

One of the "macro" ingredients in Organo Detox is raw chlorella, a green algae that aids the liver in excreting environmental toxins that the body is normally exposed to in small amounts. Organo Detox also contains milk thistle, which has been used in traditional medicines for thousands of years, and it's found in many cleanse and liver detox formulas. Unlike most other cleanses, however, the milk thistle found in Organo Detox is raw.

The real superstar ingredients are the intra-cellular antioxidant trio of glutathione, SOD, and catalase. As research continues to unveil the importance of antioxidants, none may be as important as glutathione.

Here's some background on why glutathione is so important.

We know that antioxidants work at the cellular level to combat free radicals that damage cells. If you had to define one reason why toxins are bad, it may be because they lead to oxidative stress within the body, causing a proliferation of free radicals.

Where the human body is concerned, glutathione is at its highest concentration in the liver. As the collection point of toxins, the liver is prone to oxidative stress and exposure to free radicals. Since the liver also has the ability to manufacture glutathione, four ingredients were added to Organo Detox. The four ingredients in RAW Detox are raw food-created cysteine, glycine, sulfur, and glutamic acid.

Organo Detox also contains the antioxidant enzymes SOD (superoxide dismutase) and catalase. These enzymes are active at the cellular level to balance cellular oxidation.[†] These enzymes work to balance oxygen ratios at the cellular level.[†] SOD converts superoxide radicals into hydrogen peroxide, which is then turned into water and oxygen by another intra-cellular antioxidant enzyme called catalase.

The net effect of these ingredients in the RAW Cleanse Organo Detox formula is that they support your liver to do what it was made to do—remove toxins from your body.[†] With the combination of "macro" ingredients that help remove toxins and "micro" ingredients that assist liver function, the RAW Cleanse RAW Detox formula is one of the most unique cleanses available today.[†]

Batting Clean-Up:
RAW Digestion and Elimination

Cleansing doesn't end with toxins being eliminated from the bloodstream. In fact, if you can't remove them entirely from the body, the benefits are minimal at best. To hasten the removal process, most cleanse programs contain ingredients that help facilitate the elimination of toxins from the body. RAW Digestion and Elimination serves this role within the RAW Cleanse system.

RAW Digestion and Elimination was created to systematically aid in the removal of environmental toxins from a healthy body.[†] This unique formulation starts with raw food-chelated magnesium, which attracts water to the colon, supporting the natural movement of intestinal bulk instead of "forcing" muscle contractions along the digestive tract to move waste.

RAW Digestion and Elimination also contains two superfoods—flaxseeds and chia seeds—that provide omega-3 fatty acids and fiber. Besides being highly nutritious, these bulking fibers are great for trapping toxins for removal from the body.[†] Additionally, RAW Digestion and Elimination contains four different cereal grass juices, which contain powerful nutrients that have been used for decades. Ann Wigmore would have approved.

Pound for pound, cereal grass juice may be among the most nutritionally dense foods on the planet. Where cleansing is concerned, they offer an additional benefit. They support the proper function of a healthy gastrointestinal tract and help maintain regularity, which is important when you're trying to move toxins out of the body.[†]

The Raw Truth

RAW Cleanse is a gentle, seven-day cleanse that is different from other cleanses available anywhere. RAW Cleanse works first to support the health of the entire digestive tract, and then aids the liver in removing toxins.[†] Finally, RAW Cleanse aids the digestive system in trapping the toxins and transporting them out of the body.[†]

The last thing you want your cleanse supplement to do is introduce any new toxins into the body. Raw has a purity standard that ensures that you are not adding any of the chemical byproducts associated with processing or introducing any unnecessary toxins into your body.

[†] These statements have not been evaluated by the Food and Drug Administration. This product is not intended to diagnose, treat, cure or prevent any disease.

The Forefathers of Raw Cleansing

Cleansing has become so popular over the last few years that most people probably think of it as a new concept. That couldn't be further from the truth, as I've demonstrated in this chapter, so I want to point out several other pioneers in cleansing health besides Dr. Bernard Jensen. You'll meet these Health Legends in greater depth in upcoming chapters.

Dr. John Harvey Kellogg (1852-1943) has a name that is synonymous with breakfast cereal. Indeed, he and his brother Will founded a company in 1897 that

manufactured whole grain cereals. A man of principle, John Harvey Kellogg split off from his brother when Will wanted to add sugar to their corn flake recipe. Will's new company would eventually become the wildly successful Kellogg Company. John's fame and notoriety would come from a different source.

As an experienced physician and surgeon and advocate of healthy living principles, he took over the floundering Battle Creek Sanitarium in 1878. While there, he promoted the idea that one's digestive health was directly reflective of overall health. He advocated a mostly raw vegetarian diet rich in whole grains. He believed that intestinal flora was important to digestive health, and that a well-balanced diet that included raw vegetables and fruits as well as fermented dairy was the key to overall health.

Norman W. Walker (1886–1985) was an innovator in the field of nutrition and one of the first experts to recommend vegetable juicing. He believed that a diet rich in vegetables, fruits, seeds and nuts was far superior to the cooked and processed foods that were making their way into diets in the early 20th century. He also declared that a healthy colon was the starting point of

overall great health. In 1936, he published Raw Vegetable Juices: *What's Missing in Your Body*. His legacy lives on today as the juicer he originally developed, the Norwalk Hydraulic Press, is still popular today.

Bernarr Macfadden (1868–1955) was as flamboyant as he was successful. He gained a national audience as a publishing magnate, producing everything from magazines about sports, crime, romance, and movies. His foremost passion, however, was in the field of nutrition.

Macfadden advocated a diet heavily weighted toward raw fruits, vegetables, nuts and raw dairy. He believed that white bread was one of the worst foods on earth, and he advocated periods of fasting to allow the body to cleanse itself. While he certainly wasn't the only notable at the time to recommend such a lifestyle, he was, perhaps, the most influential due to his notoriety and the sheer size of his publishing empire.

CHAPTER 2

RAW Vitamins

Health Legend:

Andy Szalay

I don't know what to be more amazed by: Andy Szalay's discovery of a special process that infuses nutrients into single-cell organisms to create vitamins and minerals that aren't isolated or synthesized but are totally raw in a whole food form; or his personal story of escaping the Iron Curtain with his family during the middle of the Cold War.

Endre "Andy" Szalay

Let's start with his personal story.

Born in a small town in Hungary in 1920, Endre Szalay grew up as the third son of a middle school history teacher. When he turned nineteen, the year was 1939, and dark war clouds were gathering over Europe. Everyone was talking about Nazi Germany and Adolf Hitler.

Endre was supposed to go into mandatory military service, but doctors told him he was half deaf in his left ear. He didn't know how lucky he was. Some friends suggested that he go to pharmacy school, so he enrolled at the University of Szeged. The first day of class was September 1, 1939, the same day the Nazi blitzkrieg stormed into Poland. He continued in school and earned his pharmacy degree in 1943, taking a job with a pharmacy near Budapest. His town was caught in between the Russian advance and the German defensive positions, and for days, he and the villagers were pounded with heavy artillery. When the Russians finally took over, soldiers raped the women and stole everything they could get their hands on, including their clothes.

Hungary became part of the Communist Bloc after the war, and pharmacies were nationalized, meaning that Endre worked for the state under oppressive conditions. He married Frida in 1946, but they were too poor to have a honeymoon. Between them, they owned two sets of clothes. They did have food, however, because many people bartered medicine for eggs, chickens, and vegetables.

The Communists who took over Hungary solidified their grip. They were totalitarians and merciless. All it took was for one person to say something wrong about you to the authorities— and you were gone. Maybe for years. Endre soon figured that anyone who had a university education like him didn't last long before they were arrested on some trumped-up charge.

In the mid-1950s, he and Frida talked about getting out of the country and starting over somewhere else. They never spoke of this secret ambition in their apartment, however, or in front of their two school-age girls. The only time they discussed escaping was when they sat on a park bench with no one around.

Then, out of the blue, the Hungarian Revolution started. On Radio Free Europe, they heard that people were getting out of the country during the chaos of the uprising. Twenty one day. One hundred the next. Two-hundred and fifty the day after. Then one day a colleague at the pharmacy told him the police had come by looking for him.

Endre got white as a sheet. Somebody had said something about him.

That very afternoon, he ran home and gathered the family. They left the apartment with no suitcases, nothing in their hands, so as not to arouse suspicion. They wrangled a ride to the Hungarian border in the back of a flatbed truck. The border patrol—these were Hungarian kids—knew there was a rebellion going on in Budapest, but they didn't know what to do with all the people dashing across the border in droves. There were too many to shoot.

That indecision provided Endre Szalay and his family with the opportunity to duck through a hole in the barbwire fence and escape into Austria on November 18, 1956. They had the clothes on their backs, and that was it.

The Austrian people were welcoming and put them into a refugee camp. The United States was allowing escaping families from behind the Iron Curtain to immigrate to this country, so within two weeks, they boarded a flight from Vienna to New York City. His family and the other refugees on the flight were put into abandoned army barracks in New Jersey. Eventually, Endre got his first job as a quality control technician at a pharmaceutical company. He spoke no English; he got the job only because the boss was Hungarian. His American co-workers called him "Andy" and taught him English. Every day, he had to pronounce a new word.

Andy scraped up enough money to move into a cramped apartment. They were starting from scratch, and every penny counted. In fact, one morning, Andy looked all over the house for enough money to pay the bus fare to go to work. All he could find was 18 cents, but the bus fare was 19 cents.

Not knowing what to do, he started walking for the bus stop, and then there it was—a penny on the ground.

When he stooped over to pick up that penny, Andy knew he and his family would be all right.

Seeing Things in a New Way

Quite a story, isn't it? Andy is still alive today, a spry ninety years old, and I was deeply moved when I met him a few years ago. But what makes his story even more remarkable is that if Andy hadn't reached American shores, you have to wonder if we in America would have raw food-created vitamins and minerals today.

After learning English and gaining confidence, Andy worked for the next twenty years for three botanical/pharmaceutical companies in the northeast corner of New Jersey, Bergen County, where Manhattan and New York City lay across the Hudson River. The family settled in the leafy town of Hackensack, New Jersey.

Andy became a poster boy for the American Dream. At all three companies, he climbed the ladder so quickly that at his last firm, he was named vice president and was running the day-to-day operations. The best research-and-development ideas came from him, the laboratory work was supervised by him, and dozens of employees and departments reported directly to him. Everyone appreciated his pioneering ideas and the products he came up with. It was a meteoric rise when you consider his humble arrival in the United States and lack of English.

Every year or two, however, he would tell his bosses that he had a great idea that he wanted to explore—an idea that stemmed from his youngest days when he studied biochemistry at the University of Szeged. No one paid attention to him, even though the companies he worked for were doing well financially because of his superior intellect and stellar abilities in the research laboratory.

Andy Szalay in his labratory

Andy was convinced that food was the most nutritious ingredient in the world, yet as he looked around in the 1950s, 1960s, and 1970s, huge pharmaceutical firms were introducing and successfully marketing nutritional supplements produced from synthetic, laboratory-derived materials. Common sense told him otherwise. Andy knew that human physiology would always distinguish the difference between the vitamin C in an orange versus ascorbic acid synthetically manufactured in a laboratory from genetically modified corn starch.

Swimming against the prevailing tide, Andy believed that if instead of these synthetically made supplements being consumed by millions of Americans in the name of health, what if he found a way to create concentrated foods in supplement form that would match the nutritive power found in real food? No one wanted to hear Andy's theories, however.

Although he was fifty-seven years old, he said to himself, *Maybe it's not too late to come up with a new discovery.* What Andy really wanted to do was develop or grow nutrients that were as close to the process by which microorganisms in healthy soil take dead, lifeless elements such as mineral salts and transform them into organic, living nutrients grown in plants such as fruits and vegetables.

Like the day he and his family stepped through a hole in the barbwire at the Austrian border and entered the Great Unknown, Andy risked everything by leaving an excellent job to start his own company in 1977. Within two weeks, he leased a small office and manufacturing plant near his hometown of Hackensack and hung out a shingle for a venture he called the Grow Company.

The Eureka Moment

Andy's original idea was to buy a large parcel of New Jersey farmland—hundreds of acres—and raise organic vegetables and fruits that he could harvest, dehydrate, then mill, extract, concentrate, and tablet the resultant whole food concentrate. Throughout the process, he would be checking for ways to improve the potency of the active ingredients as well as research the active stages of each individual nutrient found in these foods.

As he thought through this idea, Andy realized that it would take a tremendous amount of land to plant all the food he had in mind. In addition, New Jersey farmland was sure to harbor environmental problems. The Garden State was called the "Garbage State" by detractors because of 16,000 contaminated sites in the state, ranging from minor leaks at residential heating oil tanks to Superfund sites.

So Andy realized that farms were not the answer and turned his attention back to studying the active ingredients in plants and fruits. Andy knew from his studies that when a plant takes root, its roots reach into the soil and pull out inorganic nutrients such as mineral salts. When the plant is exposed to sunlight, the leaves and fruit of that plant produce vitamins and minerals through its metabolic process.

Plants, as Andy had learned back in high school biology in the 1930s, were multi-cell organisms—and vastly complicated. An idea began to percolate: What if he backed down to a simple single-cell organism or a tiny plant, if you will, and explored the possibilities with this source? After several trials, he landed upon using baker's yeast, the same type of yeast that is available in every grocery store.

Baker's yeast is a single-celled organism that can grow in a controlled environment hydroponically, or in water. The yeast grabs its nutrients from the water and starts budding and then propagating, which means the single cell goes from one cell to two cells, two cells split into four cells, four cells into sixteen cells, and so forth.

What Andy discovered is that when he fed the yeast with nutrients in their appropriate form, the nutrients traveled through the cell walls of the yeast and reacted with the protein of the yeast. Once the reaction with the protein of the yeast occurred, it became part of the yeast. Yeast, by nature, has B vitamins, vitamin D, plus minerals, which are in appropriate or "replaceable receptor sites" in the yeast.

What Andy ascertained through trial and error was that there were empty receptor sites in the yeast—empty sites that could be filled by the addition of various nutrients to the yeast. Eventually, Andy learned he could "feed" the yeast with protein chains known as peptides— which are also combined sequences of amino acids—because they could penetrate through the cell walls and deposit the vitamin or mineral into the cell structure of the yeast.

Andy's "Eureka moment" came when he learned that each vitamin and mineral had its own specific protein sequence or peptide that allowed the vitamin or mineral to pass through the yeast cell wall and embed within the food—in this case, yeast. There was no "universal" protein or peptide that worked for every vitamin, or for every mineral, however.

Undaunted—okay, maybe a *little* daunted—Andy set about trying to figure out the specific code for a single mineral, choosing selenium as his first test subject. Since Andy did not know which specific protein or peptide would allow selenium to pass through the yeast cell wall, he went about finding out the old-fashioned way, through trial and error. Andy set up his sterile lab equipment—in this case, a fish aquarium—and embedded a protein or peptide into the selenium. Then he waited for the results. When the experiment didn't work, the fish tank was left a mess. He would clean it and start all over again.

When Andy found the right peptide for selenium, he was awed. As he predicted, the peptide that he used allowed the selenium to travel through the yeast cell wall and become embedded in the yeast. When the yeast cell grew and replicated, the selenium was present. The result was the creation of a whole food nutrient—remember, yeast is food—where the selenium formed an integral part of the yeast in an organic food complex.

Andy then spent *more* years determining every protein or peptide that was necessary to grow *all* of the major vitamins and minerals. Literally thousands of tests were done, with each failure meaning a massive clean-up.

In the end, though, Andy had discovered a blueprint that he could use to manufacture a whole spectrum of nutrients in the form of food. He had done something thought to be impossible.

Endre "Andy" Szalay, the Hungarian immigrant who had come to this country with no money in his pocket, had cracked the Vitamin Code.

Producing Raw, Food-Created Vitamins

When I heard about Andy's exciting breakthrough, I saw that we now had a way to create the first multivitamins made from raw, whole food nutrients. But we didn't stop there. Since I believe that nutrients are at their most beneficial when found in a raw state, I worked with Andy and his team to ensure that his whole food nutrients were raw. This involved getting signed affidavits from each and every farmer, grower, and supplier of our fruits, veggies, sprouts, and other raw ingredients.

We could now produce multivitamins that were uncooked, untreated, and unadulterated and introduce them to consumers. I named this next generation of vitamins and minerals The Vitamin Code, and I believed it represented a breakthrough discovery that would forever change the way we take vitamins and minerals.

The food-created nutrients from Andy's laboratory were uncooked, untreated, and unadulterated, which means they were raw—never heated above 115 degrees.

This is an important distinction because our bodies were designed to take in food and then break it down into its individual nutrients. In a wonder of nature, the food actually helps in that process. The probiotics and enzymes in the food aid digestion, allowing the body to break down the food and assimilate the nutrients into the bloodstream. Other cofactors help carry the broken-down nutrients to the proper places in the body. What this means is that the whole (food) is greater than the sum of its parts.

No supplement can compare to the benefits associated with consuming raw foods. The Vitamin Code discovery gave our team at Garden of Life an innovative way to provide nutrients in their raw food-created form with their unique Code Factors intact as well as live probiotics and enzymes, amino acids, antioxidants, and other bioactive compounds, which I believe is as close to raw food nutrients that a supplement can get.

I was excited by the fact that we now had the ability to specifically target multivitamin formulations not just for men or women, but for older men and women, pregnant women, dieters, and young families. Because Andy and his Grow Company scientists had individually grown nutrients in single batches, we could put together specific Vitamin Code formulas with the exact amounts of vitamins and minerals needed to target each specific group's nutritional needs.

For instance, a Men's Formula could contain vitamins and minerals that support a healthy prostate and a healthy heart.[†] A Women's Formula could contain vitamins and minerals that support breast health, healthy skin, and bone strength.[†]

After much deliberation, we decided to launch eleven different Garden of Life Vitamin Code multivitamins. They are:

- MEN'S FORMULA
- FAMILY FORMULA
- PERFECT WEIGHT FORMULA
- RAW ONE FOR MEN
- 50 & WISER WOMEN'S FORMULA
- VITAMIN CODE KIDS

- WOMEN'S FORMULA
- RAW PRENATAL
- RAW ONE FOR WOMEN
- 50 & WISER MEN'S FORMULA
- VITAMIN CODE LIQUID

Let's take a closer look at the four most popular formulas:

Men's Formula: In developing Vitamin Code Men's Formula, Garden of Life paid particular attention to the special needs of men by selecting nutrients to support the primary areas of prostate health with added vitamin E, lycopene, selenium and zinc; mental and physical energy with vitamin B complex and chromium; and heart health with vitamin B complex, vitamins C and E.[†]

Here's a breakdown of the formulation for Vitamin Code Men's Formula:

- **Prostate health**[†]**:** vitamin E, selenium, and zinc
- **Heart health**[†]**:** vitamin B Complex, vitamins C and E
- **Mental and physical energy**[†]**:** vitamin B Complex, and chromium
- **Optimal digestion**[†]**:** live probiotics and enzymes, vitamin D and zinc
- **Stress response**[†]**:** vitamins A, C E, B Complex and selenium

Women's Formula: In developing Vitamin Code Women's Formula, Garden of Life paid special attention to the complex functions of a woman's body by selecting nutrients to support breast health with added vitamins D and E; the reproductive system with folic acid, calcium, magnesium and zinc; bone strength with appropriate amounts of vitamins A, C, and D, and calcium, magnesium, and zinc.[†]

[†] These statements have not been evaluated by the Food and Drug Administration. This product is not intended to diagnose, treat, cure or prevent any disease.

Here's a breakdown of the formulation for Vitamin Code Women's Formula:

- **Breast health[†]:** emerging science suggests that vitamins D supports breast heatlh as well as E
- **Reproductive system[†]:** folic acid, calcium, magnesium, and zinc
- **Bone strength[†]:** vitamins C, and D, calcium, magnesium, and zinc
- **Healthy skin[†]:** vitamins A, C, and copper,
- **Heart health[†]:** vitamin B Complex, C and E
- **Optimal digestion[†]:** live probiotics and enzymes, vitamin D and zinc

50 & Wiser Men's Formula: In developing Vitamin Code 50 & Wiser Men's Formula, Garden of Life paid particular attention to the needs of mature men during this special stage of life by selecting nutrients to support the primary areas of prostate health with added vitamin E, lycopene, selenium and zinc; memory and concentration with vitamin B complex and vitamins C, D, and E; and optimal digestion with live probiotics, enzymes and vitamin D.[†]

Here's a breakdown of the formulation for Vitamin Code 50 & Wiser Men's Formula:

- **Prostate health[†]:** vitamin E, selenium, and zinc
- **Heart health[†]:** vitamin B Complex, and vitamins C and E
- **Mental and physical energy[†]:** vitamin B Complex, and chromium
- **Optimal digestion[†]:** live probiotics and enzymes, vitamin D and zinc
- **Memory and concentration[†]:** vitamin B Complex, vitamins C, D, and E
- **Eye health[†]:** vitamins A, C, and zinc

50 & Wiser Women's Formula: In developing Vitamin Code 50 & Wiser Women's Formula, Garden of Life paid special attention to the complexities of a woman's body in this changing stage of life by selecting nutrients to support breast health with added vitamins D and E; bone strength with appropriate amounts of vitamins A, C, and D, and calcium, magnesium, and zinc; and cardiovascular support by adding vitamins B Complex and vitamins C and E.[†]

THE RAW TRUTH

Here's a breakdown of the formulation for Vitamin Code 50 & Wiser Women's Formula:

- **Breast health†:** emerging science suggests that vitamin D and vitamin E support breast health.
- **Bone strength†:** vitamins C, and D, calcium, magnesium, and zinc
- **Heart health†:** vitamin B Complex, and vitamins C and E
- **Optimal digestion†:** live probiotics and enzymes, vitamin D and zinc
- **Eye health†:** vitamins A, C, and zinc
- **Memory and concentration†:** vitamin B Complex, and vitamins C, D, and E

There are a several more Vitamin Code formulations that I want to tell you about:

Vitamin Code RAW B-Complex

The B group of vitamins is an eight-member family of water-soluble vitamins, which means they are not easily stored in the body and need to be replenished frequently. Their functions are so interrelated that it is suggested they be taken together so they can work harmoniously and perform at their peak levels.

Cellular energy production is the most important function of the B complex vitamins, and they are known as the catalytic spark plugs of our body. Providing mental and physical energy, supporting healthy blood, a healthy heart, immune system function and a healthy response to stress, the B complex vitamins are essential nutrients for the body.†

Vitamin Code RAW B-Complex is made with raw food-created nutrients for targeted delivery of Thiamin, Riboflavin, Niacin (as niacinimide), Vitamins B6 and B12, Pantothenic Acid, folic acid and biotin, as well as calcium, phosphorus, inositol, PABA, and choline.

† These statements have not been evaluated by the Food and Drug Administration. This product is not intended to diagnose, treat, cure or prevent any disease.

The Vitamin Code RAW B-Complex supports those who are:

- **strict vegetarians**
- **emotionally or physically stressed[†]**
- **following diets that include refined and processed foods or sugars**
- **eating cooked foods as opposed to consuming raw, uncooked foods**
- **exposed to environmental toxins**

Often recommended for healthy hair and nails, biotin, as well as folic acid, is used by the body to break down and synthesize amino and nucleic acids, which are needed to build new cells, particularly red blood cells.[†] Folic acid or folate is known to support a healthy heart when taken in conjunction with vitamins B6 and B12[†], and to support already normal homocysteine levels.[†]

Vitamin Code RAW B-12

B-12 deficiency is a growing nutritional deficiency in the developing world and in the U.S. Essential to protect the body against anemia and to support a healthy central nervous system, vitamin B12 is involved in the metabolism of every cell of the body.[†]

Since vitamin B12 is found predominantly in animal and dairy products, vegans may be especially prone to vitamin B12 deficiency, which can potentially affect the brain and nervous system. At levels only slightly lower than normal, individuals can begin to experience a range of symptoms from B-12 nutritional deficiencies.

Vitamin Code RAW Vitamin C

While most people associate vitamin C with immune support, the truth is that this powerful antioxidant, found in every cell of the body, is more far-reaching than a simple immune support vitamin. By protecting your cells against the effects of free radical damage, vitamin C helps the body ward off the effects of oxidative stress. The nutrient is critical in helping to build and maintain tissues while strengthening the immune system.

Essential for growth and repair of tissues in all parts of the body, vitamin C promotes vision health, periodontal health and collagen, bone and cartilage formation. Also needed by the adrenal glands, vitamin C helps with emotional and physical stress response. Vitamin C is also required to convert folic acid to its active form.

Vitamin Code RAW Vitamin C supports the immune system and is vital for healthy eyes, skin, bones, teeth and gums, wound healing, energy production and growth, as well as memory and concentration.[†]

Vitamin Code RAW Vitamin E

Known as a powerful antioxidant, vitamin E supports a healthy cardiovascular system while helping the immune system fight against the effect of free radicals. Determined to attack cell life in your body, free radicals may contribute to the weakening of the immune system.

A fat-soluble vitamin, vitamin E is a potent antioxidant complex composed of two classes of compounds—tocopherols and tocotrienols. These two classes of compounds work most efficiently when combined together. Whole foods contain all the vitamin E compounds, whereas most supplements contain only one part of this powerful nutrient— alpha tocopherol.

Vitamin Code RAW Vitamin E delivers seven of these compounds for maximum effectiveness along with a host of additional vital nutrients.

Vitamin Code RAW Vitamin E is a comprehensive, whole food, multi-nutrient formula that delivers vitamins E, D, K, beta-carotene, and selenium. Supporting heart, eye, digestive, prostate and breast health, Vitamin Code RAW Vitamin E also provides immune system support.[†]

Vitamin Code RAW Iron

Almost two-thirds of the body's iron is found in hemoglobin, the protein in red blood cells that carries oxygen to cells. A necessary trace element, iron is vital for producing ATP, the body's primary energy source and providing extra fuel to muscles during exertion. Iron, an integral part of many proteins and several enzymes in the human physiology, is essential for the regulation of cell growth. Playing an important role in the production of DNA, energy and cognitive function, iron is required for the health of the immune system.

Vitamin Code RAW Iron provides for the targeted delivery of iron, vitamin B12, vitamin C, and folic acid, which support mental and physical energy; heart, blood, eye, skin and reproductive health, as well as immune system support.[†]

Those who would benefit most from **Vitamin Code RAW Iron** would be:

- **vegetarians, who may have iron deficiency due to a lack of red meat, fish, and poultry in their diets**
- **women of childbearing age, who need additional iron to compensate for menstrual blood loss and tissue growth during pregnancy**

[†] These statements have not been evaluated by the Food and Drug Administration. This product is not intended to diagnose, treat, cure or prevent any disease.

The Top 10 Raw Foods

I have no doubt that the most potent form of nutrition is found in raw foods. Raw foods contain the highest levels of key nutrients, such as vitamins and minerals, as well as probiotics and enzymes that are destroyed by the process of cooking, treating, and adulterating. Cooking causes levels of fragile vitamins such as vitamin C to decrease dramatically, and while minerals are generally not destroyed by heat, the enzymes necessary for their proper utilization often are. Below is a list of exceptional raw foods loaded with vitamins and minerals.

1. Leafy greens, loaded with minerals including potassium, magnesium, calcium, and iron as well as dozens of trace elements, are a robust source of living nutrients.

2. Citrus fruits such as oranges, lemons, limes, and grapefruit are superb sources of raw vitamin C and bioflavonoids.

3. Sunflower, sesame, and pumpkin seeds are tiny nutrient powerhouses that contain B vitamins, vitamin E, and key minerals, including phosphorus.

4. Avocados are a great source of potassium and vitamin E.

5. Coconut kefir contains probiotics, enzymes and a large amount of potassium per serving.

6. Carrots are a great source of carotenoids, including beta carotene; they're also a surprisingly good source of calcium.

7. Raw yogurt, kefir and really raw cheese from grass-fed animals contain an abundance of calcium and significant amounts of B vitamins. When cows, goats, and sheep eat exclusively forage (grass, leaves, shrubs, etc.), they provide high levels of beta carotene and vitamins A, D, E, and K. Raw dairy products from grass-fed animals are also an excellent source of CLA (conjugated linoleic acid) and even contain trace amounts of omega-3 fats. Raw cheese is loaded with calcium and is an excellent source of dietary protein.

8. Celery is a first-rate source of electrolytes such as potassium and sodium, which is important for proper cardiovascular function.

9. Cultured veggies contain vitamin C, probiotics, enzymes and vitamin U, which is an active form of sulfur.

10. Watermelon and cantaloupe are two fruits rich in beta carotene and potassium, and lycopene (watermelon only).

CHAPTER 3

RAW Greens

Health Legend:

Ann Wigmore, N.D.

These days, a majority of juice bars and health food stores—plus trendy oxygen bars and even smoothie shops—seem to offer them. I'm talking about wheatgrass drinks served in shot glasses for three bucks a pop.

Made from the bright green blades of tray-grown sprouted wheat berries, a tumbler of this concentrated green juice packs a vitamin-and-mineral-rich wallop and is believed to have wonderful cleansing and rejuvenation properties. The reason why wheatgrass shots are deep green in color is due to their high concentration of chlorophyll, the green pigment found in plants.

Ann Wigmore N.D.*

To the uninitiated, a wheatgrass shooter tastes like a mouthful of backyard grass clippings, and some can't stomach the potent concoction. I'll admit that drinking wheatgrass juice is an acquired taste, but to the tens of thousands of regular wheatgrass juice consumers, nothing tastes better than feeling great. Today, wheatgrass shots are widely popular across the country.

If only Ann Wigmore were alive today to see the fruits—ah, greens—of what she started decades ago.

You see, this health pioneer is the reason why you see trays of wheatgrass in juice bars around the country. I touched on Ann's story in the Introduction, about how she literally wrote the book on wheatgrass—*How to Grow and Use Wheatgrass to Maximize Your Health and Vitality*—but this remarkable woman has an amazing life story to tell as well.

Ann Wigmore was born prematurely on the Russian steppes of Lithuania in 1909. She was a sickly infant. Her father, who had plans to immigrate to the United States after Ann was born, told his wife that since she was a frail girl, she should be put in the back of the barn with the wolves and they should leave for America without her.

Her parents packed up and abandoned her, leaving baby Ann in the care of a grandmother who nursed her with goat's milk through an eyedropper. She survived those early days and lived in the barn until she was five years old, when she moved into the house of her grandparents. Her grandfather was a raging alcoholic, however, who made life even more miserable for everyone. When World War I broke out, she and her grandmother moved out and hopscotched from village to village in an effort to stay ahead of the artillery shelling and bullets flying through the air.

***** Ann Wigmore's results were extraordinary.
You should not expect miraculous results.

THE RAW TRUTH

Most of the gardens were trampled over. Any food was stolen by the soldiers. She and her grandmother survived on grasses and weeds in the midst of two years of bloody warfare and nightmarish horrors. She saw soldiers with their limbs blown off, fires burning everywhere, and shell-blasted orchards. One time, she and her grandmother hid from the advancing armies in a dirt cellar and gnawed on tree roots to survive. If you ever saw the old 1960s movie *Dr. Zhivago*, then you have an idea of the deprivations.

She saw her grandmother clean the wounds of Russian and German soldiers with the green juice (chlorophyll) contained in wild grasses. Each morning, seven-year-old Ann would walk into the fields and swamps to collect the deepest-green grasses she could find. Then her grandmother would squeeze the juice on the solders' wounds and bandage them with leaves.

Following the war, her grandmother sent Ann to work on another farm and live with a family where the husband had died. Ann helped the mother and her five daughters with the chores, receiving the princely sum of $12 a month, which would go toward passage to the United States so that she could rejoin her family someday. Ann worked more than six years before she earned enough money to sail to America.

She arrived at Ellis Island when she was sixteen and joined her parents in Boston, but she was a slight, weak girl weighing seventy pounds. Her grandmother had told her the streets in America were paved with gold, but she soon learned otherwise. Her father made her work at his bakery and candy store from 4 a.m. until dinnertime, and family life was as hard as a crust of week-old bread. She ate the cakes and sweets in her father's bakery, and with this new American diet, Ann soon found herself battling to maintain her health.

When she was eighteen, she overheard her father making arrangements for her to marry someone she never met, so she ran away and took whatever work she could find—babysitting, house cleaning, and restaurant work. A man showed a romantic interest in her, but he came from a dysfunctional, argumentative family, and that carried right into their marriage. Ann had a very difficult time becoming pregnant—it took eleven years, but she eventually gave birth to a daughter. The marriage collapsed, however, and Ann was left penniless since he was awarded the estate as well as custody of their sixteen-year-old daughter.

It was back to the future for Ann in the mid-1950s. She scavenged for weeds and grasses in vacant lots and returned to the source of nourishment that had seen her through the darks days of World War I. She juiced with wheatgrass, weeds, and other green plants to provide her with nutrition and keep her immune system in top shape. After three years she was in great health, and she wanted to tell everyone she could about the virtues of natural living and the power

of green foods. She became a holistic health practitioner, nutritionist, and whole foods advocate, speaking and writing books with evangelical fervor about the heath benefits of cereal grass juices and eating raw "living" foods.

Ann was a tireless proponent of green foods for more than three decades. In one of those ironies of life, however, she died from smoke inhalation during a fire at the Ann Wigmore Foundation that she started in Boston. At the time of her death in 1994, she was eighty-four years young—limber, energetic, and intellectually sharp.

Capture the Power of the Sun

Why are green foods such as wheatgrass and other cereal grasses such as barley, oat, and rye so important?

My quick answer is that they are a phenomenal source of a diverse collection of nutrients, including trace minerals, that we have a hard time receiving in our diets. As the roots of cereal grasses dig into the ground, they extract nutrition from deep within the soil, which is fitting since grasses are considered to be at or near the base of the terrestrial food chain.

Grass—and all plants—turns green by utilizing the power of the sun to create nutrients through photosynthesis. If you think about it, we don't live off energy, carbohydrates, and calories, but we're really living off the sun because in order for a plant to grow, it requires the supreme source of energy—the sun, which plants convert to useable nutrients for animals and humans. Using chlorophyll and the process of photosynthesis, plants take the light from the sun and convert it into energy. That energy is then used to power the life of the plant. Without sunlight, plants that we depend on for nutrition would never reach their nutrient potential.

"The sun's rays reach the earth as an inexhaustible source of energy," said seven-time Nobel Prize nominee Dr. Johanna Budwig of Germany. "The sources of power in mineral oil, coal, green plant-foods, and fruits are based on the energy supplied by the sun's radiation."

Scientific advances tell us today that the energy from the sun comes in the form of photons, the fastest-moving, smallest units of energy ever discovered. When you plant a vegetable in dirt, it uses the power of the sun to draw nutrients from the soil and convert inorganic materials into life-giving organic substances. These nutrients are, in turn, what powers life on earth. That's why every food we eat can somehow be traced back to the sun. When you're eating a vegetable, a dairy product, a fish, or an animal that consumed some form of plant life, all of the nutrition in the food began with the sun.

Nowhere is the power of the sun more evident than in the life of green plants.

Cereal grasses, vegetables, fruits, seeds, and sprouts all depend upon the energy of the sun for their very existence, and they are the most efficient means to transfer the sun's energy to animals and humans.

I'm learning this firsthand as a budding rancher and farmer. Since we purchased our Missouri farmlands, our focus has been on the forage—the plants, legumes, herbs, and forbs eaten by our animals. I initially thought we could be called beef farmers or dairy farmers or chicken farmers or goat and sheep farmers or grape farmers, but what I've learned is that we are really grass farmers—even sun harvesters. Those ankle-high blades of grass waving in the fields are actually tiny solar panels capturing the power of the sun and transferring that energy to the animals that eat the grass, which is ultimately transferred to us humans.

What Ann Wigmore was telling anyone who would listen is that rapidly growing cereal grasses—before they become grain—contain a broad array of enzymes, vitamins, minerals, proteins, and chlorophyll, the latter being the green pigment found in plants. Chlorophyll makes life on earth possible because the oxygen we breathe comes from the chlorophyll-rich green plants.

The body transforms chlorophyll into hemoglobin, which the body requires to deliver oxygen and other nutrients to its cells. The blood-building properties of chlorophyll make scientific sense because our human blood is identical to chlorophyll with one exception: the main element in hemoglobin is iron, while the main element in chlorophyll is magnesium.

Nothing matches the nutrient density found in grasses such as wheat, barley, rye, corn, rice, oats, sorghum, millet, and spelt. They contain more nutrients relative to their size than other green foods, including wonderful veggies such as celery, parsley, and spinach.

So when you hear nutritionists talking about the importance of "eating your colors," they're referring to the idea that eating fruits and vegetables across a broad spectrum of colors will ensure that you're getting a wide variety of powerful phytonutrients contained in the colored pigments of these live foods.

Since I'm a great believer in "eating your colors," here are my Top 10 sources of dietary green foods:

1. **Wheatgrass juice** is loaded with minerals, proteins, antioxidant enzymes, and chlorophyll.

2. **Parsley,** eaten or juiced, is a great source of chlorophyll and a wonderful internal breath mint.

† These statements have not been evaluated by the Food and Drug Administration. This product is not intended to diagnose, treat, cure or prevent any disease.

3. **Cilantro** is thought by many to support the body's release of toxins.

4. **Green cabbage** has powerful sulfur compounds to support the body in detoxification.

5. **Broccoli sprouts** boast exciting research extolling the health benefits of these tiny sprouts.

6. **Asparagus** is wonderful for support of kidney function.

7. **Kale** is rich in many nutrients, including vitamin C and trace minerals.

8. **Deep green lettuce** is a great source of vitamins, minerals, and fiber.

9. **Spinach** contains some of the highest levels of antioxidants of any green veggie.

10. **Celery** is a prime source of electrolytes and a great base for fresh green juice.

Taking It to the Streets

Thanks to pioneers like Ann Wigmore, I've been a green juice fan ever since I began consuming it in San Diego. To augment my diet back then, I started taking a "green food" supplement that was a certified organic blend of barley, wheat, oat, and alfalfa grass juices. I would blend a couple of scoops of green food into a glass of water or veggie juice, and one sip would tell me that I was drinking one of the most nutrient-dense foods on this green earth. That's why many call powdered green foods "superfoods." Inspired by the benefits that green juices provided me—as well as the fact that most people will not go to the trouble of juicing fresh veggies every day—I sought to create a quick and easy way for everyone to have access to the amazing nutrients provided in two-to-three servings of green leafy vegetables.

That's why we at Garden of Life created Perfect Food. Perfect Food RAW, a certified organic* green superfood-juice powder, is derived from the highest quality raw food ingredients from every color of the rainbow. With thirty-five nutrient-dense raw organic greens, sprouts, and veggie juices dried at low temperatures to retain its powerful enzymes, Perfect Food RAW offers a wide variety of color—whole food nutrition powered by the sun that's totally *raw.*

Our Perfect Food RAW contains cereal grass juices such as barley, alfalfa, oat, wheat, and kamut, which were chosen for their outstanding nutrient profile. They are gluten-free and alive with enzymes, antioxidants, chlorophyll, and trace minerals, and they provide an abundance of energy from the captured power of the sun.

You have to catch cereal grasses at their nutritional peak, however. Just before cereal grass joints, it requires a tremendous amount of energy as it pulls nutrients from the soil.

* Organic product as certified by Quality Assurance International

The best cereal grasses are those harvested at the right time and then are quickly juiced and dried at low temperatures to preserve their raw nutrient potential. Perfect Food RAW is uncooked, untreated, and unadulterated—the raw and convenient way to get your grass-based nutrients every day!

Perfect Food RAW also contains over a dozen organic raw sprout juices. *Sprouting* is a term that refers to the process where you unlock the nutrient potential trapped within a seed. During the process, they germinate or sprout. Sprouting is a great way to increase the digestibility of seeds, nuts, and legumes while maintaining their raw nutrient density.

Finally, Perfect Food RAW contains a host of live enzymes and probiotics. Enzymes are present in all raw foods and enhance the body's ability to digest and assimilate the nutrients our food contains, while probiotics are key to the optimal function of our digestive system.[†] Perfect Food RAW was created with the belief that great nutrition is only as good as your body's ability to break down and utilize the nutrients.

After all, you're not just what you eat, but also what you assimilate.

Eating More Fruits and Veggies

Why don't we eat more vegetables? One could come up with a thousand different reasons—certainly too many to enumerate here. Suffice it to say, the vast majority of Americans do not eat nearly enough fruits and vegetables. In fact, the U.S. Department of Agriculture estimates that 91 percent of us do not eat the five-to-nine servings of fruits and veggies per day, as recommended.

Adventurous people try juicing their own fruits and veggies, but this comes with significant challenges. Anyone who has ever purchased an expensive vegetable juicer can tell you about the hassle of preparing the veggies and fruits, juicing them, and, of course, scrubbing and cleaning the juicer after use. This process also requires that you keep a large supply of fresh fruits and vegetables on hand. While nobody disputes the nutritional power of freshly juiced

[†] These statements have not been evaluated by the Food and Drug Administration. This product is not intended to diagnose, treat, cure or prevent any disease.

fruits and vegetables, convenience isn't a selling point.

You should always strive to eat the actual fruits or vegetables, preferably raw, in order to reap the most beneficial nutrients from the food; however, sometimes you need to supplement. Supplementation is not equivalent to eating actual raw food, but if you are going to supplement, you should look closely at Perfect Food RAW, which is made from fresh, low-temperature dried, juiced raw vegetables, greens, and sprouts in a nutrient-dense, great-tasting powder.

Perfect Food RAW is raw, certified organic*, whole food nutrition providing naturally occurring vitamins, minerals, antioxidants, enzymes, amino acids, essential fatty acids, and dozens of phytonutrients. This supplement is complete with prebiotics, probiotics, and soluble and insoluble fiber, and is bursting with live enzymes. Simply put, consuming Perfect Food RAW is a beneficial and convenient way to supplement veggie and cereal grass nutrients when you just can't intake enough in food form.

While it may seem obvious that eating fruits and vegetables daily is good for you, consider this:

When you take Perfect Food RAW, you're getting the following benefits:

- **raw energy†**
- **support for healthy blood sugar levels already in the normal range†**
- **healthy detoxification†**
- **immune system support†**
- **healthy digestion and elimination†**

Almost as important as what you get from Perfect Food RAW is what you're *not* getting. Perfect Food RAW is vegan, dairy-free, soy-free, gluten-free, with no fillers, added sugars, herbs, isolates or chemical additives. That means every single ingredient in Perfect Food RAW lends nutritional weight to the formula.

That's pretty powerful—almost as powerful as the sun.

* Organic product as certified by Quality Assurance International

Why Juice?

Once you harvest cereal grasses, there are two ways you can go about preparing them for use in nutritional formulas. You can either juice the grass and then dry it, or you can skip the juicing part and simply dry the cut grass, which is then milled into a powder.

Perfect Food RAW uses pure cereal grass juice, which requires between five and six times as much fresh cereal grass but yields a more nutrient-dense powder as compared to a whole grass product. If you're wondering if your green superfood uses juice powder or whole leaf powder, simply look at the label. If the ingredients say "barley grass juice powder," then you're getting a more nutrient-dense and easily digestible version of cereal grasses versus an equal weight of "barley grass powder."

RAW Probiotics

Health Legend:

Élie Metchnikoff, Ph.D.

Several years ago, I thought seriously about taking a trip to the Caucasus Mountains in Bulgaria, a country situated in southeastern Europe and bordering Romania and Serbia. Bulgarian peasants who live in remote mountain hamlets were reputed to have unusually long life spans, and I thought it would be interesting to meet these people and learn what they ate to remain so healthy.

My idea came from reading about a Russian microbiologist named Élie Metchnikof, who studied the remarkable Bulgarians for their longevity a century ago. Born in 1845 in the Ukraine, Élie was the son of a

Élie Metchnikoff, Ph.D.

military officer in the Imperial Guard and a scientific genius. He studied natural sciences at the nearby University of Kharkoff and showed that he was an academic prodigy by completing four years of university in just two years.

Armed with a doctorate in zoology, Metchnikof earned a glowing reputation for his research skills in microbiology. When Louis Pasteur offered him a post at the Pasteur Institute in 1888, Metchnikof moved to Paris to work alongside the world-renowned French chemist and top scientists of his era.

In his studies conducted on starfish, Metchnikof discovered that the amoeba-like cells in their systems engulfed foreign bodies such as bacteria. The Russian established that phagocytes—Greek for "devouring cells"—were the first line of defense against acute infection in most animals. This phenomenon, now known as phagocytosis, became a fundamental principle in modern immunology. For his work on immunity from infectious diseases, Metchnikof was awarded, together with Paul Ehrlich, the Nobel Prize for Physiology and Medicine in 1908.

Metchnikof was in his early sixties when he was catapulted to fame for winning the Nobel Prize, and like anyone getting up there in years, he contemplated his mortality. His view, abetted by research and a hunch, was that the aging process was largely abnormal in modern man. He didn't understand why normal life expectancy in humans wasn't 120 years. He was confident that scientific theories and techniques would someday prevent premature aging and senility.

Metchnikof speculated that senility might be due to illnesses caused by an abnormal ratio of intestinal bacteria, which, in turn, were caused by toxins present in the body due mainly to a poor diet. The Russian researcher laid all the blame on the large intestine, which was "the

reservoir or garbage dump of the digestive processes, and the waste stagnating long enough would rot or putrefy," he said. "The products of putrefaction are harmful."

This thinking fit in with the mindset of the early 20th century that constipation was something to be avoided at all costs. Metchnikof, born Jewish, grew up learning that the call of nature could not be delayed a minute longer than necessary, lest the bowels release more toxins into the bloodstream.

As Metchnikof continued his investigative inquiry into aging, someone told him to check into the Bulgarian peasants living in the Caucasus Mountains, who tended to live to a ripe old age. They certainly did live a long time—an average of eighty-seven years. This was double the average life expectancy of Europeans in the early 1900s, which stood in the mid-forties at the time. In the Bulgarian steppes, however, living to be 100 years old was almost the norm. Good thing the *Today Show* wasn't around back then, or Willard Scott's 100-year-old birthday shout-outs would have taken up the entire show.

Why did the Bulgarian peasants live so long, especially in an undeveloped country lacking basic medical care? What Metchnikof learned was that the Bulgarian peasants consumed large amounts of a fermented or cultured dairy beverage known simply as "sour milk."

Back in those days, the Bulgarian peasants didn't have any refrigerators, so they would lug a tin pail of fresh raw cow's milk to the family cellar. The peasants drank the raw milk, but they left the extra raw milk in the cellar, where it would culture and thicken over the next several days. The result was a tangy thick beverage they called "sour milk," whose modern-day equivalents would be the drinkable yogurt and kefir found in health food stores and high-end grocery stores today.

The Bulgarians really had a thing for this "sour milk," which became known in Europe as Crème Bulgare. According to Metchnikof's empirical observations, consuming Crème Bulgare caused the Bulgarian bowels to become acidic and thereby support the beneficial microflora of the digestive system.

Arguing that the "good" bacteria in the Bulgarian cultured dairy kept the digestive system in check, Metchnikof set off to find what it was in Crème Bulgare that sustained the intestinal flora. The Russian researcher successfully isolated a bacterium in the peasants' cultured dairy and named it *Lactobacillus bulgaricus* (pronounced just the way it looks: *lack-toh-bah-sill-us bull-gare-i-cus*) in honor of the Bulgarians. The *Lactobacillus bulgaricus* populated the intestines and colon with beneficial intestinal flora, he claimed.[†]

Lactobacillus bulgaricus is an example of live lactic acid bacteria that is commonly referred to as a probiotic, which is very important for your digestive system. By definition, probiotics—whose Latin roots mean "for life"—are microscopic organisms that help maintain the natural balance of microflora in the intestines necessary for the proper digestion and assimilation of food. These "good germs" help keep your bowels healthy and running smoothly.

For his groundbreaking work, Metchnikof is known today as the "Father of Probiotics" and is a health legend in my book.

Probiotics are not to be confused with antibiotics, which are better understood by the public. Antibiotics are one of the main weapons that physicians employ to kill harmful bacteria that have invaded the body. Since their discovery in the 1930s, antibiotics have cured millions worldwide suffering from pneumonia, tuberculosis, and meningitis by killing the "bad germs." Consequently, many parents believe that bacteria are bad for you. In fact, I would wager that every time people hear the word bacteria on a TV ad, the adjective *harmful* has been placed in front of it. Case in point: one popular mouthwash says their product "kills harmful bacteria on contact."

For all the good that they do, the downside to antibiotics is that they do not discriminate between good germs and bad germs in the body. This means that while taking the course of an antibiotic, the good bacteria are destroyed along with the bad. Since we live in a culture where folks routinely take an antibiotic for whatever ails them, we need to look for ways to add probiotics to our diets as well as the diets of our children.

Keep in mind that 400 species of microorganisms are said to live inside your body's "terrain"—or internal environment—so when probiotic bacteria are circulating in your gut in the numbers they should be, your body maintains health. Good intestinal flora can aid occasional bloating and gas by controlling the pH level of the intestines through the production of lactic acid.[†] (The pH level refers to the level of acidity versus alkalinity.)

Top Probiotic Foods

Cultured dairy foods like yogurt and kefir (a tart and refreshing beverage similar to a drinkable yogurt) have been the traditional go-to foods for probiotics—the "originals," if you will.

Europeans seem to understand this better than Americans do. Whenever I travel to France, Italy, or Switzerland, I love browsing supermarket aisles where the refrigerated cases are filled with cow's milk yogurt, sheep's milk yogurt, goat's milk yogurt, a hundred varieties of raw cheeses, and several varieties of kefir. The raw dairy products get stacked high into my cart when I'm doing the shopping.

Yogurt is an example of a lacto-fermented food. Fermentation—the culturing or natural processing of foods with the intentional growth of bacteria, yeast, or mold—has a long history. Anthropologists tell us that cultured dairy has been around for thousands of years, from Iran to Greece to Finland, but we get our word *yogurt* from the Turkish word *yoğurt*. Up until Metchnikof's time, though, the only people eating cultured yogurt in abundance were farmers and their families in Eastern Europe and Central Asia—places like Bulgaria.

Yogurt is milk that has been fermented with a culture containing lactic acid-producing bacteria that includes *Lactobacillus bulgaricus*. These friendly bacteria are known for facilitating proper digestion and a healthy gastrointestinal system.[†] Yogurt is high in calcium and potassium, and one cup has more protein than an egg or an ounce of meat.

Yogurt has a tart taste that puckers lips, but much of the commercial yogurt sold in this country is pasteurized and sweetened with natural and artificial sweeteners. Consumers can buy yogurt in flavors like maple syrup, blueberry cheesecake, cinnamon, and piña colada, but the latest trend from commercial yogurt makers is fortifying their yogurt with additional probiotics and selling them at a premium to cash in on the craze for probiotic foods.

While adding probiotics to commercial yogurt sounds like a good thing, the truth is that many of the *real* probiotics were lost during the pasteurization process. Lacto-fermented yogurt made from raw milk that has not been pasteurized or homogenized can be healthier for you because you'll be consuming more beneficial probiotic bacteria.

While whole organic yogurt from cow's milk is beneficial, I highly recommend purchasing yogurts derived from goat's milk and sheep's milk, which are easier on stomachs because they do not contain the same complex proteins found in modern cow's milk. (Most cow's milk produced in America today has an abundance of a protein that can be an allergen or irritant to many individuals. Heritage breeds of cattle are more likely to have greater health benefits.) Goat's milk and sheep's milk yogurts are readily available at natural grocers, although my personal favorite—yogurt made from sheep's milk—is more difficult to find. Ask the store dairy manager to order some.

If you are able to find raw cow's milk yogurt from grass-fed cattle that come from a breed other than a Holstein—for example, a Jersey, Guernsey, or Brown Swiss—that would be more beneficial for your health.

Let's Hear It for Kefir

I've noticed that when I talk to audiences about kefir, I receive some blank looks. It amazes me that many people still don't know what kefir is. Maybe it's due to the fact that there are no national advertising campaigns for kefir—like you see for certain brands of yogurt—and many supermarket chains don't carry the product at all. You usually have to go to natural food grocers or health food stores to find kefir.

It's worth the effort, though. Raw, organic whole milk kefir, sold in ready-to-drink quart bottles, is a tart-tasting, thick beverage containing naturally occurring bacteria and yeasts that work synergistically to provide superior health benefits. Kefir is also a great base ingredient to build smoothies around: just add eight ounces of kefir into a blender, an assortment of frozen berries or fruits, a spoonful of raw honey, and you're well on the way to churning up a delicious, satisfying breakfast or afternoon snack.

When people ask me the difference between yogurt and kefir, besides the drinkability of the latter, my reply is that kefir differs from yogurt in that it has healthy yeasts in addition to healthy bacteria, which is why some have called kefir the "champagne of milk." Besides the beneficial bacteria and yeast, kefir contains calcium, phosphorus, magnesium, and vitamins A, B2, B12, D, and K. Tryptophan, one of the essential amino acids abundant in kefir, is well known for its relaxing effect on the nervous system.[†]

Whatever you add to your diet—yogurt or kefir or both—you'll be consuming a healthy product that's more nutritious than milk. Cultured dairy is much higher in B vitamin content and vitamin C, and the protein is the very highest quality available in human consumption. Dr. William Campbell Douglass, author of *The Milk Book*, wrote that yogurt and kefir can help to balance the microorganisms in the gut and may support the cardiovascular and immune systems as well.[†]

Kefir originated in ancient times when Eastern nomadic shepherds discovered that fresh milk carried in leather pouches would eventually ferment into a deliciously effervescent

[†] These statements have not been evaluated by the Food and Drug Administration. This product is not intended to diagnose, treat, cure or prevent any disease.

beverage. The word "kefir" (pronounced kee-fur) is thought to originate from another Turkish word *keif,* meaning "good feeling"—no doubt for the sense of well-being you experience after drinking it.

During fermentation, peptides and exopolysaccharides produced by a variety of lactic acid bacteria have been shown to have bioactive properties. According to Canadian researcher Edward R. Farnworth, clinical studies have shown that kefir supports the immune system, balances microflora in the gut, and supports healthy cholesterol levels already in the normal range.[†]

Thank goodness I discovered raw kefir when I was in San Diego back in the mid-1990s. More than fifteen years later, I still drink raw milk kefir regularly because I want to keep my immune system in balance and my gut populated with health-supporting microbes.[†] I've found a wonderful source of raw kefir from a Pennsylvania farm, and I often make my own kefir at home from raw milk. I make sure I keep my garage refrigerator stocked—just like I kept kefir on hand in my coolers back in my motor home in San Diego.

If you don't have access to raw milk, you can purchase or make your own kefir from coconut water, which is the sweet liquid found inside coconuts. Raw coconut kefir is a delicious and healthy effervescent beverage that provides billions of probiotics and a significant amount of potassium.

When it comes to consuming the best probiotic foods for yourself and your family, I've compiled a great list that will flood your body with powerful enzymes and billions of friendly bacteria.

So here's my list of Top 10 Probiotic Foods:

1. **Kefir** trumps yogurt for reasons I just mentioned. Look for plain whole milk kefir, or make it yourself from raw milk you buy at your local farm.

2. **Yogurt** is milk that has been fermented with a culture containing the lactic acid-producing bacteria *Streptococcus thermophilus* and *Lactobacillus bulgaricus*, which are friendly bacteria known for supporting proper digestion and a healthy gastrointestinal system.[†]

3. **Really raw cheese,** made from raw milk that has not been heated above the body temperature of a cow, is a great source of probiotics as well as vitamins and minerals.

4. **Sauerkraut** is an example of a fermented vegetable that contains digestive enzymes that help break down food and increase its digestibility.[†] Too bad you see this fermented cabbage on American plates only around Oktoberfest time or on top of a sodium-laden, highly processed food affectionately known as a "hot dog."

5. **Pickled carrots, beets, and cucumbers** are fermented vegetables that may be greeted with upturned noses at the dinner table, but these foods help reestablish natural balance to your digestive system.[†]

6. **Coconut kefir** is a delicious and healthy effervescent beverage that provides billions of probiotics and beneficial compounds including minerals. Coconut kefir was popularized by health author and nutrition expert Donna Gates, author of *The Body Ecology Diet*, and it's a wonderful tonic to promote digestive wellness.[†]

7. **Miso** is a well-known form of fermented soybean paste, and miso soup often accompanies meals served in Japanese restaurants in this country.

8. **Soy sauce,** also derived from soybeans, is a probiotic-rich food.

9. **Kimchi,** a staple of the Korean diet for centuries, is a peppery fermented cabbage that is served at almost every meal in South Korea.
   Low in calories and high in fiber, kimchi is an excellent resource for lactic acid bacteria, which aids in digestion.[†]

10. **Pickled ginger,** the world's most widely cultivated spice, contains compounds that support healthy, balanced intestinal microflora.

The Need for RAW Probiotics

I think everyone can agree that our bodies need a good dose of probiotics every day. It's getting them into your system that can be a real challenge.

Let's start with yogurt and kefir, the "sour milk" if you will, that Metchnikof found so promising for longevity. Raw cultured dairy is very difficult to purchase in this country, and like I mentioned earlier, illegal in a majority of states. I have to buy my raw dairy products directly from a farm in Pennsylvania and have everything shipped to my Florida home, which makes it inconvenient, to say the least.

What about those folks who want raw dairy but have no access to dairy farmers who raise cows on grasses and organic feed or find out-of-state shipments too expensive? Where does someone in downtown New York and Chicago even begin to shop for raw cultured dairy?

I know how difficult it is to find raw dairy because I've crisscrossed this country dozens of times and have stayed in more than a hundred different cities and towns. Unless the city or suburb is legally allowed to sell raw dairy or local farms and coops are nearby, raw dairy won't be available.

[†] These statements have not been evaluated by the Food and Drug Administration. This product is not intended to diagnose, treat, cure or prevent any disease.

As of the writing of this book, the most widely available and beneficial source of raw dairy is really raw cheese. Really raw cheese is rich in probiotics and important fat-soluble vitamins, and it's usually available at fine health food stores nationwide (see the Raw Truth Resource Guide). Please note that many important cheeses are made from raw milk, but it's hard to determine if the cows were grass-fed.

If you're having a difficult time procuring raw dairy products, however, I have the no-brainer solution to help you get the powerful probiotics, raw food vitamins, minerals, enzymes, and beneficial compounds found in yogurt and kefir each and every day, and that's by supplementing with one of the brand-new probiotic formulas called RAW Probiotics from Garden of Life. First of all, RAW Probiotics are raw, meaning they are uncooked, untreated, and unadulterated.

When we set out to formulate a line of probiotic supplements at Garden of Life, I told my team that I wanted these formulas to nutritionally match, if possible, what the Bulgarians peasants were receiving in their "sour milk" during Metchnikof's time. I wanted to create probiotic supplements from the "original source," and we did just that.

First, we made inquiries and found—in Eastern Europe—original yogurt and kefir cultures that have been handed down for thousands of years, from one family to the next. These dairy cultures contain a diverse amount of probiotic-created vitamins and minerals, including the same probiotic that Metchnikof discovered and later named *Lactobacillus bulgaricus*.

In addition, due to the fact that cultured dairy and its organisms create digestive enzymes to help break down milk protein and milk sugar lactose, we made sure we provided high amounts of these enzymes to aid in the digestion of dairy foods.[†] To achieve the robust health of the Bulgarians, Metchnikof recommended consuming sixteen or more ounces of the "sour milk." RAW Probiotics contain a similar number of probiotic cultures found in sixteen ounces of fermented dairy.

We found a source for a wild Eastern European kefir culture as well, which gave us the unprecedented diversity of more than thirty species of probiotics in each RAW Probiotics formula. We also included raw fruits and vegetables directly from the region of the legendary long-living Bulgarians, and RAW Probiotics contain carefully selected species and strains of probiotics.

Each RAW Probiotics formula is "full spectrum," meaning we have the probiotics and enzymes found in raw, cultured dairy products such as yogurt and kefir as well as vitamins and minerals created from the same probiotic first discovered by Metchnikof,, *Lactobacillus bulgaricus,* plus eight different raw fruits and vegetables.

Arrive Alive!™ Potency Promise

One other important aspect of RAW Probiotics is the care we take in making sure that the probiotics you purchase **Arrive Alive!™** One of the reasons so many probiotic supplements have such large CFU counts (colony-forming units per gram—a potency measure) is due to the fact that there is an expected die-off of some of the probiotics between the time they are manufactured and the time they are consumed. When you see the words "50 billion CFU per serving," that statement is often followed by the phrase "at time of manufacture." It is very hard for the consumer to know—and have confidence in—the number on the bottle.

For RAW Probiotics, we wanted to remove the doubt. That is why we use our own Arrive Alive process, which ensures our probiotics are handled in such a way that you can feel confident that you're getting a full 85 billion CFU in every serving.

Our exclusive eight-point Arrive Alive!™ system—a "fresh approach" on how probiotics are delivered from the manufacturer to you—works like this:

1. **RAW Probiotics are grown in a state-of-the-art, temperature-controlled culturing facility.**
2. **When the probiotics are fully grown, they are immediately put into frozen storage.**
3. **The probiotics are packed in dry ice and then shipped overnight to our manufacturing facility.**
4. **Upon arrival, the probiotics are immediately transferred to freezer units and stored below 39 degrees.**
5. **RAW Probiotics are blended and encapsulated in a facility that is exclusively dedicated for that purpose—meaning it is kept cold and at the proper humidity (below 40 percent) throughout the process.**
6. **After blending and encapsulating, the probiotics are immediately moved back into cold storage.**
7. **Finished bottles and cartons are picked and placed into special containers, along with desiccants (moisture-absorbing agents) and ice packs so that they remain at optimal temperature and relative humidity all the way to the store.**
8. **Upon arrival, retailers are instructed to immediately place RAW Probiotics™ in the cooler for display.**

The Arrive Alive!™ Potency Promise requires a great deal of extra time and cost—but our promise to you is that we will do everything we can in our power to ensure that what you see on the label is what you get in the bottle.

RAW Probiotics

Below is a list of the what Raw Probiotics formulas support:

- supports colon health, bowel regularity and overall digestive function[†]
- supports gut-related immune system function and overall immune system health[†]
- supports healthy microbial balance by promoting healthy bacteria in the gut[†]
- supports healthy nutrient absorption and assimilation[†]
- relieves occasional gas and constipation[†]

The following RAW Probiotics are available in your local health food store:

RAW Probiotics™ Men contains 85 billion probiotic cultures from thirty-one species of probiotics as well as vitamins, minerals, enzymes, Bulgarian yogurt concentrate, and Eastern European wild kefir culture to support the unique digestive and immune system needs of men, including increased energy and stamina.[†]

Targeted benefits for men:

- supports healthy stress levels, as well as prostate and heart health[†]

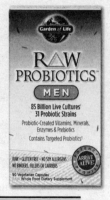

RAW Probiotics™ Women contains 85 billion probiotic cultures from thirty-two species of probiotics as well as vitamins, minerals, enzymes, Bulgarian yogurt concentrate, and Eastern European wild kefir culture to support the unique digestive and immune system needs of women, including support for the female urinary tract and reproductive system.[†]

Targeted benefits for women:

- supports vaginal health and healthy thyroid function[†]
- emerging science suggests vitamin D supports breast health[†]

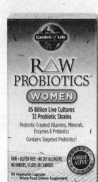

RAW Probiotics™ Men 50 and Wiser contains 85 billion probiotic cultures from thirty-two species of probiotics as well as vitamins, minerals, enzymes, Bulgarian yogurt concentrate, and Eastern European wild kefir culture to support the unique digestive and immune system needs of men fifty years of age and older.[†]

Targeted benefits for
Men 50 & Wiser:

- helps maintain healthy blood sugar levels that are already in the normal range[†]
- helps maintain healthy cholesterol levels that are already in the normal range[†]

RAW Probiotics™ Women 50 and Wiser contains 85 billion probiotic cultures than thirty-three species of probiotics as well as vitamins, minerals, enzymes, Bulgarian yogurt concentrate, and Eastern European wild kefir culture to support the unique digestive and immune system needs of women fifty years of age and older.[†]

Targeted benefits for
Women 50 & Wiser:

- helps maintain healthy cholesterol levels that are already in the normal range[†]
- emerging science suggests vitamin D supports breast health[†]

RAW Probioitcs™ Kids

RAW Probiotics™ Kids is a great-tasting certified organic probiotic powder containing clinically studied probiotic cultures to support the unique digestive and immune system needs of infants and children.[†]

Now you have the option to consume probiotic-rich foods when you can find them *and* supplement with a raw, whole food, original source, full spectrum, high potency probiotic supplement—RAW Probiotics.

[†] These statements have not been evaluated by the Food and Drug Administration. This product is not intended to diagnose, treat, cure or prevent any disease.

CHAPTER 5

RAW Enzymes

Health Legend:

Edward Howell, M.D.

THE RAW TRUTH

Back in the 19th century, the baseline of scientific knowledge relating to the human diet was that we needed to consume the proteins in meat, the carbohydrates in grains, the fats in dairy, and a little salt to stay healthy. No one had discovered enzymes yet, which are small bioactive proteins that act as catalysts, meaning they start and speed up chemical reactions in the body.

Dr. Edward Howell

That started to change in the late 1800s when German biochemist Wilhelm Kühne uncovered a biological catalyst in pancreatic juice that degraded or broke down other substances. He called this catalyst an *enzyme* after the Greek words *en*, meaning "in," and *zyme*, meaning "yeast" or "leaven."

As scientific inquiry advanced the knowledge of enzymes in the early 20th century, researchers learned that enzymes were essential for digestion, cellular energy, tissue and organ repair, and brain activity. A Chicago medical doctor, Edward Howell, who lived from 1898 to 1988, was fascinated by the complex role that enzymes played in the body. From 1930 until his retirement in 1970, Dr. Howell made enzymes the focus of extensive clinical and laboratory research. Because he was the first person to "get it" when it came to recognizing the vital role that enzymes from raw foods play in our health, Dr. Edward Howell deserves recognition as a health legend.

Not much is known about the personal life of Dr. Howell, who earned his medical degree in 1924 in the state of Illinois. He was on the professional staff of Lindlahr Sanitarium in Elmhurst, Illinois, for six years before branching off on his own and establishing a private facility for the treatment of chronic ailments by nutritional and physical methods. For four decades, Dr. Howell treated patients and studied the role of enzymes and how they act as catalysts for all chemical reactions in the body. For his body of work, he leaves behind a legacy as the "Father of Food and Digestive Enzymes."

When Dr. Howell started his quest eighty years ago, scientists had identified eighty enzymes; today, more than 5,000 enzymes have been discovered, and researchers are learning more each day about enzymes and their profound effects on our health. Our minds can barely comprehend how complex enzymes are when you consider that a single human liver cell contains at least 1,000 enzyme systems.

What's notable about Dr. Howell is that he was the first researcher to recognize the importance of enzymes in food. He wrote *The Status of Food Enzymes in Digestion and Metabolism* in

1946, and then he spent the next twenty years completing his seminal work, *Enzyme Nutrition*. His extensive clinical and laboratory research prompted him to sound the alarm about the importance of consuming raw foods to ensure a proper level of enzyme activity.

Enzymes are the driving forces behind virtually every biochemical reaction that occurs in the human body. Made of tiny proteins, or amino acids, enzymes turn food into energy and unlock this energy for use in the body. Without enzymes, life would slow to a standstill because chemical reactions inside our bodies wouldn't happen fast enough. In addition, any minerals, vitamins, and hormones inside the body could not work without the help of enzymes.

The body's digestive system produces a substantial number of different enzymes, but the body needs specific enzymes that can only be obtained directly from raw foods in the diet, which I'll get into in a moment.

For now, let's take a closer look at the three different types of enzymes:

- **Metabolic enzymes** are produced by the pancreas and perform a wide variety of functions. Breathing, eating, sleeping, digestion, absorption of nutrients, moving around, working, growth, blood circulation, immunity build-up, sexual function, and sensory perception—all are dependent on metabolic enzymes.
- **Digestive enzymes** are found in the mouth and the digestive tract, where they aid in the digestion of food. Digestive enzymes are secreted by the stomach, pancreas, and small intestine.
- **Food enzymes** are found only in raw foods and help initiate the process of digestion in the mouth and stomach. So while our digestive organs produce enzymes internally, the rest must come from *uncooked foods*—I've italicized the words for emphasis—such as fresh fruits and vegetables, raw sprouted seeds and grains, and unpasteurized dairy products. Food enzymes can also be consumed in the form of raw food enzyme supplements.

Food enzymes are vital to the body because they can help you pre-digest the food before it reaches the small intestine, thereby reducing the need of the pancreas to produce more digestive enzymes. Enzymes do their work by making it easier for two proteins to react together, which is important since hundreds of thousands of reactions take place in your body every minute.

For example, your central nervous system is busy processing information while your digestive system is breaking down the foods from your last meal. Your immune system is fighting off germs and toxins that have entered the body. Your brain is thinking, your heart is beating, and millions of cells are being made and replaced as other internal systems carry out a multitude of intricate processes. All of these functions involve numerous enzymes, which explains why they are essential to the life process.

Breaking Down Enzymes

The total number of enzymes in our bodies can only be speculated, and the number of individual enzyme molecules is virtually inestimable.

That said, the following food enzymes are critical for our overall health:

- **Protease** is a member of a large group of enzymes that have a variety of functions in the body, the primary one aiding in the digestion and assimilation of protein.[†] In other words, without protease, the body would not be able to digest the protein in food.

- **Bromelain** is a protease enzyme that comes from either the stem or the fruit of pineapple. Bromelain aids digestion and supports healthy and natural inflammation response in the body.[†]

- **Papain** is a protease enzyme found naturally in unripe papayas and has been used for centuries in South America to support digestion.[†]

- **Peptidase** is a naturally occurring enzyme that helps metabolize proteins in the body and plays an important role in the digestive, immune, and circulatory systems.[†]

- **Dipeptidyl peptidase IV** is a digestive enzyme that detoxifies gluten and beta casein in the digestive tract.[†]

- **Amylase** breaks down starch and converts it into sugar. You'll find amylase in saliva, where it begins the chemical process of digestion by breaking down food before it's swallowed and sent into the digestive tract.[†]

- **Invertases and sucrases** break down sucrose, or what we call table sugar.

- **Glucoamylase** is a digestive enzyme that breaks down components of starches into sugars.

- **Maltase** is an enzyme that breaks down maltose into the simple sugar glucose.

- **Xylanase** is an enzyme that breaks down a component of plant cell walls containing a compound known as xylose.

- **Beta glucanase** is an enzyme that acts on glucan, which is a fiber component found in barley and oats.

- **Cellulase** refers to a class of enzymes that humans don't naturally produce but must consume from raw foods in their diet. Cellulase breaks down the plant fiber cellulose for better digestion and absorption of nutrients.[†]

[†] These statements have not been evaluated by the Food and Drug Administration. This product is not intended to diagnose, treat, cure or prevent any disease.

- **Hemicellulase** is an enzyme that breaks down a plant's cell wall interior, which is known as hemicellulose.

- **Pectinase** breaks down pectin, which is a component in certain fruits and vegetables such as grapes and apples.

- **Phytase** is an enzyme that breaks down the indigestible parts of grains.

- **Lactase** is an enzyme in the small intestine that digests lactose, the sugar in milk and other dairy products.

- **Alpha galactosidase** breaks down the sugars in the complex carbohydrates found in vegetables, grains, and legumes, including beans. It's a process that often leads to the reduction of gases that causes the occasional case of bloating and flatulence.[†]

- **Lipase** is an enzyme that the body uses to break down fats in foods so they can be absorbed in the intestines.

Okay, the college chemistry class is over. I hope you were taking notes because I would like to give you a pop quiz about your digestive health.

Answer true or false to these statements:

- PEOPLE TELL ME I EAT TOO QUICKLY AND WOLF DOWN MY FOOD.

- I OCCASIONALLY FEEL BLOATED AFTER FINISHING MY MEAL.

- AFTER EATING, I CAN USUALLY COUNT ON BURPING OR PASSING GAS.

- I EAT A LOT OF MEAT—AT LEAST TWO MEALS A DAY.

- I ENJOY SWEET FOODS REGULARLY.

- I LOVE TO EAT AT LEAST ONE LARGE MEAL A DAY.

- I FREQUENTLY EXPERIENCE LOW ENERGY THIRTY MINUTES AFTER EACH MEAL.

- I'M MORE THAN THIRTY YEARS OLD.

If you answer "true" to at least five of these eight questions, then you should be very excited to learn more about the benefits of enzymes, which break down fats, promote protein utilization, and help detoxify the body.

To ensure your body is functioning optimally, make sure you're continually stocked up on enzymes by consuming raw foods and raw digestive enzyme supplements so that your body has what it needs to break down food and utilize the nutrients contained within that food.

Before we go any further, let's examine how enzymes facilitate the digestive process. When food is chewed and swallowed, it moves to the stomach and then to the small intestine, followed by the large intestine. At each step along the way, specific enzymes break down different components of food, starting with enzymes in your saliva that begin to break down food before it enters the digestive tract, where other enzymes will get to work breaking down the protein, fats, and carbohydrates within the foods.

Ideally, all the enzymes work together, digesting food and delivering nutrients to cells to maintain your health. Equally as important, by breaking down components of food, enzymes prevent undigested material from traveling to the colon, where it could be a potential breeding ground for toxicity.

To make sure that your body has the digestive enzymes it needs to break down the proteins, fats, and carbohydrates in your meals, Dr. Howell declared that it's very important to eat raw foods and fermented raw foods that are high in raw enzymes. Raw foods are the best source of raw food enzymes because when you cook or heat food, many enzymes are deactivated—a nice way of saying destroyed—at a wet-heat temperature as low as 118 degrees Fahrenheit and a dry-heat temperature as low as 150 degrees. It could be a design of nature that foods and liquids at 117 degrees can be touched without burning you, but liquids over 118 degrees will burn you. Thus, there is a built-in mechanism for determining whether or not the food you eat still contains its enzyme content.

While heating fruits, vegetables, meats, eggs, and dairy does a number on enzymes, *boiling* food is a complete obliteration. "Whenever a food is boiled at 212 degrees, the enzymes in it are 100 percent destroyed," Dr. Howell said.

Whether boiled, heated, or left alone, enzymes are delicate dynamos. Since enzymes begin to be destroyed when they reach a temperature of 118 degrees Fahrenheit and stay at that temperature for a period of time, eating steamed and cooked vegetables—or any other food—gives you far fewer of the these powerful biochemical catalysts necessary for digestion, breathing, talking, moving, cellular energy, tissue and organ repair, neutralization of toxins, and brain activity.

† These statements have not been evaluated by the Food and Drug Administration. This product is not intended to diagnose, treat, cure or prevent any disease.

Dr. Howell pointed out in his writings that humans and animals on a diet comprised largely of cooked food, particularly grains, had poorer health that became evident when certain organs were examined postmortem.

Sally Fallon Morell, author of *Nourishing Traditions*, wrote that Dr. Howell formulated the following Enzyme Nutrition Axiom, which is that the length of life is inversely proportional to the rate of exhaustion of the enzyme potential of an organism. In other words, when your enzyme bank account is empty, life ceases to exist.

"Another sage rule can be expressed as follows: Whole foods give good health; enzyme-rich foods provide limitless energy," said Sally Fallon Morell.

Top Enzyme Foods

Based on Dr. Howell's research, the best way to insure adequate enzyme activity in the body is through the consumption of raw fruits and vegetables, fermented raw foods, and raw enzyme supplements.

Did you know that the standard American meat-and-potatoes diet of broiled streak, baked potato, and steamed vegetables has little if any enzymes? And let's not even discuss fast food meals.

A great way to bolster your enzyme bank account is to regularly consume my Top 10 Enzyme-Rich Foods:

1. **Raw cultured dairy yogurt and kefir** from grass-fed cows has sixty known fully intact and functional enzymes. Some of the enzymes are native to raw milk, while others come from the beneficial bacteria growing in the milk. A few of the many enzymes are amylase and bacterial-produced lactase, lipases, and phosphatases that break down lactose (the milk sugar), fat like triglycerides, and starch, making milk more digestible and freeing up key minerals such as calcium.

2. **Wild salmon ceviche,** which is marinated in lemon or lime juice, is loaded with proteases, which are protein-digesting enzymes.

3. **Raw butter** is a supreme source of lipases—fat-splitting enzymes that support our health in the areas of immune function and brain and nervous system health.[†]

4. **Raw sauerkraut** is a fermented veggie that is consumed as a healthful food in various cultures around the world, but here in this country, most commercially available sauerkraut is processed with heat and made with vinegar, which eliminates the naturally occurring enzymes beneficial to the digestive tract.

5. **Avocados,** with their creamy, rich texture, provide protein, healthy unsaturated fats, and enzymes galore, especially lipase. If my salad doesn't have avocado, I feel like something is missing.

6. **Bananas** are another enzyme-rich food, but note of caution: the more bananas ripen, the more enzymes that are disintegrated in the process. Try to eat bananas before they are overripe.

7. **Pineapple** is the main source of bromelain, a protein-digesting enzyme, which has been used for centuries to support healthy inflammation.† The less ripe the pineapple, the more enzymes.

8. **Papaya**, another fruit native to Central America and tropical latitudes, contains papain, a digestive enzyme more abundant in green, unripe fruits. Papain has a mild and soothing effect on the stomach.† When isolated, papain is used as a meat tenderizer because of the way it breaks down proteins.

9. **Raw coconut kefir** is a delicious and healthy effervescent beverage that provides billions of probiotics and is loaded with enzymes and beneficial minerals such as potassium. Two ounces of raw coconut kefir before a meal is great for digestion.†

10. **Alfalfa sprouts** contain enzymes like lipase to break down fat; amylase to break down carbohydrates and convert them into sucrase; pectinase to digest starches; and protease to digest proteins.

Sprouting is a process that has been used for centuries to make seeds and grains easier to digest—and to increase the bioavailability of their nutrients. During his research, Dr. Howell observed that sprouted food increased enzyme and nutrient activity. These enzymes acted upon the seeds and grains to make them more digestible. In essence, the enzymes activated in the sprouting process work to pre-digest the food, making it more body friendly.

Sprouting also deactivates a compound known as phytic acid, which is found in the coats of many seeds. Phytic acid can bind with minerals that are important to the body and block their absorption into the bloodstream.

Let me finish this section with a riddle, and it goes like this: Can you name the only vegetable or fruit that is never sold frozen, canned, processed, cooked, or in any other form except fresh?

Give up? The answer is *lettuce.*

Introducing RAW Enzymes

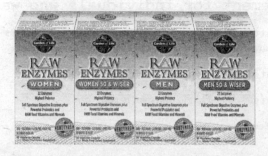

As I mentioned earlier, Dr. Howell poured *twenty* years into researching and writing a single book known as *Enzyme Nutrition*. I have a copy of this health classic, which is actually a condensed version of a work that once was as long as 700 pages with 160,000 words.

To help the body with digestion, the answer is to eat more raw food in its natural, unprocessed state, but that isn't always possible, especially if you're traveling and dining out or have a heavy social schedule back home. If you're having trouble finding a way to eat enough raw, fresh foods like raw cultured dairy products (which are difficult to obtain), if you can't stand the taste of raw sauerkraut, if certain fresh fruits are out of season, or if each cooked meal you eat ends with a five-alarm fire in your gut, then I urge you to try RAW Enzymes with your next meal.

RAW Enzymes—a whole food enzyme formula providing raw enzymes and powerful probiotics that serve as "enzyme factories"—work overtime for your digestive health.† RAW Enzymes support the digestion of proteins, fats, carbohydrates, and fiber as well as difficult-to-digest components of dairy and grains such as lactose such as gluten.†

I've been using digestive enzymes since I learned about them during my digestive health journey. What I've gleaned from personal experience is that without the proper levels of enzymes in foods—either raw or fermented—and supplementing your diet with a raw, full spectrum, whole food enzyme supplement, people become more susceptible to occasional post-meal gas and bloating as well as low energy levels.†

RAW Enzymes is the first gender- and age-specific raw enzyme formula with higher-potency digestive enzymes per capsule than any other product available today. Ideal for high-protein or high-carbohydrate and fiber diets, RAW Enzymes contain enzymes to help with the digestion of a wide variety of proteins and carbohydrates, including soluble and insoluble fiber.†

RAW Enzymes is a perfect digestive health supplement for individuals who want to:

- **support the digestion process of difficult-to-digest foods such as dairy, grains, sugars, nuts, seeds, beans, broccoli, and cabbage[†]**

- **support colon health and overall digestive function[†]**

- **support gut-related immune system health[†]**

- **reduce occasional post-meal gas and bloating[†]**

We've found RAW Enzymes to be ideal for anyone who wants to support digestive health as well as the other important systems of the body.[†] When stress is reduced in the digestive system, which has a heavy workload breaking down and assimilating the food that comes its way, more energy and thus more metabolic enzymes are made available to other systems of the body responsible for overall health.[†]

As the highest potency, raw plant-based enzyme blend on the planet, RAW Enzymes is the best choice for those who are lipase deficient and need enzymes help to break down fats that can be absorbed in the intestines.[†] Encapsulated in easy-to-swallow capsules, RAW Enzymes is a full-spectrum formula for the entire meal, meaning that the full complement of enzymes for proteins, carbohydrates, fats, and sugars are made available to the digestive system.

Our proprietary enzyme formula is raw, plant-based, and vegetarian, making it ideal for anyone seeking a source of powerful enzymes that would be otherwise available only from raw animal foods and organs and fermented raw dairy foods. RAW Enzymes is non-GMO, meaning no genetically modified organisms were used, and it contains digestive enzymes produced through controlled fermentation of select microbial species. This full-spectrum, high-activity digestive formula is enhanced with specialized enzymes for the digestion of fibers, sugars, and other normally indigestible plant constituents.

A Host of Benefits

Like RAW Probiotics™, RAW Enzymes™ has a long list of incredible benefits. Here's what these totally raw, whole food enzyme formulas can do for you:

- **help your body process difficult-to-digest foods such as dairy, grains, sugars, nuts, seeds, beans, broccoli, and cabbage[†]**

- **support colon health and overall digestive function[†]**

† These statements have not been evaluated by the Food and Drug Administration. This product is not intended to diagnose, treat, cure or prevent any disease.

- support gut-related immune system health[†]

- reduce occasional post-meal gas and bloating[†]

- pH-optimized enzyme support for the entire digestive tract[†]

RAW Enzymes come in various unique formulas for the complex health needs of each individual:

RAW Enzymes™ Men is a raw, whole food enzyme formula that contains twenty-two vegetarian digestive enzymes, raw food vitamins and minerals, antioxidant enzymes, and powerful live probiotics to support the unique digestive system needs of men.

Targeted benefits for men:

- **supports prostate health, heart health and a healthy metabolism[†]**

RAW Enzymes™ Women is a raw, whole food enzyme formula that contains twenty-two vegetarian digestive enzymes, raw food vitamins and minerals, antioxidant enzymes, and powerful live probiotics to support the unique digestive system needs of women as well as breast health and the female reproductive system.[†]

Targeted benefits for women:

- **supports bone health and a healthy metabolism[†]**
- **emerging science suggests that vitamin D supports breast health[†]**

THE RAW TRUTH

RAW Enzymes™ Men 50 and Wiser is a raw, whole food enzyme formula with twenty-two vegetarian digestive enzymes, raw food vitamins and minerals, antioxidant enzymes, and powerful live probiotics to support the unique digestive system needs of men fifty years of age and older as well as prostate health.

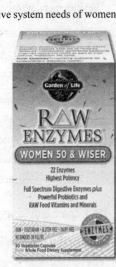

Targeted benefits for Men 50 & Wiser:

- supports prostate health, heart health and a healthy metabolism†

- as men age, they tend to experience a drop in stomach acid production ,which impacts protein digestion. This formula provides amplified strength of fat-digesting enzymes plus the highest available potency of protein-digesting enzymes

---

RAW Enzymes™ Women 50 and Wiser is a raw, whole food enzyme formula that contains twenty-two vegetarian digestive enzymes, raw food vitamins and minerals, antioxidant enzymes and powerful live probiotics to support the unique digestive system needs of women fifty years of age and older.†

Targeted benefits for Women 50 & Wiser:

- supports bone health and a healthy metabolism†

- emerging science suggests that vitamin D supports breast health†

- as women age, they tend to experience a drop in stomach acid production, which impacts protein digestion. This formula provides amplified strength of carbohydrate-digesting enzymes plus the highest available potency of protein-digesting enzymes

RAW Enzymes™ is the next generation of enzymes, formulated to address the complex digestive needs of men and women of all ages.

† These statements have not been evaluated by the Food and Drug Administration. This product is not intended to diagnose, treat, cure or prevent any disease.

RAW Fiber

Health Legend:

Denis Burkitt, M.D.

It was a childhood tragedy that would cause sleepless nights for any parent.

Denis Burkitt, born in 1911, grew up in the picturesque county of Fermanagh, now in Northern Ireland. The centuries-long tension between Protestants and Catholics was strong as ever one hundred years ago on the Emerald Isle.

Dr. Denis Burkitt

Raised in a Protestant family, Denis was eleven years old and walking to school when a group of Catholic boys attacked him. They pummeled him with punches and beat him so savagely that he lost one eye. It's hard to imagine how boys could be so cruel, but the loss of one eye would shape Denis's life, and in a way, help us understand the importance of fiber in our diets.

Denis grew up in a deeply religious family, so his faith helped him through the tragedy of losing an eye. His parents imbued him with a strong tradition of service to others, and an uncle who served as a medical missionary in Kenya influenced the young man as well. When Denis attended Trinity College in Dublin with the idea of becoming an engineer, his heart wasn't in it, however. He sensed God was leading him into medicine.

He completed his medical training at the Edinburgh Royal College of Surgeons in 1938 and applied for a position overseas in one of the British colonies. When his application was rejected because of his glass right eye, he suspected that he was turned down because of his religious zeal. Then World War II started, and surgeons of any stripe were in high demand. The British Army posted him and his wife, Olive, in Kenya, Somalia, and Uganda throughout the war. He showed his superiors that even with one eye, he could save lives in the operating room. Following the war, the talented surgeon applied to the Colonial Medical Service for work in East Africa and was posted to Uganda in 1946 as a government surgeon.

From 1949 to 1964, Dr. Burkitt noticed a few things. One was that the British residents in Uganda showed a high incidence of constipation, hemorrhoids, and diverticula (pouches in the colon). The native Ugandan population, however, rarely displayed any signs of any of those health challenges.

Dr. Burkitt theorized that dietary differences were the reason for the high incidence of serious digestive problems in Westerners. The British ate a meat-and-potatoes diet with very few fruits and vegetables, and they built a social life around afternoon tea, which was really an excuse to snack on cakes and scones with a spot of sugared tea and milk. The native

population, however, consumed plenty of fruits and vegetables. Processed flour and white sugar were either too expensive or generally unavailable to them.

The Irish surgeon made detailed observations of his patients' bowel habits and noted how the Africans produced much more feces than the Brits. Western diets were so dense in calories and low in bulk that their intestines didn't pass enough volume to remain healthy, while the feces of Ugandans was soft and produced with negligible discomfort. Why was this happening?

The conclusion that Dr. Burkitt arrived at was the lack of fiber in the British diet. The Irish doctor, who was quick with a quip, said, "If you pass small stools, you have to have large hospitals."

Today, just about everyone knows about the importance of fiber in the diet, but fifty years ago, Dr. Burkitt's contention that we should eat plenty of fiber-rich foods was revolutionary. The spike in digestive-related diseases in England and the United States, Dr. Burkitt said, could be traced back to 1890 following the introduction of a new milling technique that removed fiber from whole grain to produce white flour. We were merely reaping what we sowed, he said.

In a sense, Dr. Burkitt saw things with his one eye that others missed in plain sight: he was the first to link the emergence of intestinal problems, colon, and heart health issues with a low intake of dietary fiber. Dr. Burkitt claimed he could predict the number of a patient's hospital visits from the size and frequency of their bowel movements. Those who ate charred steaks, pan-fried potatoes, and ice cream for dessert were strong candidates to come down with the "diseases of civilization," as Dr. Burkitt called constipation and hemorrhoids. Those with high intakes of fiber-rich fruits and vegetables, like the Ugandans, had more frequent and bulkier stools and less digestive issues.

Dr. Burkitt was known for taking pictures of piles of human feces during his early morning walks in the African bush and showing them at medical conferences. During one talk before an audience of gastroenterologists, he asked, "How many of you have any idea of the size of your spouse's stool?" After the rumblings of laughter died down, Dr. Burkitt drove home the message that more fiber in the diet would increase stool weight and reduce stool density, two variables that were epidemiologically linked with the reduction in the incidence of several diseases.

"Western doctors are like poor plumbers," he said. "They treat a leaking tube by cleaning up the water. These plumbers are extremely adept at drying up the water, constantly inventing new, expensive, and refined methods. Somebody should teach them how to close the tap."

Dr. Burkitt's insight and advocacy moved "the fiber hypothesis" from obscurity to the forefront of science with the publication of an important study called "Dietary Fiber and Disease" in the *Journal of the American Medical Association (JAMA)* in 1974. In the decade following publication of this groundbreaking research, a consensus developed in the United States and Great Britain that fiber was missing in modern diets and needed to be reintroduced.

Dr. Burkitt came frequently to the United States to lecture following the *JAMA* study, telling audiences that America was a constipated nation because of the modern habit of eating carbohydrate sugars and starches in refined form, stripped of the bulky, fibrous coverings. "Better to build a fence at the top of the cliff than park an ambulance at the bottom," he said. In other words, you're better off working to maintain your body while it is already in a healthy state.

Another thing Dr. Burkitt liked to do at his lectures was ask those in the audience if their stools floated or sank—a simple guide to whether they were eating enough fiber. Stools, he believed, should sink because of their bulk and fiber content.

Until his death in 1993, Dr. Burkitt forced the world to take dietary fiber seriously, which is a remarkable achievement for someone with a glass eye shipped off to the African continent for the first two decades of his medical career. He was fueled by a strong desire to ease the sufferings of humanity, based on a deep faith in God and mankind.

For the world, his legacy is a healthier way of eating, which is why Denis Burkitt is a health legend in my book.

Fiber Facts

Fiber became a household word in the 1970s, thanks to Dr. Burkitt. Fiber is the indigestible remnants of plant cells found in fruits, vegetables, whole grains, nuts, seeds, and beans. Foods that contain fiber help keep you regular. As fiber works its way through the digestive tract, it increases the elimination of waste matter in the large intestine and gives you an urge to have a bowel movement. That's why native Africans' stools were larger.

Not enough fiber in the diet means increased transit time for the food to wend its way through the small and large intestines before being expelled through the colon. When high-fiber diets cut down on that transit time, however, food has less time to putrefy in the colon. Toxins are quickly flushed out of the system.

Fiber, however, is not a uniform material. One way to classify fiber is by how easily it dissolves in water. Soluble fiber, which is found in oatmeal, nuts and seeds, beans, apples, pears, strawberries, and blueberries, partially dissolves in water. Soluble fiber from these foods, as part of a healthy diet, may reduce the risk of heart disease[†].

Insoluble fiber, which cannot be broken down by water, is found in whole grains, barley, brown rice, cereals, carrots, cucumbers, zucchini, and tomatoes. Insoluble fiber provides the "bulk" needed for proper functioning of the stomach and intestines..

While different in nature, both types of fiber contribute important elements to a healthy lifestyle, which makes the consumption of both soluble and insoluble fiber an essential part of any effective nutrition plan.

Foods containing soluble and insoluble fiber are loaded with phytochemicals, which are naturally occurring substances that give fruits and vegetables their characteristic flavor, color, aroma, and resistance to the sun's rays, pests, and disease. Most phytochemicals—also known as phytonutrients—have antioxidant activity and support our cells. One of the phytochemicals found in plants is lignans, which are obtained through the consumption of fruits, vegetables, whole grains, legumes, and seeds—especially flaxseeds.

The hulls of flaxseeds contain mega-amounts of lignans, which reduce excess estrogen from binding to receptor sites in breast tissue. For men, lignans convert to enterolactones in the intestine, which are then absorbed into the bloodstream, where they have demonstrated significant biological effects for the aging prostate gland.

Pectin is another noteworthy phytochemical found in the cell wall of plants. You may have heard of pectin because it's often available in a powdered form that's used in making jams or jellies. Pectin is the phytochemical found just underneath the peel of apples—remember my "applesauce" story in the Introduction?—as well as in grapefruits, oranges, and apricots. Generally speaking, 60 to 70 percent of the dietary fiber in citrus fruits is pectin. Other sources include bananas, beets, cabbage, and carrots.

Lignans and pectin are examples of components of fiber that can make a real difference in your health.

I've compiled an inventory of the Top 10 Raw Fiber Foods, but I'm dividing the list in half between seeds and nuts and fruits and vegetables:

The Top Raw Seeds and Nuts

1. **Chia seeds** come from edible seeds that grow abundantly in desert plants found in southern Mexico and parts of South America—and have nothing to do with those

kitschy, sprout-covered Chia Pets. High in fiber, chia seeds swell from seven to nine times inside the stomach and go to work inside the intestinal tract. Sprinkling chia seeds on salads or yogurt is a good way to get these seeds into your diet.

2. **Flaxseeds** contain natural dietary fiber that is not digested in the stomach but instead passes to the large intestine, where it acts like a sponge, drawing water that softens the stool and promotes bowel movements for relief from occasional constipation.[†] Flaxseeds can be ground and added to juices or smoothies.

3. **Sesame seeds**, which add a nutty crunch to many Asian dishes, have plenty of health-promoting lignans and are a top source of dietary fiber. Ground sesame seeds are delicious in hummus and contain sesamin and sesamolin, which are types of lignans.

4. **Pumpkin seeds** are usually thrown away after carving a pumpkin to make a Jack O'Lantern, but these flat, green seeds are highly nutritious and flavorful.

5. **Almonds**, one of those perfect snack foods, are higher in fiber than all other nuts and contain 50 percent more total fiber than peanuts as well as healthy omega-9 oleic fatty acids.

The Top Raw Fiber-Rich Fruits and Vegetables

1. **Blueberries** are high in the soluble fiber pectin and contain no cholesterol or fat and are also low in calories. We're fortunate to have relatively easy access to blueberries because they are native to North America and grown in the woods and mountainous regions of the Northeast and Canada.

2. **Pears** contain more fiber than many other fruits, including my favorite— blueberries. The gritty fiber content, which is insoluble, works to keep things moving in the colon. Pear skin also contains the majority of the fruit's antioxidants.

3. **Carrots** have a thick, deeply colored root that grows underground and are brimming with soluble and insoluble fiber following harvest time.

4. **Blackberries, raspberries, and strawberries**—and just about any berry you can find at your natural grocer or farmer's market—are dietary fiber superstars.

[†] These statements have not been evaluated by the Food and Drug Administration. This product is not intended to diagnose, treat, cure or prevent any disease.

5. **Coconut** is neither a fruit nor a vegetable but is classified as a fibrous, one-seeded drupe. The coconut meat is off-the-charts high in dietary fiber—four times as much fiber as oat bran and twice as much fiber as wheat bran or flaxseed meal. You can easily add coconut to beverages, smoothies, and juices. A great way to boost your family's fiber intake is to consume raw cookies and crackers made with raw coconut. My kids love these high-fiber cookies that are also loaded with healthy fats, vitamins, minerals, and probiotics.

So take another look at my list. Are you eating enough of these fiber-rich foods? If you're not, I understand. Americans rarely consume enough fiber on a daily basis, eating only around ten grams a day, when we should be eating double or triple that amount.

The Ugandans, according to Dr. Burkitt's research, were consuming sixty-five grams of fiber in their daily diets, which is why he stumbled across piles of human feces during his morning walks in the African bush.

Many Great Benefits

Whenever Denis Burkitt spoke at medical meetings in rural outposts in Great Britain, two things were likely to happen: there would be a record turnout to hear from a learned doctor who could muster much persuasive power about the benefits of dietary fiber, and the local grocery store would run out of bran by noontime the following day.

The story draws a smile, and I can only imagine Dr. Burkitt having a field day talking up the benefits of fiber.

Fiber is helpful to the body in many ways, but here are the three main ones:

*   **Fiber helps maintain regular bowel function and relieves occasional constipation.[†] Since fiber absorbs large amounts of water in the bowels, this benefit makes stools softer and easier to pass.**

*   **Fiber can help reduce risk factors for cardiovascular disease. Evidence is growing that fiber in the diet can lower the risk of developing heart disease because the soluble fiber found in oats, barley, and beans can have a positive effect on cholesterol, triglycerides, and other particles in the blood that affect the development of cardiovascular challenges.**

*   **Adequate fiber in the diet can help maintain healthy blood sugar levels already in the normal range.[†]**

Most people, when they move away from refined and processed foods found in the Standard American Diet and eat fruit instead, end up consuming fewer calories because the fiber-rich fruits fill them up more. But what if you're running late in the morning and don't feel like an apple for breakfast or just don't shop for fruits and vegetables like you know you should?

Then consider adding the organic fiber supplement RAW Fiber, a brand new formula from Garden of Life, to your dietary plan. RAW Fiber is great for those with a busy lifestyle or looking to make sure they get the recommended 25 to 35 grams of fiber into their daily diets. What I really like about RAW Fiber is that it provides both soluble and insoluble fiber.

While both types of fiber are important in maintaining good health, it's not difficult to overdo it. Too much soluble fiber (nuts and seeds, beans, apples, pears, strawberries, and blueberries) can cause constipation or create a gas problem for some people. Too much insoluble fiber (whole grains, brown rice, cereals, carrots, zucchini, and tomatoes) can bring on a case of the runs.

Maintaining the right balance of soluble and insoluble fiber is easy when you take RAW Fiber, which contains a soothing and nourishing blend of organic flaxseeds, chia seeds, sprouted seeds such as sesame and pumpkin, sprouted gluten-free grains, legumes, and live probiotic cultures in every serving. The blend of raw, organic, vegan, gluten-free, soy-free, and dairy-free ingredients in RAW Fiber were specially chosen for their exceptional ability to support and maintain optimal bowel health and function.[†] The powerful whole food formula is an excellent source of dietary fiber with the right balance of soluble to insoluble fiber that nature intended. Vegans will appreciate knowing that RAW Fiber is a strong source of protein from sprouted seeds, grains, beans, and legumes.

Each of the ingredients was chosen for its ability to support normal gut balance, regular bowel function, and overall health.[†] RAW Fiber doesn't contain any added sugars or artificial ingredients such as sweeteners, colorings, or flavorings, unlike many popular mass market fiber supplements.

[†] These statements have not been evaluated by the Food and Drug Administration. This product is not intended to diagnose, treat, cure or prevent any disease.

Experience a Turnaround

Here's what this RAW Fiber, an organic, convenient source of fiber, can do for you:

- provide an excellent source of dietary fiber with 9 grams per serving

- provide naturally occurring omega-3 fatty acids

- provide health-promoting phytonutrients like lignans and pectin

- support healthy gut flora balance, regular bowel function, and overall health[†]

- support healthy elimination of toxins[†]

- help relieve occasional constipation[†]

- support healthy cardiovascular function[†]

- help maintain healthy blood sugar levels and healthy cholesterol levels that are already in the normal range[†]

- supply certified organic fiber, which does not reintroduce toxins in the body[†]

RAW Fiber™ comes in a powder that can be sprinkled on soups and salads, or you can top your yogurt and granola with a couple of teaspoons. Two servings of RAW Fiber™ provide over 50 percent of the Daily Value for fiber and add a pleasant, nutty flavor to your favorite foods—or your beverages, if you prefer to add RAW Fiber™ to your juices or smoothies.

RAW Protein

Health Legend:

Bernarr Macfadden

Long before there was Arnold Schwarzenegger, there was Bernarr Macfadden.

Called the "Father of Bodybuilding" by *Time* magazine, Macfadden, who lived from 1868 to 1955, was an influential proponent of physical culture with a body that once posed as Michelangelo's *David* and a litany of nutritional and health theories that still resonate today.

Biographer Clement Wood put Bernarr Macfadden on the same pedestal as American titans who changed the course of history at the turn of the 20th century. Between

Bernarr Macfadden

1839 and 1870, Clement wrote, eight boys born to impoverished families rose to unprecedented achievement and wealth. They were John D. Rockefeller, Thomas Edison, Henry Ford, Charles Sumner Woolworth, Harvey S. Firestone, Amadeo Peter Giannini (founder of Bank of America), Asa G. Candler (founder of Coca-Cola), and Bernarr Macfadden.

Many of the names we recognize, so why was Macfadden mentioned in the same breath as these captains of industry and inventive minds? The answer is contained in his life story, which begins in Mill Spring, Missouri, not far from my farming and ranching operation in the southern part of the Show Me state.

Bernarr was born into a dysfunctional family. His father was an abusive alcoholic, and his mother was a despondent woman in poor health. Both parents died by the time he was eleven years old, leaving him an orphan. After spending a year in an orphanage, the young boy was sent out on his own.

He went to work for a farmer and learned how to labor with his hands. While cutting down trees, plowing fields, and slaughtering pigs, his young body grew strong and healthy. Two years of tilling in the fields did wonders for the boy's torso as well as his confidence.

The teenage Macfadden found work as an office boy, but his muscles atrophied from the lack of strenuous activity in the fresh air. Sensing intuitively that he should do something to get back in shape, Bernarr bought his first set of dumbbells, which had to have been quite primitive in the 1880s. But he exercised religiously with the dumbbells and started walking three to six miles a day to gain stamina.

Macfadden was not tall, standing just five feet, six inches and weighing 145 pounds, which sounds like a pipsqueak today but was fairly average for the time. But with his washboard abs and muscular appearance, the young man developed an unshakable self-confidence that he was on the right road in life. A strong body, mental tenacity, and unyielding determination were his calling cards.

He moved to St. Louis and started working out at a gymnasium, where he became a highly skilled gymnast. A champion wrestler named George Baptiste taught him some moves in the ring, and before long, Macfadden was wrestling before crowds, pinning men much heavier than he was. They said he was a real showman in the ring and loved playing to the fans.

He spent his free time in libraries making up for the school he missed growing up. Macfadden was a voracious reader, drawn to subjects like fasting, eating whole foods, and drugless health treatments. All this "book" education would provide a solid foundation when he struck out for New York City in 1894 with $50 in his pocket. He was twenty-six years old with a dream of making a name for himself.

The first thing he did was change his name from Bernard McFadden (his given name) to Bernarr Macfadden because he thought "Bernarr" sounded like the roar of a lion, and Macfadden sounded more masculine to his ears. He hung out his shingle as a personal trainer and physical therapist, taught wrestling, and began publishing his own pamphlets on health and physical training.

Little did Macfadden know that those booklets would lead to a publishing empire worth tens of millions of dollars.

Publishing Magnate

Prior to the turn of the 20th century, only the upper class could afford to purchase and read magazines. But advances in printing presses lowered costs dramatically, and suddenly "pulp" magazines were affordable for the masses. Circulation rose dramatically, and city corners were dotted with kiosks.

Macfadden had an idea: publish his own magazine. He launched *Physical Culture* magazine in 1899, which initially focused on bodybuilding before branching out with articles on health and fitness. A single copy cost a nickel. Word of mouth quickly boosted circulation to 100,000 copies a month.

Next, he launched a magazine targeted at women called *Beauty & Health*, which encouraged women to exercise, play tennis, swim laps, and even tan in the sun. Such an editorial focus was revolutionary. At that time, no self-respecting woman would be caught breaking a sweat; in proper society, it wasn't ladylike to perspire. Not in Macfadden's world, though, where he campaigned against corsets, high heels, and constricting clothing.

Macfadden was a dynamic and charismatic man filled with abundant energy, a young man in the right place at the right time—New York City at the turn of the century in the midst of the Industrial Revolution. His publishing empire grew by leaps and bounds, aided by a decision to publish "true" articles in which average people told their stories. *True Story* magazine reached 300,000 readers within the first year, which spawned more "confession" magazines: *True Detective, True Romances, Dream World, True Ghost Stories, Midnight, Dance,* and *Photoplay*.

By 1924, Macfadden had become the most successful publisher of magazines in history. His circulation numbers even topped the publications of William Randolph Hearst. Even though he became a very wealthy man, the Great Depression, a string of bad business decisions, and a divorce conspired against him. By the time he died in 1955 at the age of eighty-seven, he had lost it all.

When he was in his prime, though, Macfadden inspired millions to make life-altering decisions about health and nutrition, including one of my health heroes, Paul Bragg.

Milk of Human Kindness

In the early 1920s, Bernarr Macfadden believed that raw milk was a foundational food that could take place of all other nourishment. He began promoting something he called "The Milk Diet" in which the participants would drink nothing but raw milk exclusively, whether it be for several days, several weeks, or several months. The length of time the person needed to be on the Milk Diet varied according to their nutritional profile and needs.

J.E. Crewe, M.D., one of the founders of the Mayo Foundation (which was the forerunner of the world-famous Mayo Clinic), recommended in 1929 that patients drink raw milk as a treatment for certain conditions. According to Dr. Crewe, milk was the most convenient and acceptable form of raw protein available, capable of supplying the enzymes, antibodies, and nutrients needed to recover from disease. Patients who could not stomach a bite of raw beef, raw fish, or raw chicken could follow a raw milk diet that would meet their protein needs and maintain a strong body, Dr. Crewe contended.

Even though we know today that a nothing-but-milk diet shouldn't be the way to go, we do know that drinking raw milk is a superb way to meet your protein needs. So what is protein? Why is protein important?

Protein, along with carbohydrates and fat, is an essential macronutrient that has a big job to do in the body:

- Protein is the major building block for muscles, blood, skin, hair, nails, and the internal organs, including the heart and the brain.

- Protein increases stamina and fuels most of the biochemical activities of the body—building muscle strength and supporting the immune system.

- Protein is needed for hormone formation and controls bodily functions such as growth and metabolism rate.

Enzymes, antibodies, and hormones are made primarily of protein. Responsible for building and repairing tissue, protein is one of the most plentiful substances found in the body—after water. Protein adds up to one-fifth of your body weight and is the major constituent of most living cells and body fluids.

Since the body's other macronutrients—fat and carbohydrates—are unable to build strong bodies, burn fat, repair the daily wear of vital muscles, and replace body chemicals, it stands to reason that providing your body with a healthy source of protein is vital. The key word here is *healthy*. So now the question becomes: *What are healthy sources of protein?* I love answering this question.

Here are my Top 10 sources of protein that you should think about incorporating in your diet:

1. **Raw milk yogurt or kefir** have predigested amino acids, along with probiotics, enzymes, and fat-soluble vitamins, which make these raw cultured dairy foods a superb source of protein (not suitable for vegans).

2. **Really raw cheese,** produced from grass-fed cows fed no grain, is perhaps the best food protein source available nationwide. The proteins contained in really raw cheese are practically predigested due to the aging process, which makes them extremely high quality. Really raw cheese is loaded with healthy fats,

probiotics, vitamins, and minerals, making it a wonderful protein source for all ages (not suitable for vegans).

3. **Wheatgrass juice** has high-quality proteins within the raw cereal grass juice that have been shown to build excellent health.[†]

4. **Microalgaes** (spirulina, chlorella, and AFA) contain high-quality vegan proteins in whole food form.

5. **Leafy greens (such as spinach or kale)** and their juices
   contain healthy proteins, along with critical trace minerals, that can make the body strong (think Popeye).[†]

6. **Sesame seeds** are a good source of vegetarian protein and are renowned for their blood-building abilities in Eastern medicine.

7. **Avocados** contain high-quality protein, fats, and fat-soluble vitamins.

8. **Salmon ceviche,** a popular preparation from South America, uses citrus juice to ."cook" the salmon, keeping intact all of the high-quality protein, enzymes, fats, vitamins, minerals, and the antioxidant astaxanthin (not suitable for vegans).

9. **Raw eggs,** which should be consumed only from organic and preferably local sources, contain wonderful complete proteins, vitamins, minerals, and omega-3 fats. Great in smoothies and homemade ice cream (not suitable for vegans).

10. **Raw coconut cream** contains high-quality, easily digested, vegan-friendly protein as well as powerful fats and potent enzymes.

The Much-Needed Amino Acids

As you can tell from my list, animal sources are some of the best suppliers of protein. Beef, chicken, fish, eggs, and milk are called complete proteins because they supply all the essential amino acids. Vegetables and fruits are called incomplete proteins because (in most cases) they do not supply all of the essential amino acids. There are instances where you can combine several top-quality vegetable proteins together to form a complete protein, but that certainly takes work and knowhow.

The concept of a complete protein is fairly easy to understand. First of all, it's generally regarded that eight amino acids are essential for healthy living. These eight amino acids are essential because the body cannot manufacture them on its own, requiring that they must come through the diet. A complete protein source then is one that contains all eight of these amino acids in the amounts your body requires.

When you eat protein, the body breaks it down into amino acids that can be used by the body. If any of these eight essential amino acids are missing or insufficient, then the body's ability to synthesize the protein it needs can be severely inhibited. In addition, not receiving the amounts of amino acids and protein necessary can have adverse effects on the body. Proteins called immunoglobulins, for instance, are key elements of your immune system.

While everyone agrees that protein is a great thing to eat, eating raw protein is a tough sell. When audiences watched Sylvester Stallone down a pitcher-full of raw eggs in his *Rocky* movies, there were collective gasps in the movie theaters. The last time I was in a casual restaurant, I didn't see much *carpaccio* (raw beef) on the menu.

Raw fish is another roadblock. I know that sashimi and sushi has its fans, but I don't see many Americans making either of these raw foods part of their daily meal plan as they do in Japan. But anthropologists who've studied remote cultures cut off from the outside world say that many of them thrived on diets made up primarily of animal proteins, nuts, seeds, and grains. Some of them—like the Eskimos—ate their salmon catches raw and even buried raw fish, allowing them to ferment for consumption weeks and months later.

These raw sources of protein were loaded with enzymes, probiotics, and fat-soluble vitamins—and were *not* loaded with antibiotics and added hormones. Today, cows and chickens chew and peck on feed with added antibiotics, and "farm-raised" salmon spend all their lives swimming in concrete tanks snapping up pellets of ground-up fish.

Since few of us can stomach an entirely raw diet and cooking animal protein destroys many of the nutrients and alters others, I felt our team at Garden of Life needed to create a convenient easy-to-use raw protein formulation that would deliver a full complement of nutrients and beneficial compounds that could compare to the list of nutrients that raw protein-rich foods offer.

† These statements have not been evaluated by the Food and Drug Administration. This product is not intended to diagnose, treat, cure or prevent any disease.

Since many people choose not to include animal foods in their diets, we wanted to create a complete protein formulation that was vegan friendly. Our goal was to produce a supplement adhering to the "raw standard"—uncooked, untreated, and unadulterated. That also meant live probiotics and enzymes, but no binders, fillers, synthetic ingredients, or isolates. Raw truly defines pure, even more so if the product is USDA certified organic.

It was not an easy task finding a quality, pure, raw, and organic form of protein. When you consume raw protein found in nature, you get a lot more than just protein. Raw protein foods contain enzymes and probiotics as well as beneficial fat-soluble vitamins like A, D, E, and K.

Eating raw food is superior to taking a supplement.

That said, we can attempt to emulate the constituents of a raw, healthy protein food in nature by requiring the following four components in a protein supplement:

1. The protein must come from a raw, un-denatured source.

2. The protein must contain live enzymes, including proteases aiding in the digestion and utilization of protein.[†]

3. The protein must contain probiotics to support digestion and elimination.

4. The protein must contain raw food-created, fat-soluble vitamins A, D, E, and K.

The importance of consuming live probiotics and enzymes with your protein is critical. In order for your body to get the most out of it, you must first break down and then absorb the protein. Certain enzymes, known as proteases, help digest protein so that your body can properly use it.[†] While your body can produce protein-digesting enzymes, raw foods provide both the protein and the enzymes for utilization together as they should be.[†]

Probiotics, on the other hand, are needed after the enzymes go to work. Probiotics aid digestion by making it easier for the nutrients from our diets to be absorbed—and later used—by the body.[†] Again, raw protein foods contain probiotics that aid this process. So should your raw protein supplement.

When it comes to fat-soluble vitamins, nature once again shows its perfection. A look at the most powerful food sources of vitamins A, D, E, and K—foods like fish and fish liver, beef liver, dairy, eggs, avocados, and green leafy vegetables—is also a list of some of the best sources of protein for your body. It's no accident that high protein foods are some of the richest sources of fat-soluble vitamins. Therefore, the importance of consuming live fat-soluble vitamins, along with probiotics and enzymes with your protein, is critical.

Introducing Garden of Life® RAW Protein™

If you're looking to supplement your diet with a quality source of protein, look no further than Garden of Life RAW Protein™, the first certified organic, raw, and vegan protein powder containing live probiotics and enzymes and fortified with raw food-created fat-soluble vitamins.

Featuring thirteen raw and organic sprouts, RAW Protein™ is a good source of complete protein, providing 18 grams per serving, or 35 percent of the Daily Value, plus all essential amino acids. RAW Protein™ contains Vitamin Code® fat-soluble vitamins A, D, E and K, and supports digestive health and function with protein-digesting enzymes and powerful probiotics.†

RAW Protein™ is suitable for almost anyone, including those on a vegan or vegetarian diet, those on low carbohydrate diets, or those with gastrointestinal sensitivities to milk, whey, soy, or other protein sources. This nutritional supplement comes complete with essential amino acids, probiotics, enzymes, and fat-soluble vitamins. RAW Protein™ contains no fillers or synthetic ingredients and is always uncooked, untreated, and unadulterated. It is dairy- and gluten-free with no soy allergens.

If Bernarr Macfadden were alive today, I have a feeling that he'd be a big fan of RAW Protein™.

RAW Meal

Health Legend:

John Harvey Kellogg, M.D.

Chances are you've heard of Kellogg's cereal.

The story begins with John Harvey Kellogg, who was born in 1852 to a farming family in rural Michigan. Early in his childhood, his parents became Seventh Day Adventists and moved to Battle Creek, where the denomination started. Seventh Day Adventists are known for their emphasis on diet and health as well as a holistic understanding of the person. They recommend a largely vegetarian diet and discourage members from the use of alcohol, tobacco, or beverages containing caffeine.

John Harvey Kellogg, M.D.

By the time John Harvey was twelve years old, he had totally bought in to the Adventist lifestyle. He worked as an apprentice in the Adventist print shop, where he set type for various Adventist books and pamphlets and became deeply interested in the issue of health and hygiene. He decided he wanted to go to medical school so that he could change the direction of medicine. Kellogg attended the prestigious Bellevue Hospital Medical College in New York City, and in 1875 he earned his M.D. He promptly returned to Battle Creek to start his practice.

Dr. Kellogg became a highly skilled surgeon who operated on thousands of colons (he said that only 1 percent were healthy) and became a prolific author on a variety of health topics. Remember, he always wanted to change the direction of health care. Kellogg wasn't a shrinking violet afraid to share his opinions, and many of his ideas were ahead of his time. He recommended eating whole grain foods, urged urban families to get enough sunlight, warned of the dangers of eating pork, and believed longevity was directly related to a healthy diet, exercise, vitamins, and reducing stress.

Other opinions were a bit more "out there": he determined that oysters were covered in germs, bouillon was basically poisonous, coffee harmed the liver, and tea was the primary cause of insanity, according to the *Britannica Concise Encyclopedia*. Kellogg's nutritional ideas, which were influenced by both science and religion, recommended that dietary intake should be limited to primarily nuts, grains, legumes, and fruit.

These views were certainly right up the Adventist alley, so it was no surprise that denominational leaders turned to Kellogg to take over a floundering health institute founded by the Adventists. After changing the name to the Battle Creek Sanitarium, Kellogg set a course to transform the institute into the most famous health retreat of its time. By 1900, "The San," as it was called, had grown to 700 beds. Kellogg enticed the famous and powerful

people to come to Battle Creek, including John D. Rockefeller, Henry Ford, and Harvey Firestone—industrialists mentioned in the previous chapter on Raw Protein.

Biographers often use the adjective "quirky" to describe Dr. Kellogg, but what I want to focus in on was his unwavering belief in the power of whole raw foods as a great breakfast.

Kellogg had traveled to Europe, where he found extremely healthy people eating an amazing combination of raw grains, raw seeds, and raw dried fruit mixed with a raw cultured dairy product known as quark, which is like a combination of yogurt and sour cream. He returned to Battle Creek and began experimenting with ways to serve more whole grain foods as the first meal of the day.

John Harvey, who liked to tinker around the kitchen, stirred a mixture of oatmeal and corn meal and baked it into biscuit size, then ground it to bits. He called the whole grain concoction Granola, which was a play on the only other commercially produced cereal at the time called Granula. Guests at the Battle Creek Sanitarium liked the crunchy taste, and John Harvey's Granola was a hit.

Meanwhile, he had hired his younger brother, Will, to do the grunt work around the sanitarium, which was a step up from Will's last job as a broom salesman. His brother kept the books, bought supplies, answered the mail, and cleaned the enema rooms, which had to be an onerous chore.

One day Will was making Granola for the guests when he left a batch of the boiled paste out overnight. The next morning, instead of throwing the dried mixture out, Will ran it through rollers. Out came thin flakes, which Will baked. The Battle Creek clients loved those even *more* than the Granola, and they told him so.

Will saw dollar signs. *We can start our own cereal company, John. People will love our cereal.* Back then, city dwellers and rural folks often began the day with a bland fare of porridge, farina, gruel, and other boiled grains. A flaked, crunchy cereal would hold wonderful appeal to the masses, Will contended.

John Harvey Kellogg wasn't interested in starting a cereal company or even keeping their discovery a secret. In fact, he allowed anyone at the sanitarium to drop by the kitchen and watch how they made their flake cereal. One guest, C.W. Post, was so intrigued that he copied the process and started Post Cereals and later General Foods. (And now you know the rest of the story.)

Will eventually convinced John Harvey to produce and sell their whole grain flakes, but they faced stiff competition; there were around one hundred cereal companies in Battle Creek alone. Then something happened that changed the course of history—and the way we eat breakfast in America.

One day, Will, looking to sweeten profits, tinkered with the corn flake recipe by adding cane sugar—a forbidden ingredient at the sanitarium. Sweetening a cereal with sugar was a deal-breaker for John Harvey, and the two brothers went their separate ways. Will started his own company in 1906 and called his sweetened cereal Kellogg's Toasted Corn Flakes, and John Harvey dropped out of the cereal business.

Word got around about the sweet taste of Kellogg's Toasted Corn Flakes. Sales soared, and the rest is history. Today, breakfast cereal is a mature $9 billion business, and hundreds of different brands fight for attention on supermarket aisles.

The market is certainly huge: nearly half of the U.S. population eats cold or hot cereal seven days a week, and Americans eat 160 bowls per capita each year.

Starting Out Your Day

One hundred years ago, breakfast for the upper class involved a banquet of steaks, roasts, chops, oysters, and grilled fish accompanied by fried potatoes, scrambled eggs, biscuits, breads, and coffee. No wonder the wealthy and titled descended upon Battle Creek for a colon cleanse.

No one eats breakfast like that anymore—unless they pay for an expensive brunch at a country club on a Sunday morning. Today, breakfast usually means eating something fast and not necessarily nutritious: a bowl of sugar-frosted cereal with skim milk before running out the door; a grapefruit-sized blueberry muffin in the car; or a drive-thru stop at a donut shop on the way to work.

That's if any food gets eaten at all. Breakfast is the most skipped meal of the day, especially for busy moms and weight-conscious women and girls. The culprits are time—people always seem to be in a rush today—and a lackadaisical attitude about the benefits of breakfast. Others believe that skipping breakfast will help them maintain a trim figure.

Nothing could be further from the truth. You're *more* likely to become overweight if you skip breakfast, and if you start the morning with a meal, you'll reap the

daylong beneficial effects on your appetite, blood sugar, and energy metabolism.

Here's how your body works. Your metabolism—which resembles a furnace—doesn't get fired up until it's stoked with fuel. If you don't eat breakfast, the body turns to its own muscle mass, not those fat cells parked in your midsection, for energy. As the metabolism slows to a crawl, the body conserves energy because it doesn't know when it's going to receive fuel again. That's why you lack energy when you don't eat.

But let's say the morning break time comes along, and you drop by the vending machine for a bag of chips and a soda. Or you take an early lunch and grab a turkey sandwich on white. When these events happen, the body doesn't burn the food but stores it as fat because it can't be totally sure if the stomach will be fed again in a few hours.

Eating a healthy meal in the morning, however, will stoke your furnace and get you burning calories, a healthy way to start your day. But what about those occasions when you really don't have time to prepare yourself a healthy breakfast, or you're out of your favorite breakfast foods, or you're trying to "be good" but load up on a lot of empty calories after you wake up in the morning?

Those were the questions that I challenged our product development team at Garden of Life with, and our answer was the first raw, certified organic, vegan, whole food, gluten-free meal replacement that satisfies hunger, provides energy, and furnishes the body with protein, fiber, healthy fats, vitamins, minerals, probiotics, enzymes, and nearly thirty superfoods. Fittingly, we called our new creation Garden of Life® RAW Meal™. If you really don't have time to eat breakfast, then RAW Meal™ is a great option for you.

When you mix a serving of RAW Meal™ into water, you're receiving twenty-six superfoods from raw organic seeds, sprouts, and greens as well as Vitamin Code® raw food-created vitamins and minerals. You'll also receive nutrient Code Factors™ such as beta-glucans, superoxide dismutase (SOD), glutathione, and CoQ10.

Besides offering the nutrition of a well-balanced, healthy meal that satisfies hunger and provides energy, RAW Meal™ provides:

- **34 grams of protein, including all eight essential amino acids**
- **9 grams of soluble and insoluble fiber**
- **thirteen non-gluten organic sprouted grains and seeds**
- **four raw organic cereal grass juices**
- **five raw organic fruits, plus spirulina and chlorella**

- twenty RAW Food-Created Nutrients™ and RAW Food-Chelated Minerals™ that enable targeted delivery and natural recognition by your body
- live probiotics and enzymes for healthy digestion
- no trans fats

RAW Meal™ is suitable for almost anyone, including those on vegetarian or vegan diets, those on low carbohydrate diets, or those with gastrointestinal sensitivities to milk, whey, soy, or other protein sources. RAW Meal™ also dampens the munchies an hour or two before lunch or dinner, and this nutrient-rich meal will likely fill a stomach that others have described as bottomless.

A Great Chance to Eat a Raw Meal

Say what you want, but John Harvey Kellogg must have been a dynamic personality. How else could he have convinced the richest people of his day that a breakfast of groats—the hulled grains of various cereals such as oats, wheat, barley, and buckwheat—or his beloved Granola would be better for them than a sirloin steak and boiled potatoes in the morning?

Dr. Kellogg saw the value of consuming a raw or a mostly raw meal to start the day, which means that if he was alive today and running the Battle Creek Sanitarium, I think you would find RAW Meal™ somewhere on the campus. I believe that RAW Meal™ with its raw, certified organic, gluten-free and vegan-friendly ingredients loaded with live probiotics and enzymes would receive his seal of approval.

My Top 10 Raw Meals

This chapter on John Harvey Kellogg and RAW Meal™ wouldn't be complete without a listing of my favorite raw meals. I've done my best to keep some of these meals simple to ensure easy digestion. Others fall into the dessert category, but due to their caloric level and abundance of nutrients, they are a meal unto themselves.

The recipes for each meal can be found in Chapter 16. Take a look at these combinations, and I urge you to give at least one a try this week:

1. Avocado and tomato
2. Flaxseed crackers and really raw cheese
3. Blueberries and almonds
4. Salmon ceviche with avocado
5. Raw-blended salad/soup
6. Raw pizza
7. Raw apple pie
8. Raw coconut pie
9. Raw smoothie
10. Paul's Powerful Salad

CHAPTER 9

RAW Calcium

Health Legend:

Richard Carmona, M.D.

You may have never heard of our health legend for this chapter, Dr. Richard Carmona, a surgeon with an extensive background in public health. It's even more unlikely that you've heard about the work that should have made him world famous.

Before I get to his noteworthiness, the first thing you need to know is that Dr. Carmona was the U.S. Surgeon General during the Bush Administration. But you still don't remember him, do you?

Here's what he did to gain legendary status, at least in my book. Back in the fall of 2004, Dr. Carmona released the first-ever Surgeon General Report on bone health with a shot-across-the-bow warning that by 2020, half of all American

Dr. Richard Carmona

citizens older than 50 years old were at risk of developing osteoporosis due to low bone mass if no immediate action was taken by individuals, medical doctors, and government policy makers. "We all need to take better care of our bones," Dr. Carmona declared.

You'd think the media would be all over this headline-grabbing story, but the Surgeon General's *2004 Bone Health Report* got buried. The media was fixated on the U.S. presidential campaign between George Bush and John Kerry as well as the Boston Red Sox' improbable World Series victory—the first since 1918.

It's too bad that Dr. Carmona's *2004 Bone Health Report* was relegated to the back pages of our nation's newspapers and ignored by the 24-hour news channels. Dr. Carmona's thesis statement that widespread and serious bone health issues will likely happen to both men and women at the relatively young age of 50 deserved much more media attention because osteoporosis has become a common condition among many—especially postmenopausal women, though men can suffer from bone loss as well. What happens is that as we age, the renewal of bone structure slows, causing bones to lose density and become more porous and brittle.

Doctors call osteoporosis the "silent thief" because this insidious condition drains away bone mass so slowly that many aging adults are unaware their bones have weakened considerably until there is a pronounced stoop in posture or a fall resulting in a fracture.

Osteoporosis afflicts 44 million Americans—80 percent of them older women. Shrinking height is also a revealing sign of osteoporosis.

So how did we reach this point where Dr. Carmona felt compelled to sound the alarm about our national decline in bone health? Like most health issues, you can point to several factors robbing our bodies of healthy bones, starting with our diets and sedentary lifestyle. Where diet is concerned, we have become more reliant on cooked and processed grains that can actually inhibit absorption of key minerals, while raw foods richer in calcium and other important minerals—such as dark, green leafy vegetables—have been sent to the sidelines.

Basically, this means we are eating less calcium-rich foods and more acid-forming foods. Cooked and processed meats and grains have an acidic effect on the body. In order to combat this, the body has to release minerals to balance pH levels. What is the primary mineral the body releases? Calcium—which is leeched from the bones and teeth. We also consume an inordinate amount of carbonated soft drinks. Many brands contain phosphoric acid, which robs our bones of calcium.

It's not helping matters that our lives have become more sedentary. Watching TV and the increased use of computers and hand-held devices negatively impact physical activity, which is an extremely important factor in bone health. Being sedentary often equates to being indoors, away from the rays of the sun. Our bodies are designed to transform sunlight into vitamin D, another key element in bone health.[†]

Therefore, nutrition, as well as consistent exercise, is essential for good bone health. There is no known cure for osteoporosis, which points to the importance of taking preventative measures to maintain—or at least slow—bone loss[††]. That means making sure your body is getting enough calcium, which is an essential mineral.

The body can manufacture some vitamins, but it cannot manufacture a single mineral—including the mineral calcium. All tissues and internal bodily fluids contain varying quantities of minerals, and minerals are components of bones, teeth, soft tissue, muscle, blood, and nerve cells, making them crucial to overall physical and mental well-being.

Calcium is not only the most abundant mineral in the body, but it's also one of the most important since it plays a key role part in many body functions. Calcium is noted for ensuring strong bones and teeth.[†] Ninety-eight percent of the body's calcium is found in the bones, 1 percent in the teeth, and 1 percent in blood and tissues. When the body is at rest, calcium is pulled out of the bones to be used elsewhere, establishing the importance of daily adequate intake of this essential mineral.

The Surgeon General's *2004 Bone Health* report specifically called for dietary changes to enhance the health of our bones. Not surprisingly, Dr. Carmona's list of foods considered important for bone health read like a catalog of the healthiest foods on the planet—and appears to be the very foods missing from many people's diets. Dr. Carmona's report recommended green leafy vegetables, nuts and seeds, dairy products, and wild-caught fish.

I concur, so here is my list of the Top 10 Raw bone-building raw foods:

1. **Green leafy vegetables** such as broccoli, collard greens, Chinese cabbage, and kale are rich sources of plant-based calcium and other minerals.

2. **Raw, full-fat dairy products such as milk, cheese, and yogurt** are also great sources of calcium, particularly cultured dairy such as yogurt and kefir. Dairy from exclusively grass-fed animals contains fat-soluble vitamins, including vitamins D and K2. Raw cheese contains approximately 200mg of calcium per single ounce, along with high quality protein and fats.

3. **Raw salmon ceviche** is a rich source of vitamin D and essential fatty acids.

4. **Bean sprouts** are high in the bone-building minerals such as phosphorus.

5. **Sesame seeds and sesame butter (tahini)** are good sources of calcium and phosphorus.

6. **Almonds** are a good source of calcium, phosphorus, magnesium, and omega-9 fatty acids.

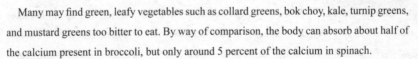

7. **Mushrooms** are rich in minerals and vitamin D2.

8. **Parsley and dill (fresh or juiced)** are good sources of calcium, magnesium, and potassium.

9. **Seaweeds such as hijiki, wakame, and kombu (soaked to rehydrate)** are loaded with trace minerals.

10. **Natto (cultured/fermented soybeans)** is the richest natural source of vitamin K2 available today.

Many may find green, leafy vegetables such as collard greens, bok choy, kale, turnip greens, and mustard greens too bitter to eat. By way of comparison, the body can absorb about half of the calcium present in broccoli, but only around 5 percent of the calcium in spinach.

Black-eyed peas have the most calcium of any legume, but navy beans and kidney beans are also brimming with calcium. The most popular raw calcium-rich foods are really raw cheese, cultured dairy products, sesame seeds, almonds, and salmon with edible bones.

Of course, many people looking to boost their bone health choose to supplement their diets. It is in this area that one of the most common myths associated with bone health is found.

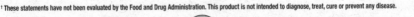

The Role of Calcium

Over the years, clinical studies have underscored the importance of calcium and bone health, including a *New England Journal of Medicine* study showing that taking calcium and vitamin D supplements tends to improve bone density and maintain strong bones and teeth.[†] So in addition to eating calcium-rich foods, if you want healthy bones, you should take calcium in a supplement form, right?[†]

That seems like a no-brainer, but what many consumers don't know is where their calcium supplements are coming from—or their composition. Today, 90 percent of calcium sold in supplemental form comes from . . . rocks. That's right: the leading calcium sources derive their calcium from ground-up, pulverized limestone, usually dug out of a rock quarry. These sources of calcium are known as *calcium carbonate* and *calcium citrate* (carbonate reacted with citric acid). Calcium carbonate is the most abundant form of calcium found in nature.

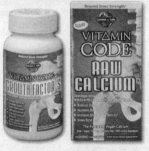

If you've ever taken over-the-counter antacid products, then you've been consuming calcium carbonate, which acts as a buffering agent for the accumulated acids in the stomach. Calcium is an alkaline-forming mineral, meaning that it requires extra stomach acid for better absorption. That's why calcium carbonate is recommended to be taken with meals since the acidity of the stomach is greater when food is being digested.

Another type of calcium supplement is *calcium citrate*, which is basically rock calcium that has been chemically reacted with citric acid to make it easier for the body to absorb.

To confuse you even further, there are other forms of calcium—*calcium acetate, calcium gluconate, calcium lactate*, and *calcium phosphate*. These names are rock calcium that has been reacted with other chemicals to differentiate it on store shelves with some sort of marketing advantage.

There is, however, a type of calcium that comes from a natural, raw, organic, whole food source, and this calcium is produced from a special type of marine algae known as *Lithothamnion superpositum,* which is harvested from coastlines in South America.

When my team at Garden of Life began to develop a two-part system featuring a raw, organic, whole-food source calcium to stimulate bone growth, increase bone strength, and build bone mineral density for adults of all ages, we decided to use *Lithothamnion superpositum* in the pair of formulas known as Vitamin Code RAW Calcium and Vitamin Code Growth Factor S.

The Grow Bone System starts with Vitamin Code RAW Calcium. As mentioned earlier, the raw calcium in the Grow Bone system is a patented form of *Lithothamnion superpositum.* After the marine algae is harvested in South America, it's rinsed in fresh water, dried in the sun, and then milled into a powder. This is the only organic, raw, pure plant-source of calcium available today.

When you take a plant-source supplement, you get the added benefits of naturally occurring plant-based trace minerals. While calcium is an important bone-building mineral, there are other nutrients vitally important to bone health.[†] The consumption of bone-building co-factor minerals such as magnesium, silica, boron, vanadium, and strontium have all been linked to healthy bones.[†] And all of them are either naturally occurring or added to Vitamin Code RAW Calcium.

Let's take a closer look at some important bone nutrients:

- **Vitamin K2:** Vitamin K belongs to the star-studded fat-soluble compounds called anphthoquinones and includes vitamins K1, K2, and K3. Simply put, vitamin K plays a leading role in bone growth.[†] Vitamin K activates at least three proteins involved in osteoblasts—the cells that generate bone—and that's significant. Vitamin K2 is needed to produce one of these proteins, osteocalcin, which also assists to incorporate calcium into the bones.[†] Vitamin K2 truly rocks the house in bone metabolism and bone growth.[†]

- **Vitamin D:** A veteran in the bone-building world, vitamin D needs little introduction. Vitamin D is critical for building strong, healthy bones and is required for the body to absorb calcium.[†] Unfortunately, 70 percent of women ages fifty-one to seventy and 90 percent of women over seventy don't get enough vitamin D from food and supplements. Low levels of vitamin D are linked to osteoporosis, reduced calcium absorption and bone loss.[††].

- **Magnesium:** Calcium may be the star of the show, but magnesium controls calcium's fate in the body. If magnesium levels are insufficient, then calcium could just pass right on through the body and not find its way to the bones.[†] A worse

[†] These statements have not been evaluated by the Food and Drug Administration. This product is not intended to diagnose, treat, cure or prevent any disease.

scenario is that if magnesium isn't along for the ride, then calcium might get way off track and go for the soft tissues, including the arteries and kidneys.[†] That's something you don't want to happen.

- **Vanadium:** Research suggests that the lack of vanadium may be detrimental to proper skeletal development.[†] Additionally, vanadium appears to jumpstart the synthesis of collagen, essential for bone strength and flexibility.[†]

The second formula in the Grow Bone System is Vitamin Code Growth Factor S, which is a combination of important bone health minerals such as strontium and probiotics, enzymes, and raw organic fruits and vegetables. Strontium is a superstar mineral that is found naturally in your bones in trace amounts of approximately 100 micrograms in every gram of bone. Closely related to calcium, strontium is believed to support bone cells to build bone mineral density, while inhibiting cells that break down bone tissue.[†] Clinical trials conducted on strontium found it most effective at 680mg per day—the same amount contained in Growth Factor S.[†]

Closing Thought

It's hard to believe that seven years have passed since the Surgeon General's warning about the state of bone health in our nation—a warning that is even more valid today. If you want the best for your body, begin a regimen of regular exercise, seek out adequate sunshine, consume bone-building raw foods, and supplement with the Vitamin Code Grow Bone System.

Maybe, just maybe we'll see to it that Dr. Carmona's prediction never comes to pass.

[††] Adequate calcium and vitamin D throughout life, along with physical activity, may reduce the risk of osteoporosis in later life.

RAW Sunshine

Health Legend:

Weston A. Price, D.D.S.

The health legends that I've picked for *RAW Truth* are individuals I highly respect for their contributions to healthy living. I shudder to think where our nation's health—as poor as it is these days—would be without these courageous men and women who swam against the cultural tide, fighting for our good health, when they were alive.

There's one bust in my Health Heroes Hall of Fame, however, that shines a bit brighter than the others, and that one belongs to Dr. Weston A. Price, a Cleveland dentist who lived from 1870 to 1948. I've long been a fan of Dr. Price and the Weston A. Price

Dr. Weston A. Price

Foundation, which carries on the work he started more than eighty years ago.

Dr. Price was a scientifically curious individual who wondered why he was so busy filling more and more cavities of patients sitting in his dental chair each and every year. The more he considered the reasons why, the more he believed it was due to poor nutrition. Just as Henry Ford's invention of the assembly line revolutionized the way cars were made, innovative food manufacturing companies in the early 20th century were discovering ways to streamline the production of canned and frozen foods as well as boxed cereals, assorted candies, and sweet pastries. Instead of housewives preparing food from scratch—peeling potatoes, shucking peas, plucking chickens, or grinding flour—they could purchase the same foods at their nearby general store or corner market already prepared for them.

"Modern" foods like boxed cakes, ice cream bars, sugar-coated cereals, and glazed doughnuts, Dr. Price sensed, were the main reason why frightened children had to be dragged kicking and screaming into his dental chair. Every young mouth he peered into revealed increasingly deformed dental arches, crooked teeth, and enough cavities to keep him busy drilling.

Dr. Price suspected that the "diet of commerce," as he termed the newfangled processed foods flooding the marketplace, was the reason why his young patients—as well as their parents—were suffering from more and more tooth decay as well as chronic and degenerative diseases. But how could he prove it?

That fundamental question challenged Dr. Price until he came up with an idea: why not go out and find the world's healthiest populations and study what they were eating to stay healthy?

At sixty years of age and being rather well off, Dr. Price had the financial means to take an extended sabbatical and search out healthy people untouched by civilization and modern foods. For most of the 1930s, he and his wife, Florence, traveled around the world on steamships, prop planes, trains, automobiles, canoes, and on foot, befriending and then studying indigenous people whose teeth and gums had no evidence of malformation or other problems associated with the "diet of Commerce."

This wasn't some half-baked Indiana Jones expedition but a serious scientific quest that led to his authorship of the seminal work *Nutrition and Physical Degeneration*, a groundbreaking book that has been a textbook in every naturopathic college in North America and is experiencing a resurgence in today's new generation of natural health practitioners.

Dr. Price's mission took him to hundreds of cities in fourteen nations on five continents. He and Florence globetrotted to some of the most isolated parts of the world, visiting tribes and villagers in the backwoods and bayous, in the rainforest and the Alps. His investigative spirit took him to islanders in the South Pacific, the Maoris in New Zealand, the Aborigines in Australia, the tribesmen in Africa, the Swiss in remote Alpine villages, the Peruvian and Amazonian Indians in South America, and the Eskimos living south of the Yukon.

He came into contact with primitive cultures who not only displayed row after row of healthy teeth, but these smiling men, women, and children also lived healthy lives. As he asked questions and conducted research, Dr. Price discovered that healthy tribal groups fed special foods to young couples before conceiving and during pregnancy and to children during their growing years. He analyzed the foods they ate (mainly seafood, organ meats, eggs, and bright yellow cheese and butter, mostly raw) and determined that they were rich in fat-soluble nutrients such as vitamins A, D, E, and K. The diet of the so-called primitive peoples contained "at least ten times" the amount of fat-soluble vitamins found in the average American diet of his day.

Vitamin D is the superstar fat-soluble vitamin that will be the focus of this chapter. Vitamin D keeps bones healthy for young and old and plays a vital role in regula ng cell growth, maintaining a healthy immune system, and supporting blood pressure already in the normal range.[†] Besides being a critical nutrient for strong, healthy bones, vitamin D must be present for the body to fully absorb the all-important mineral calcium.[†]

This essential vitamin has other benefits, too. Over 900 genes and several areas in the body—the brain, heart, blood vessels, muscles and intestines—have vitamin D receptors, or proteins that bind to vitamin D. Studies show positive health effects when vitamin D binds to these receptors. Perhaps that's why research indicates vitamin D's key role in maintaining immune, cellular, brain and cardiovascular health.[†]

[†] These statements have not been evaluated by the Food and Drug Administration. This product is not intended to diagnose, treat, cure or prevent any disease.

Dealing with Deficiencies

I touched on vitamin D in the previous chapter and how low levels of vitamin D are linked to osteoporosis in older men and women.†† Our sons and daughters are experiencing vitamin D deficiencies as well. Mothers are loading their kids with fruit juice, sodas, and sports drinks, which are empty calories offering nothing on the nutritional front. You also don't find many parents serving their children fatty fish like wild-caught salmon, which is also high in vitamin D. Another avenue for getting vitamin D is through the rays of the sun, but children aren't playing outside like they used to in past generations.

Letting the sun warm your skin is extremely important because skin synthesizes vitamin D from the ultraviolet rays of sunlight. You need to expose your face, arms, hands, and back to the sun to provide your body with adequate vitamin D—the "sunshine vitamin." The American Lung Association, however, estimates we spend a majority of our time indoors, and that byproduct of our modern culture is robbing us of this significant hormone vitamin.

No matter what our age, we're spending too much time indoors, and that goes especially for children. Latch-key kids get even *less* sun exposure because their working parents prefer they stay inside the home and not play outside for safety reasons. Even if kids go outside to play with their friends, that's no guarantee that they'll be bathed in sunlight. Those of you living in northern latitudes—that imaginary line that runs from the northern border of California all the way to Boston—must contend with gray overcast skies and shorter days from the late fall to early spring. In the dead of winter, people can go for weeks without seeing the sun, which is why I see "snowbirds" rolling into my Florida hometown just before Thanksgiving.

Summer is just the opposite throughout much of the country: the sun is too hot, so people stay indoors. It used to be that nothing could be done about the searing heat, but now we generally live inside air-conditioned comfort, whether we're driving, shopping, eating out in a restaurant, or attending church. When families *do* go outside in the summer, everyone gets lathered in sunscreen.

The National Institutes of Health (NIH) says that ten to fifteen minutes of sunlight *without* sunscreen allow adequate time for vitamin D synthesis to occur, after which you can apply a natural sunscreen with an SPF of at least 15 to protect the skin. But watch how you shower— or where you soap up—when it comes to vitamin D synthesis! Vitamin D experts point to research showing that the body needs up to forty-eight hours to absorb the majority of the vitamin D that was generated when you went outside in the sun. That means if you go for an energetic Sunday afternoon walk on a hot day and come home and jump in the shower because you're sweaty, you very well could wash away much of the vitamin D your skin generated, thus decreasing the benefits of your sun exposure.

So don't shower for two days.

I'm kidding, of course, but here's what you can do so that your vitamin D doesn't run down the drain. When you take a shower, just lather up with soap underneath your arms and groin area and shampoo on your hair. This way you avoid soaping up the larger areas of the body that were exposed to sunlight and are still synthesizing the ultraviolet rays.

You really do want to think about how much you soap up because a deficiency of vitamin D could carry health consequences. In fact, an estimated 75 percent of the U.S. population is deficient in vitamin D, which portends serious implications for our national health.

The benefits of vitamin D are staggering, and there is a growing body of scientific studies backing that up. Besides supporting bone health, increasing your vitamin D levels supports healthy blood pressure already in the normal range, supports proper cell replication, and supports healthy immune system function and colon health.[†]

There's More to Vitamin D Than Meets the Eye

So how can you increase your levels of vitamin D?

Before I answer that question, you need to know that our understanding of vitamin D exploded about fifteen years ago when scientists determined that vitamin D comes in two forms important to human health:

- **vitamin D2 (ergocalciferol), which come from plant foods**

- **vitamin D3 (cholecalciferol), which comes from sunlight and from animal sources like fatty fish and grassfed dairy products**

While both vitamin D2 and D3 have been shown to be effective in raising vitamin D levels in the blood, vitamin D3 is preferred since it metabolizes much better in the body and is considered more bioactive.

Because of vitamin D3's ability to supply the body with the vitamin D it needs, *The American Journal of Clinical Nutrition* argued in 2006 that D2 should no longer be considered as a nutrient suitable for fortification or supplementation. We kept that advice in mind when we started working on a raw vitamin D formula at Garden of Life. Our research and development team zeroed in on D3 because the D2 sources are less well-utilized by the body.

† These statements have not been evaluated by the Food and Drug Administration. This product is not intended to diagnose, treat, cure or prevent any disease.

This is why vegans and vegetarians have to be careful to get enough sunlight because their main source of vitamin D is vitamin D2, which comes from a relatively small number of plant sources, including mushrooms. If you're not a fan of animal foods, then you'll be happy to learn that Vitamin Code RAW D3 is the perfect resource for you because it's the only raw, vegetarian, whole food vitamin D3 formulated with raw food-created nutrients as well as live probiotics, antioxidants, enzymes, and nutrient-specific peptides.

These raw food-created nutrients support:

- **healthy bones and joints**[†]
- **memory and concentration**[†]
- **healthy immune system balance**[†]
- **healthy colon and digestion**[†]
- **breast and prostate health**[†]

While Vitamin Code RAW D3 is a great source of this powerful nutrient, below are ways in which you can receive vitamin D from eating and lifestyle habits.

1. **Get plenty of sunshine.** Make an extra effort to get out in the sun during the day. You don't have to take a walk; just puttering around in the garden or reading a newspaper in the backyard—even on your iPad—will help tremendously. Fifteen minutes a day can work wonders.

2. **Eat certain plant foods and animal foods.** Vitamin D isn't found in a wide variety of plant foods, but the raw foods you'll want to include in your diet are citrus fruits and juices (fresh raw juice), green peppers, mushrooms, tomatoes, broccoli, turnip greens and other leafy greens, and sweet and white potatoes. (While eating raw potatoes may sound strange, they can be marinated in citrus, which will soften them, or they can be juiced as part of a blend.) These foods don't quite match up to what vitamin D3 can do, but they can help increase vitamin D utilization in the body.

3. **Include raw animal sources of vitamin D3.** Those who eat raw meat and dairy products receive vitamin D3, which is a superior form of vitamin D. Raw, citrus-marinated wild salmon is a great source of vitamin D3 and omega-3 fatty acids. Raw, organic eggs and raw full-fat dairy products such as really raw cheese, butter, yogurt, kefir, and cream are great sources of fat-soluble nutrients, including vitamin D. Sheep's milk dairy contains between two-to-four times more vitamin D per serving than cow's or goat's milk.

RAW Antioxidants

Health Legend:

Norman Walker, N.D.

One time when I was in New York City, I walked by the Stage Deli, a famous delicatessen on Seventh Avenue patronized by numerous celebrities as well as the tourist crowd.

Norman Walker, ND

Sorry, but a humongous white bread bun filled with six inches of processed pastrami and corned beef is nothing I'd ever eat, but the Stage Deli is known for naming sandwiches after celebrities—like Joe DiMaggio, Adam Sandler, Dolly Parton, and Sarah Jessica Parker—who've dined there.

I was thinking of the way the Stage Deli names their famous triple-deckers after celebrities because my next health legend, Norman Walker, deserves to have some type of juiced drink named after him at smoothie shops and juice bars across the nation. Known as the "Father of Juicing," Norman Walker was the first to promote the amazing health benefits of extracting the juices from fruits and vegetables.

Born the son of a Scottish Baptist minister, young Norman grew up with a family that lived in Italy and France during his early years. The year of his birth is open to speculation. He is believed to have been born in 1886 and lived until 1985, making him ninety-nine years old at the time of his death, but some claim Walker lived considerably longer—109, 113, 116, 118, or even 119 years.

Even if he lived "only" ninety-nine years, Norman Walker left behind quite a health legacy. He was a pioneer in raw foods, juicing, and eating a vegetarian diet, but he's most remembered for his invention of the Norwalk Hydraulic Press Juicer, a machine well known for producing great juice quality and its ability to extract the greatest amount of antioxidants from fruits and veggies. Even today, the Norwalk Press is the gold standard, and while holding a reputation as being difficult to clean, you can certainly taste and feel the difference in the juice quality coming from Walker's invention.

Walker's health story begins when he was a young adult and suffered a breakdown from stress and overwork. While convalescing in the French countryside, he watched the woman of the house peeling carrots one day. He was struck by the moistness on the underside of the peel and thought there might be something to it. He politely asked if he could have the carrot peelings since they were sure to be discarded. Then he began grinding the carrot peels by hand, which gave him some juice. His first cup of carrot juice tasted great and helped Norman feel "alive," and that incident made a huge impression on him.

THE RAW TRUTH

He immigrated with his family to the United States in 1910, arriving at Ellis Island on the *RMS Lusitania*, a ship made famous when she was later sunk by a German torpedo in 1915, killing 1,198 of the 1,959 passengers aboard. He married an American in 1913 and worked odds jobs but remained interested in nutrition and good health. When he and his family moved to the Los Angeles area, he opened a juice bar and taught the benefits of colon cleansing and drinking fresh juices.

In the 1930s, he designed a machine that slowly grinded fruits and vegetables with a press that extracted the juice. He named it the Norwalk Hydraulic Press and began manufacturing the juicer. He also wrote eight books that shared his views on healthy eating and living.

Walker was a vegan long before the word became popular and advocated a diet of fresh fruits and vegetables as well as an abundance of raw juices to anyone who would listen. He regarded cooked food as dead food and believed it contributed to deteriorating health, energy, and vitality. As a strict vegan, he did not recommend eating any meat, fish, dairy products, or eggs. He also counseled against eating any grains.

Walker considered a healthy colon fundamental to wellness and surmised that 80 percent of all disease began in the bowels. He started his own health magazine, *The New Health Movement Review*, operated a health ranch in Arizona for a number of years, and remained physically active and mentally alert, eating raw foods and drinking live juice, until his death in 1985. He died peacefully in his sleep, which sounds like a great way to make a graceful exit.

Walker is remembered for his Norwalk Press Juicer, which is still available today. When I said this stainless steel juicer is the gold standard, I wasn't kidding. One costs as much as $4,000. The machine has two operating mechanisms, one for grinding and the other for pressing and squeezing liquid out of fruit and vegetables. The Norwalk can grind wheat berries, seeds, and nuts and handle hard and soft fruits and vegetables. It's the two-step method that makes the Norwalk complicated and difficult to use, but you can juice larger quantities in one session.

Juicing with raw fruits and vegetables is an incredibly healthy practice because of the antioxidants found in brightly colored produce, which are loaded with vitamins and minerals. The antioxidants are found largely in the pigments that color fruits and vegetables, and the idea of "eating your colors" is critical to good health. You'll never go wrong consuming raw fruits and vegetables exhibiting the pulsating, radiating colors of the rainbow. The pigments are chock-filled with phytochemicals, which offer antioxidant protection as well as other health benefits.

Pigments with health-promoting properties color every fruit and vegetable on display at your local health food store or farmer's market. Green vegetables, as I mentioned in an earlier chapter, owe their pigment to chlorophyll. Tomatoes and watermelon are red because of a carotenoid antioxidant known as lycopene. Blueberries—a favorite in the Rubin household—are colored by the phytochemical anthocyanin, which is also found in "red" fruits like strawberries, raspberries, and red grapes.

Lycopene and anthocyanins act as powerful antioxidants, which are nature's soldiers against cellular oxidation—also known as free radicals—in the body.[†] Free radicals are something you don't want running rampant within your molecular system, although every day tens of thousands of these unstable molecules are generated within the body. This means you really have to pay attention to eating a wide variety of fruits and veggies, or free radicals will gain the upper hand, and that's not good for your long-term health.

I've compiled a list of twenty of the top commonly available high antioxidant fruits and veggies, and I'm including an analysis called ORAC (Oxygen Radical Absorbance Capacity), which measures the total antioxidant power of foods. Next to each food, I've included the ORAC units per 100 grams, or about three-and-a-half ounces, as measured in studies conducted at Tufts University in Boston on behalf of the United States Department of Agriculture (USDA).

Leading nutritional researchers believe that you should strive to consume approximately 10,000 ORAC units daily to promote health, wellness, and longevity.

When you include the following foods in your diet, that should be a cinch:

Fruits:

- **blueberries (2400)**
- **blackberries (2036)**
- **strawberries (1540)**
- **raspberries (1220)**
- **plums (949)**
- **oranges (750)**
- **red grapes (739)**
- **cherries (670)**
- **kiwi fruit (602)**
- **pink grapefruit (483)**

Vegetables:

- **kale (1770)**
- **spinach (1260)**
- **Brussels sprouts (980)**
- **alfalfa sprouts (930)**
- **broccoli (890)**
- **beets (840)**
- **red bell pepper (710)**
- **onion (450)**
- **corn (400)**
- **eggplant (390)**

As you can see, blueberries top the leader board when it comes to antioxidant power, another reason why blueberries should become as popular in your home as they are in mine. If you can find ways to include kale and spinach, which are slightly bitter-tasting greens, into your salads and juices, then you'll really give your body a huge antioxidant boost.

Checking Out the Best Antioxidants

The most well-known antioxidants are vitamins E and C and carotenoids such as beta-carotene, lycopene, and lutein. Through scientific research, we've learned that:

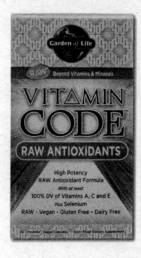

- **Vitamin E** is a fat-soluble vitamin present in whole grains, corn, leafy green vegetables, spinach, broccoli, asparagus, almonds, peanut butter, sunflower seeds, olives, egg yolks, fruits like kiwi and mangos, organ meats, and seafood.

- **Vitamin C** is a water-soluble vitamin present in green peppers, cabbage, spinach, broccoli, kale, cantaloupe, kiwi, strawberries, and citrus fruits and their juices.

- **Beta-carotene** is a precursor to vitamin A (which means the body converts beta-carotene to vitamin A) and is present in butter from grass-fed cows, spinach, carrots, cereal grasses such as wheat and barley, squash, broccoli, yams, tomatoes, cantaloupes, and peaches.

- **Lycopene** is a carotenoid found in watermelon, pink grapefruit and most of all, tomatoes.

- **Lutein** is found in a variety of fruits and vegetables including kale, spinach, peaches, and oranges.

Scientific research "demonstrating" the benefits of antioxidants on the body is fairly extensive these days. These superstar compounds show great potential as amazing health promoters. For instance, we know that vitamin E has a powerfully positive support brain function and helps the maintain proper red blood cell formation.[†] Vitamin E has the ability to maintain cholesterol and blood pressure levels already in the normal ranges, which may have a positive impact on cardiovascular health.[†] Research also suggests that lycopene may support blood pressure already in the normal range and bone health, and a Harvard study of more than 28,000 women showed that those with the highest blood lycopene levels were also where also the most heart healthy after five years.[†]

I know juicy red organic tomatoes aren't readily available year-round and can be on the expensive side, but you really need to make them part of your everyday salad or blended

[†] These statements have not been evaluated by the Food and Drug Administration. This product is not intended to diagnose, treat, cure or prevent any disease.

drink. Tomatoes are great in blender drinks because pulverizing the red flesh of the tomato and combining it with a healthy fat can aid the absorption of lycopene. I make a blended drink daily that consists of raw tomatoes, cucumbers, raw honey, lemon juice, apple cider vinegar, and coconut cream. Lycopene is also present in watermelon, papaya, pink grapefruit, and guava, but not at the same levels as tomatoes.

And what about lutein? Raw sources such as green leafy vegetables like spinach and kale, along with carrots, are great additions to a healthy diet. Lutein is a powerful antioxidant. Researchers at Tufts University analyzed the composition of the human lens and discovered concentrations of lutein in the eye. This finding suggests a strong correlation between carotenoids and macular health.[†]

One of the great things about the Vitamin Code's raw food-created nutrients and their unique Code Factors is that we now have the ability to produce a raw, gluten-free, dairy-free antioxidant formula. In addition, the Vitamin Code raw food creation process (which is described in Chapter 2 in RAW Vitamins) creates companion compounds such as CoQ10 and glutathione—powerful antioxidants in their own right—in each and every nutrient complex.

Our research led to the creation of a comprehensive antioxidant formula containing raw food-created nutrients that delivers vitamin A, vitamin C, vitamin E, and selenium, along with a raw antioxidant blend that includes raw glutathione and raw superoxide dismutase, or SOD. RAW Antioxidants contains a blend of over twenty raw, certified organic fruits and veggies, providing a broad array of antioxidant phytochemicals. Vitamin Code RAW Antioxidants supports heart, skin, eye, prostate, and breast health as well providing memory, concentration, and immune system support.[†] Working best when taken together, the components of RAW Antioxidants are carefully selected to provide a powerful maintenance tool to maintain good health.[†]

We see vitamin A working in conjunction with vitamin E and selenium to provide immune system support.[†] Vitamin C, which is integral to fighting free radicals against oxidative stress, supports the body's natural process of building and maintains collagen, which holds the body's blood vessels in place and supports a healthy heart.[†] We also like how vitamin C supports healthy eyes, skin, bones, teeth and gums, energy production, and growth.[†]

The vitamin E in RAW Antioxidants supports breast and heart health and acts very much like a "big brother" to vitamins A and C.[†] Selenium, an essential trace mineral known for its antioxidant properties, supports normal growth and a healthy immune system.[†]

If Norman Walker were alive today, I think that he would like to swallow a few RAW Antioxidant capsules with his daily raw juice.

RAW Fats

Health Legend:

Mary Enig Ph.D.

I graduated from high school with the class of '93, a time when girls in my class were obsessed with not eating *any* fat in their foods. You should have seen the popular girls and cheerleaders obsessing about the fat grams in their salad dressings or favorite flavor of ice cream. I knew classmates who were borderline anorexic because of their phobia of fat.

Dr. Mary Enig

At that time, teenage girls were heavily influenced by articles in tabloid magazines that described in vivid detail how bad fat was for you. These stories drummed a similar theme: if you want to lose weight, then you better not eat any foods containing fat because fat makes you fat. Millions of young women took that advice to heart, believing if they eliminated fat from their diets, they would be as thin as Jennifer Aniston or Courtney Cox, stars of the hit sitcom *Friends*, which began airing in 1994.

In a demonstration of the law of unintended consequences, however, this country saw an unprecedented leap in anorexia and bulimia among weight-conscious teen girls and, surprisingly, an increase in obesity. It turns out that it wasn't fat that was making them fat—it was eating foods with excess carbohydrates, especially processed foods. Cakes and cookies (especially the fat-free versions) seemed to be the culprit.

Nonetheless, since they bought into the lie that foods with fat automatically caused weight gain, these teenage girls and young women began avoiding all foods containing fat. Food manufacturers immediately picked up on this trend, and it wasn't long before we saw foods with the magic words "fat-free" or "reduced fat" stamped on the packaging. Suddenly, overnight, you could buy cheese, crackers, cookies, yogurt, and ice cream with no fat or very little fat in the product. Restaurants revamped their menus with low-fat and fat-free entrees to suit the changing tastes of "health-conscious" consumers. The best-selling diet books in the 1990s extolled a low-fat, high-carbohydrate diet, and low-fat diets especially appealed to women. By 1995, 44 percent of urban women were on a low-fat diet, according to the consumer research firm Decision Analyst, Inc.

So did low-fat blueberry muffins and reduced-fat rocky road ice cream make anyone any thinner? I'm afraid not. We continued to become fatter as a nation in the 1990s, which carried right into the new millennium.

Unfortunately, I fell prey to the fat-free hype as a freshman at Florida State University. During the year immediately preceding my Crohn's diagnosis, my dietary goal was to consume as few grams of fat per day as possible and largely avoid or minimize saturated fat. Reading from a dietary journal that I kept in those days to track my nutritional progress, I saw my fat intake drop to less than 10 grams on many days with carbohydrate levels of more than 800 grams.

I consumed a multitude of fat-free "natural" cookies, muffins, granola bars, and cereals. Not only did they taste like cardboard, but this diet was also the virtual opposite of the diet I now follow and recommend, which is loaded with healthy raw fats and proteins and is complemented with healthy carbohydrates from raw fruits, veggies, nuts, seeds, and honey. Whether or not a low-fat, high-grain diet contributed to my illness, we'll never know. I will say this: if I were to prescribe a diet that could lead to a multitude of health challenges of every kind, it would be one with limited fats and high in starchy, processed foods.

None of this would surprise Dr. Mary Enig, a research scientist and nutritionist who subscribes to a traditional eating approach. I first became aware of Dr. Enig when she was listed as a contributing editor on the cover of *Nourishing Traditions: The Cookbook that Challenges Politically Correct Nutrition and the Diet Dictocrats* by Sally Fallon, which was released in 1996. This thought-provoking, groundbreaking book contained a startling message: animal fats and cholesterol were *not* villains but were vital factors in the diet: necessary for normal growth, proper function of the brain and nervous system, protection from disease, and maintaining optimum energy levels.

Sally Fallon, who had no formal nutrition training, recruited Dr. Enig to co-write *Nourishing Traditions* because the licensed nutritionist had authored numerous articles on fats and oils in various scientific journals, including the *Scientific Journal of Clinical Nutrition*, where she served as a contributing editor. Dr. Enig was also a consulting editor of the *Journal of the American College of Nutrition*.

Born in 1931, Mary Enig married and raised three children in Maryland before returning to school and earning a Ph.D. in Nutritional Sciences from the University of Maryland in 1984. Her expertise was in the field of lipid biochemistry. She went on to head a number of studies on the content and effects of trans fatty acids and authored over sixty technical papers and presentations. She then became a popular lecturer and author, thanks to *Nourishing Traditions* and *Know Your Fats: The Complete Primer for Understanding the Nutrition of Fats, Oils, and Cholesterol*, which she wrote in 2000. Today, at the age of eighty, Dr. Enig is still going strong as vice president of the Weston A. Price Foundation and continuing to work on the exploratory development of complementary therapies using medium-chain fatty acids from

whole foods such as coconut and palm oils.

Her legacy, however, will be for busting the myth that saturated fats are bad for you. In her view, low-fat diets failed to distinguish between the so-called "good fats" in foods (including olives and flaxseed; tropical oils such as coconut oil; and fats from pastured-raised beef, lamb, bison, poultry, and eggs, as well as fish oils) and the "bad fats" (hydrogenated oils found in margarine and most packaged goods), which are often associated with clogged arteries, cardiovascular disease, and other health problems.

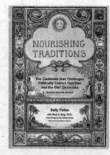

The reason why low-fat diets never worked over the long haul is because they had several things working against them, Dr. Enig said. First, most people could not stay on a low-fat diet for any length of time, especially teen girls in the throes of adolescence and hormonal changes. In addition, "Those who possessed enough willpower to remain fat-free for any length of time developed a variety of problems, including low energy, difficulty in concentration, weight gain, and mineral deficiencies," she wrote in *Nourishing Traditions*.

The raw truth is that we need certain fats in our diet to provide a concentrated source of energy and building material for cell membranes and various hormones. Extra-virgin olive oil, raw coconut and coconut cream, and flaxseed oil—as well as almonds, avocados, really raw cheese, and organically produced butter—contain the fats that you want to include in your diet. The fats you *don't* need are the hydrogenated and partially hydrogenated fats found in processed foods such as dry cereal for breakfast, a glazed doughnut at break, fried corn chips and chocolate chip cookies for lunch, and breaded chicken nuggets for dinner.

The Importance of Fat

What is fat and why is it important?

Whatever we eat—good or bad—is a protein, carbohydrate, or a fat. These macronutrients are essential for health, and our diets need to include a healthy balance of all three.

Protein, as I've described earlier, is required for the structure, function, and regulation of the body's cells, tissues, and organs. Protein is constantly being broken down and replaced in our bodies. The protein in the foods we eat is digested into amino acids that are later used to replace these proteins in our bodies.

Carbohydrates are the starches, sugars and fibers produced by plant foods such as fruits, vegetables, nuts, seeds, legumes, and grains. When carbohydrates are eaten, the digestive tract breaks down the long chains of starches into single sugars, mainly glucose, which becomes an immediate source of energy. If these calories are not expended, however, the body converts them to fat—which is one of the main reasons why our country is so overweight.

Fats, meanwhile, are a concentrated source of energy and building material for cell membranes and various hormones. Healthy fats help maintain the heart, play a vital role in the health of our bones, support the immune system, support normal liver function, and support balanced digestive flora.

Aajonus Vonderplanitz, a raw foods advocate and author of the book *We Want to Live: The Primal Diet,* has the following to say about the importance of raw fats: "Because fat cleanses, fuels, lubricates, and protects the body, it is needed more than any other single nutrient. Fat is a necessary catalyst for utilizing minerals and protein." I would hasten to add that fats add wonderful taste to food and give us that full feeling of satisfaction when we leave the dinner table. Without fats in our foods, we would be raiding the refrigerator for a midnight snack.

The problem with the standard American diet is that we eat too many of the wrong foods containing the wrong fats and not enough of the right foods with the right fats. "Wrong fats" are hydrogenated oils containing trans fats, which increases LDL cholesterol (the "less healthy" blood fat).

As for the "right fats," I'm referring to foods loaded with omega-3 and omega-6 polyunsaturated fats, monounsaturated (omega-9) fatty acids, conjugated linoleic acid (CLA), and my favorite of all fats—healthy saturated fats containing short- and medium-chain fatty acids, which are found in raw dairy products and coconut. These good fats are found in a wide range of foods, including salmon, lamb, and goat meat; in dairy products derived from goat's milk, sheep's milk, and cow's milk from grass-fed animals; and in flaxseeds, walnuts, olives, macadamia nuts, and avocados.

Let's take a closer look at the types of fat that you want to include in your diet:

- **Omega-3 fatty acids.** Considered to be essential fatty acids for the body, omega-3s are necessary for human health, playing a crucial role in brain function as well as normal growth and development.[†] The body can't make omega-3s, however; we have to get them from our food. Omega-3 fatty acids are found in wild-caught fish such as salmon, tuna, and halibut; organic beef such as grass-fed red meat; free-range eggs from chickens; and from walnuts, flaxseeds, and chia seeds. Raw green algae contains the omega-3 fatty acid DHA.

[†] These statements have not been evaluated by the Food and Drug Administration. This product is not intended to diagnose, treat, cure or prevent any disease.

Raw, marinated wild fish (ceviche) is one the best sources of omega-3 fatty acids known to man, containing high-quality protein, vitamin D, and a pair of long-chain polyunsaturated fats known as eicosapentaenoic acid (EPA) and docosahexaenoic acid (DHA) that play a very important role in the function of our bodies.

These nutrients support the formation of neural transmitters, which are vital for brain function.† EPA and DHA are converted into hormone-like substances called prostaglandins, which regulate cell activity and maintain healthy cardiovascular function.† DHA plays a key role during fetal development and early infancy.†

Another omega-3 fatty acid worth noting is alpha linolenic acid (ALA), which is present in flaxseed and its oil, chia seed, hemp seed, and pumpkin seed. ALA is a key player in the support of immune system health, vision, cell membranes, and the production of hormone-like compounds.†

- **Omega-6 fatty acids.** Fatty acids such as linolenic acid (LA) and gamma linolenic acid (GLA) are found in foods containing omega-6 fatty acids. Like their omega-3 cousins, LA and GLA are essential fatty acids (EFAs) that our bodies must have.

The problem is that omega-6s fatty acids are often found in processed foods and refined grains. Thus, most people consume too many omega-6 fatty acids in comparison to omega-3s because they don't eat foods like wild-caught fish and free-range eggs. They prefer to eat chicken nuggets and French fries, which are deep-fried in safflower, corn, and soybean oils—all high in omega-6 fatty acids. A diet heavy in omega-6s impacts your health for the worse by increasing the likelihood of inflammatory and autoimmune disease.

Since the typical American diet is weighted heavily toward omega-6 fatty acids instead of omega-3s, we typically have a ratio of 20 omega-6s to one omega-3, or 20:1. That's way too high. We need to greatly improve our omega-6 to omega-3 ratio to something like 4:1, which is the bull's eye to shoot for. Some excellent sources of omega-6 fatty acids include raw sunflower seeds and its oil, hemp seeds and its oil, poppyseed oil, evening primrose oil, borage seed oil, and blue-green algae such as spirulina and chlorella.

It's important to maintain an appropriate balance of omega-3 and omega-6 fatty acids in the diet so that these two substances can work together to promote good health.

- **Omega-9 fatty acids.** This non-essential unsaturated fat is commonly found in vegetable and animal sources. Unlike omega-3 and omega-6 fatty acids, the body produces omega-9 fatty acids, but they are also beneficial when obtained in food. These fatty acids are known as oleic acids or monounsaturated fats and can be found in olives, olive oil, avocados, and macadamia nuts. Omega-9s are known to support the health of the heart and promote healthy blood sugar levels already in the normal range.†

Although omega-3, omega-6, and omega-9 fatty acids all serve different functions within the body, it's important to consume a balanced portion of these essential and non-essential fatty acids for maintaining overall health and general wellness. According to the American Dietetic Association, adults should receive 20 to 35 percent of their energy from dietary fats and avoid trans fats. I believe that recommendation is way too low. When you're on a primarily raw diet, consuming healthy fats is of paramount importance.

Everyone, it seems, has heard of trans fats, which are produced during the hydrogenation process. Food manufacturers inject hydrogen into safflower, corn, cottonseed, or soybean oil under high pressure to make the oil solid at room temperature, which prevents the oil from becoming rancid too quickly. A nice thought, but adulterating the oil carries a price since trans fatty acids are produced. Trans fats have been associated with a host of maladies and are found in zillions of processed foods.

Believe it or not, there is a healthy trans fatty acid known as CLA (conjugated linoleic acid), which is found in the fats of grass-fed red meat such as beef, lamb, bison, and venison as well as dairy products such as butter and cheese produced by pasture-raised cows, sheep, and browsing goats.

The Top 10 Raw Fats and Oils

As you'll soon see, I've divided my list of Top 10 Raw Fats and Oils into four separate categories. If you make an effort to eat any and all of these healthy foods, you'll be supplying your body with the healthy fats it needs.

According to research reported by Dr. Mary Enig and scientists like her around the world, the fats in these foods are not likely to add pounds to your midsection or put your health at risk. These fats will help you live in extraordinary health.

The top raw omega-3 fats are found in fish, flaxseeds, and chia seeds.

- **Salmon and tuna** caught in the wild are rich sources of omega-3 fats and should be consumed liberally. I'm a fan of raw salmon ceviche that's been marinated in lemon juice, which is quite edible in its raw form. Those of you who've come to enjoy sushi or sashimi, which is sliced raw fish, can benefit greatly from the omega-3s found in wild-caught tuna and salmon. Another notable raw fish dish is halibut or tuna tartar with Sun Gold tomatoes, extra virgin olive oil, and limes. Not only are these types of

raw fish superior sources of omega-3 fatty acids, but they also supply much-needed animal protein. Dr. Enig, who studied the work of Dr. Weston A. Price, promotes the eating of raw meat such as fish for those not following a vegan lifestyle.

- **Flaxseeds**, as well as flaxseed oil, have an abundance of omega-3 fatty acids. Available year-round, flaxseeds are slightly larger than sesame seeds and have a smooth, hard shell. When eaten whole, however, flaxseeds are difficult for the body to digest. Low in calories and rich in alpha linolenic acid (ALA), flaxseeds also contain antioxidants and fiber. Ground-up flaxseeds can be easily mixed with the juice or smoothie of your choice. Ground flaxseeds should be stored in an airtight, opaque storage container that is not exposed to any heat or light.

- **Chia's fiber-rich seeds** have the highest percentage of omega-3s of any plant, including flaxseeds. A half-ounce serving of chia seeds has the same amount of omega-3 fatty acids as found in nine ounces of salmon. The small, grayish seeds can be mixed in water or juice or sprinkled on cereal or salads. The nut-like flavor is pleasing to the palate.

The top raw omega-6 fatty acids are found in sunflower seeds and borage seeds.

As I mentioned before, **omega-6 fatty acids** are an interesting group of fats because they can be good for you as well as bad for you—if you're consuming a high ratio of omega-6s to omega-3s. Still, omega-6s fatty acids are essential, and my favorite sources are sunflower seeds and borage seeds as well as their oils.

- **Sunflower seeds**, delicious to eat, are a gift from the beautiful sunflower with its ray of petals radiating from its bright yellow, seed-studded center. The flower produces grayish-green seeds encased in tear-dropped gray-and-black shells that baseball players love to pop into their mouths and spit out after consuming the nutty seed.

- **Borage seeds** aren't as well known, but borage seed oil is something you want to seek out. Known as the richest dietary source of gamma-linolenic acid (GLA) and containing linolenic acid (LA), borage seed oil is found in numerous nutritional supplements but is best consumed as a cold-pressed, raw oil. Borage seed oil, which has one of the highest amounts of omega-6 GLA of any seed oil, is known to support the body's healthy inflammation response and promote healthy skin.[†]

The top raw omega-9 fatty acids are found in avocados, olives, olive oil, and macadamia nuts.

One of the most nutritious of all fruits, the **avocado** is high in monounsaturated fats and omega-9 fatty acids, making this a superfood in my book. When you make a salad, add an avocado and chop up a few olives, which are also high in omega-9 fatty acids.

- **Extra virgin olive oil** requires less pressure and lower temperatures during the pressing process than oil from seeds, which preserves its nutritional qualities. Olive oil is rich in oleic acid, an omega-9 fatty acid, which is thought to play a protective role for the heart. Be sure to choose extra virgin olive oil, which guarantees that the oil was not put through a heat process that curtails its health benefits.

- **Macadamia nuts** are a delicious snack food that wins high marks for its rich, buttery flavor and crunchy texture. This high-energy food is full of protein and fiber and contains high amounts of monounsaturated fats as well as omega-9 fatty acids.

The top raw saturated fats are found in cheese, butter, coconuts, and coconut cream.

"Butter is better," says Dr. Mary Enig, who has made it her life's goal to fight a misinformation campaign from "Diet Dictocrats" who assert that naturally saturated fats from animal sources are the root cause of heart disease and other ailments.

"Butter bore the brunt of the attack and was accused of terrible crimes," wrote Dr. Enig. "The Diet Dictocrats told us it was better to switch to polyunsaturated margarine, and most Americans did. Butter all but disappeared from our tables, shunned as a miscreant."

It's time to bring butter back.

The notion that butter causes weight gain is another sad misconception, said Dr. Enig. "The short- and medium-chain fatty acids in butter are not stored in the adipose tissue, but are used for quick energy," she said. Fat tissue in humans is composed mainly of longer-chain fatty acids, which comes from refined carbohydrates.

Really raw cheese is another great source of high-quality protein and fat, along with being a concentrated source of beneficial minerals. Really raw cheese contains powerful short-chain fatty acids, and because it's produced by grass-fed cows, it's a great source of CLA (conjugated linoleic acid), which supports a healthy immune system and healthy weight management.

Really raw cheese also contains vitamin K2 (MK-7), which is also known as the X Factor or Price Factor in honor of Dr. Weston A. Price. This grass-fed dairy product is the subject of exciting and emerging research pointing to cardiovascular and bone health support.

Much of the raw cheese available in health food stores is made from milk that has been heated to just under 150 degrees, which is technically not pasteurized but isn't raw in my book either. My friend and master cheese maker Trent Hendricks is an award-winning farmstead and artisanal cheese maker who creates my favorite really raw cheese in a number of varieties. Really raw cheese is made from raw milk produced by grass-fed cows that have been fed no grain and raised organically.

My family enjoys really raw cheese virtually every day. Really raw cheese can be found in better health food stores nationwide, but in order to receive the true health benefits from this wonderful source of healthy fats, you must find a source of raw cheese that has been made from milk that has never exceeded the body temperature of a cow that has consumed no grain. This ensures a high amount of vitamins, minerals, and healthy fats, including omega-3 and CLA. (See the RAW Truth Resource Guide for more information.)

The Wonderful Superfood: Raw Coconut Cream

For several years now, my family and I have enjoyed a superb source of healthy fats from delicious and nutritious raw coconut cream. My oldest son, Joshua, and I consume raw coconut cream in our morning smoothies, use it as an ingredient for raw popsicles, and make the best-tasting raw piña colada ice cream you've ever tasted.

In the last two years, I have been purchasing raw coconut cream from my friend Renee Ainlay, who began making fresh-pressed raw coconut cream for her personal use to maintain her own health. When Renee discovered the health benefits, she began to share the raw coconut cream with family and friends. Since raw coconut cream was perishable and not available commercially anywhere in the U.S. at the time—all canned coconut cream, coconut ice cream, yogurt, and coconut milks have been heat treated or pasteurized—the demand grew. Renee eventually purchased special equipment from Asia and started a small business creating and selling raw coconut cream, which she now supplies to people across America. The Rubin family is among her top customers.

Raw coconut cream should not be confused with coconut milk or puréed young coconut meat. Raw coconut cream is created by pressing or "juicing" the meat of the mature coconut, creating a food loaded with medium-chain fatty acids that are easily absorbable. Because most of the coconut fiber is removed, raw coconut cream has the consistency of cream cheese and has a smooth texture, making it ideal as a healthy snack or as an ingredient in a raw dessert or smoothie.

Let me tell you more about why I think raw coconut cream is one of the most important foods in my family's diet.

The saturated fat contained in coconut cream, when eaten in moderation, is a healthy fat that your body can easily metabolize and turn into quick energy, all done without raising your blood cholesterol level or adding pounds to your frame. The main saturated fat—or fatty acid—in coconut cream is lauric acid, which is the same type of saturated fat found in a mother's breast milk. For those on a raw vegan diet or who are unable to acquire or choose not to consume raw dairy products, I believe raw coconut cream could be the most important food to include in your daily diet.

Raw coconut cream is difficult to produce at home (see sidebar for instructions) but can be purchased in its raw form. (Please see the the RAW Truth Resources Guide for more information).

The benefits of coconuts and coconut cream have been known for centuries. Early Spanish explorers, who called the hairy nut a *coco* (meaning "monkey face") because of the three indentations or "eyes" on the shell, soon discovered that coconuts provided a nutritious source of water, juice, milk, meat, and even oil. Many island civilizations in the Caribbean and South Pacific depended upon the coconut as a staple in their diet. From India to Indonesia, the coconut nourished growing populations and was even used as currency for purchasing goods on the Nicobar Islands in the Indian Ocean. The native populations understood that the coconut fruit had many uses for its water, milk, meat, and oil, and the shell even functioned as its own dish and cup.

Highly nutritious and rich in fiber, vitamins, and minerals, Dr. Enig classifies coconut as a "functional food" because it provides many health benefits over and beyond the basic nutrients. Rich in protein, the meat of the coconut is low in carbohydrates, low in sugars, and high in lauric acid, which is key.

I urge you to get the healthy fats you need by consuming foods such as raw coconut and raw coconut cream, raw avocado, flaxseed oil, and really raw cheese.

† These statements have not been evaluated by the Food and Drug Administration. This product is not intended to diagnose, treat, cure or prevent any disease.

Do-It-Yourself Raw Coconut Cream

Making raw coconut cream at home is a very difficult but rewarding chore. I initially made a batch or two at home, but then I decided thereafter to order raw coconut cream and store several jars in the freezer. (See the The RAW Truth Resources Guide for ordering information.) Since my family consumes several jars per week, I purchase a few dozen jars at a time, which last me a few months.)

If you're going to try making raw coconut cream yourself, start by choosing a coconut and inspecting its shell. If you find any cracks or dark watermarks—small or large—or any black spots, the coconut has probably soured. You should also inspect the three small dark circles grouped together at the top, which are called the eyes. If one of the eyes is open or shrunken, then the coconut has soured. If the coconut is without any of the above, the odds of having a good coconut are nine out of ten.

You will need leather gloves and an ice pick, hammer, curved-ended oyster knife, plus a juicer—such as a Green Star juicer—to separate cream from the pulp. Poke the coconut eyes until you find the eye that is soft. Do not puncture it yet, however. Puncture one of the hard circles with the ice pick and hammer. Then puncture the soft circle with the ice pick. Pour the coconut water into a glass. Taste the coconut water. If it is sour, the coconut may be partially or completely soured. If the coconut water is good, then you can drink it as a wonderful source of hydrating electrolytes.

Put on your gloves. To loosen the meat from the shell, firmly tap coconut all around for two minutes but not hard enough to crack it yet. Now, crack the coconut shell at the end opposite from the three eyes. Hammer the coconut into many pieces. (If you find some of the meat yellow or discolored, then the coconut has partially soured.) Pry the meat from the shell with the oyster knife.

If black spots appear on the brown skin, the coconut has molded where the spots appear. Separate the non-soured meat from the soured meat. If it is completely soured or moldy, begin again with another coconut.

Slice good coconut pieces into strips that are approximately ¼-inch thick by ½-inch thick width and any length. Or—easier!—drop the chunks of coconut into a food processor and grind.

Place the coconut meat slices or ground coconut into a juicer that separates cream from pulp, such as a Green Star or Champion juicer. The result is coconut cream that will thicken as hard as butter when refrigerated. Use the pulp to fertilize your garden or air-dry it for use in a raw dessert. Do not mix the coconut water with the coconut cream unless you intend to drink it within twenty-four hours, or it will sour.

It is best to store coconut cream in many four- or eight-ounce glass jars and freeze if you don't plan to consume the coconut cream within seven days. Each coconut renders six-to-eight ounces of pure cream, plus several ounces of coconut water.

RAW Beverages

Health Legend:

F. Batmanghelidj, M.D.

Like Dr. Mary Enig, Fereydoon Batmanghelidj was born in 1931, but half a world away in Iran, where he was raised by wealthy parents who had the means to send him abroad to St. Mary's Hospital Medical School in London, where he specialized in gastroenterology.

He eventually returned to his homeland to help in the development of hospitals and medical centers in the 1970s, but years of living abroad made him politically suspect when the Shah of Iran was deposed during the 1979 revolution. Dr. Batmanghelidj was thrown into Evin Prison, along with thousands of other political prisoners, when the Ayatollah Khomeini grabbed the reins of power.

Dr. Fereydoon Batmanghelidj

The guards, who knew that he was a physician, would ask him to take a look at prisoners in various states of agony. Dr. Batmanghelidj was not sure what he could do; after all, there were no medications available at the prison. One day, he was asked to see a prisoner complaining of excruciating stomach pain, so much so that two friends had to help him to his feet as he doubled over in pain.

The only thing Dr. Batmanghelidj could give the poor soul was a couple of glasses of water. Within minutes, his stomach pain subsided and eventually disappeared after drinking additional water. This prisoner was severely dehydrated.

More hurting prisoners asked to see Dr. Batmanghelidj. In fact, over the next two and a half years, he treated hundreds, if not thousands of prisoners suffering from stomach pains caused by the stress of being falsely imprisoned with a regimen of water drinking. As he noted their physical recuperation after hydrating themselves with plenty of water, Dr. Batmanghelidj began writing his clinical observations on the effect of water as a treatment for various stress-induced health problems.

Here's where the story takes another twist: after nearly two years in prison, the warden told Dr. Batmanghelidj that he was free to go. The Iranian physician, instead of walking out the front gate, asked the warden if he could stay in prison a while longer to complete his scientific study of the link between drinking water and prisoners' health.

I'm sure a guard had to pick the warden off the floor, but he granted Dr. Batmanghelidj's request. The Iranian doctor stayed four extra months and finished his study, which he announced in the *Iranian Medical Association Journal*.

The rest is history, and Dr. Batmanghelidj's clarion call to drink more water was eventually heard by health-minded readers of his books, *Your Body's Many Cries for Water* and *You're Not Sick, You're Thirsty!*

I was one of those readers, and I can remember gulping down *Your Body's Many Cries for Water* in the late 1990s, thirsty for information about the importance of keeping myself thoroughly hydrated. I nodded my head to Dr. Batmanghelidj's assertion that people around the world, especially in Western cultures, did not drink nearly the amount of water they need to keep themselves properly hydrated. Replenishing the body with water throughout the day is vital because fluids in urine eliminate waste products, keep the digestive system from becoming clogged, dissipate excess heat, and cool the body.

How much water does the body need to stay hydrated? The most oft-quoted advice in health books is to "drink eight glasses of water a day," which is easy to write and hard to do. Many think that if they drink that much water, they'll be running to the bathroom every twenty minutes. Others sense they need to drink something, but instead of water, they ply their bodies with mocha coffees, flavored sodas, and sport drinks.

Yes, you do go to the bathroom more often when you're well hydrated, but is that so bad? Our bodies need water. "Every twenty-four hours, the body recycles the equivalent of forty thousand glasses of water to maintain its normal physiological functions," said Dr. Batman, which is what many call him. "If you think you are different and your body does not need eight to ten glasses of water each day, you are making a major mistake."

I've heeded Dr. Batman's advice for the better part of fifteen years by staying hydrated with pure water and raw foods and beverages.

I also make it a point to drink raw beverages before each meal and before, during, and after exercise, knowing that I need extra fluid to offset perspiration. I've learned through personal experience that if I fail to drink enough fluids before or during my exercise periods, my body goes into the tank.

I'm thankful that I've heeded the hydration message that health legend Dr. Batmanghelidj felt so passionate about. He is no longer with us, having died in 2004 from complications related to pneumonia, but his legacy lives on in seven books with his message that proper hydration plays a key role in regulating body temperature, carrying nutrients and oxygen to the cells, cushioning joints, protecting organs and tissues, and removing toxins from the body.

Caution: you must independently test all spring water before you make the decision to consume it. The findaspring website is simply a source for locating springs, and no one can validate water safety.

Water—which, in its pure form, is odorless and colorless—is the perfect fluid replacement. But how can you drink "raw" water—meaning water that has been uncooked, untreated, and unadulterated? And are there "raw beverages" that we should look for?

Well, water isn't normally cooked or boiled, although that's often necessary in many Third World countries where water supplies are often contaminated by pollution, sewage, and garbage. Even though municipal water treatment plants in the U.S. do not boil our water, they do routinely *treat* our water supplies with chlorine, which is a potent bacteria-killing chemical. Since the water coming out of the tap is chemically treated to make it safe to drink, many choose to "process" their tap water with a water filtration system. If you're like me, you probably have some sort of water-filtration system at home that removes chlorine and other impurities from the water. That's a smart thing to do, but an even better source of hydration come from the "raw" water pouring forth from natural springs, which I'll describe in greater detail in the next section.

I'll also talk about how the most hydrating, most organized water comes from raw foods and beverages, including fruits and vegetables and their juices, and introduce several excellent raw beverages from raw milk kefir, raw coconut water, kombucha, and the lacto-fermented grape beverage I call "new wine." When it comes to keeping the body properly hydrated, pure water and raw beverages are the only game in town.

The Top Raw Beverages

A good place to start is with **raw, natural spring water.**

My earliest memory of consuming raw water, so to speak, happened when I was seven or eight years old. Every summer, my parents would take me to visit my paternal grandparents in Long Island, New York. Grandpa Jerry and Grandma Ann had a summer home in Mountaindale, a hamlet around ninety miles from New York City near the Catskill Mountains. Mountaindale isn't far from George Washington's home in Monticello.

I loved Grandpa Jerry. Born Joshua Rubin, my grandfather "Americanized" his name to Jerry to escape persecution for being Jewish. He was a dentist who saw patients in the basement of his home and had a keen interest in natural health in his early twenties. He enjoyed studying the works of Herbert Shelton, one of the founders of the science hygiene movement, otherwise known as natural hygiene, as well as the work of Dr. Royal Lee.

Whenever we visited Papa Jerry in Mountaindale, he'd call me into the kitchen and hand me an empty gallon plastic container. "We're going to get some spring water," he'd say.

With empty containers in hand, we'd set off on a short drive, followed by a fifteen-minute walk that would take us the side of a small mountain, where a fresh spring gushed forth the purest, most refreshing, best-tasting water you'd ever find. We'd fill up our gallon containers and tote them back home to drink.

Spring water—unadulterated by filtration, chlorine, ultraviolet rays, or ozone to kill bacteria—is your best chance to drink raw water. A friend of mine, Daniel Vitalis, can help you find raw sources of water in your area. He has helped put together a website called www.findaspring.com, which helps you locate a natural spring close to your home. Then you can do what Papa Jerry and I did—go on a hike and bring home a gallon of spring water. Of course, fetching your own water is a bit idealistic these days, and

for most people, not a realistic way to keep yourself properly hydrated. That's why I want you to consider drinking **raw milk, yogurt, kefir and probiotic whey,** which are not only loaded with nutrients but are also extremely hydrating. I've already talked in some detail about the health benefits of raw cultured dairy products in Chapter 7 on RAW Protein, but consuming raw milk and cultured dairy products from cows, goats, and sheep will go a long way to keeping your body properly hydrated.

Raw dairy contains the right fats, including omega-3 fats and conjugated linoleic acid (CLA), which is abundant in milk from grass-fed animals. With vitamins, minerals, enzymes, and probiotics, fresh, unprocessed raw milk supports the body's digestive and immune systems.[†] Raw milk contains lactic acid bacteria that creates a healthy intestinal environment while providing more calcium, magnesium, phosphorus, and sulfur than pasteurized, homogenized dairy.

The best dairy products are the lacto-fermented kind—yogurt, kefir, hard cheeses (preferably aged), probiotic whey, cream cheese, cottage cheese, and cultured cream. You can shop for them at natural food supermarkets in certain states, but the best sources of raw, cultured dairy are found at local farms. (Visit www.RealMilk.com for a farm near you.) Another advantage to consuming cultured dairy is that those who are lactose-intolerant can often stomach fermented dairy products because they contain little or no residual lactose, which is the type of sugar in milk that many find hard to digest.

Kefir, believed to have originated in Turkey and meaning "feel good" in Turkish, is a cultured raw milk. This tart-tasting, effervescent beverage contains naturally occurring

bacteria and yeasts. Kefir is also a great base ingredient to build smoothies around: just add eight ounces of kefir into a blender, an assortment of frozen berries or fruits, a spoonful of raw honey, and you're well on the way to churning up a delicious, satisfying, and hydrating beverage. What a great drink to start the day!

Yogurt, when made without the use of thickeners, often has the consistency of a beverage. Consuming yogurt from grass-fed cows, goats, or sheep is wonderful for your health and shows its versatility as a component of blender drinks, snacks, and meals. You can find raw dairy from cows, goats, and sheep by visiting www.RealMilk.com.

Probiotic whey is a new twist on an ancient beverage. Raw probiotic whey is a byproduct of cheese making and contains pre-digested protein in the form of whey protein, vitamins, minerals, organic acids, and, of course, powerful probiotics. Raw probiotic whey can be consumed in small amounts to support healthy digestion, elimination, and immune system function.[†] Raw probiotic whey can be made by straining raw yogurt or kefir through a cheese cloth. Used daily as a health beverage or as a key ingredient in many recipes or as a starter culture to make several lacto-fermented beverages mentioned in this chapter, whey is an indispensible item in your culinary arsenal.

Another raw beverage I enjoy drinking every day is **fresh veggie juice**. What a great way to start the morning—with a hydrating and detoxifying dose of greens. When you wake up in the morning, your body is acidic and dehydrated, the natural consequence of sleeping for an extended period of time. Each exhalation of breath results in the loss of a small amount of water, and if it was warm in your bedroom overnight, sweating also depletes the body's water.

That's why hydration should be a priority after you wake up and get dressed. Start by drinking a glass of spring water with raw lemon juice—at room temperature so as not to shock the body—and give yourself at least fifteen minutes for the water to reach the body's cells. Or you can do what I do as soon as your feet hit the floor—reach for a glass of fresh vegetable juice.

Carrots, celery, parsley, and spinach—these are just a few of the vegetables that can be juiced together into a wonderful blend of healthy nutrition. If you want to be more adventurous, you can add ginger, garlic, jalapeno pepper, radish, or turmeric to your vegetable juice, but many like to also add fruits like lemons or apples to improve the taste.

Raw fresh juice not only provides hydration through the water in the vegetables and fruits, but fresh veggie juice also supplies vitamins, minerals, enzymes, and phytochemicals, which have amazing overall health properties. Unlike dehydrating beverages like coffee, soft drinks, and alcohol, raw fresh juices hydrate you and supply your body with the fluids it needs from daily activities and exercise.

Of course, you can drink fresh fruit juice as part of your breakfast, or as a snack later in the day. Whenever I stayed at Grandpa Jerry's as a youngster, I could count on him having a quart or two of fresh-squeezed orange or grapefruit juice waiting for me at the breakfast table. Many people, including myself, enjoy juice made from their favorite fruits. What can taste sweeter—or be better for you—than a glass of fresh-squeezed juice made from organic oranges or a mixture of several fruits?

Raw fruit juices and raw veggie juices shouldn't be a breakfast-only item. After these juices are made in a juicer, you can drink them any time of day, but they are best consumed on an empty stomach at least twenty minutes before eating other foods. When you consume the whole fruits and vegetables found in a juice, you receive easily absorbable nutrients, along with enzyme co-factors. Since the nutrients and enzymes have been liberated, so to speak, from the fiber pulp—and without any heat, I might add—the cells of your body can take in the nutrition quickly and easily. Keep in mind that the body's cells are made up mostly of water, which is why good hydration is essential for proper cellular nutrition.

Another raw beverage I want to throw into the mix is **raw nut milk such as raw almond milk, raw cashew milk, or raw hazelnut milk.** Various raw nut milks can be found in better health food and natural grocery stores, but those are sterilized and not beneficial to health. Nut and seed milks can be healthy if you make your own raw versions at home with a high-performance blender. You will need to soak the nuts or seeds in filtered water overnight and then blend them with water and some type of raw sweetener like raw honey or dates.

Nut milks are a dairy alternative for vegans or for those who don't drink raw dairy. Raw nut and seed milk are a good source of nutrients such as protein and healthy fats.

Lacto-Fermented Beverages Are a Kick

Looking for an effervescent beverage that is loaded with probiotics and enzymes? The following beverages may not be familiar to you, but they should be. **Lacto-fermented beverages such as kvass, kombucha, kefir, and new wine** are relatively unknown in this country, but you can be the first on your block to derive great hydration and health benefits from these unfamiliar drinks.

Kvass and kombucha are Russian in origin and have been around for centuries. Kvass (pronounced *kuh-VAHSS*) is a fermented beverage that's made from rye, barley, or beets and tastes like a bit like beer or ale—but kvass isn't alcoholic. Kombucha (pronounced *kom-BOO-cha*) is a fermented beverage made from black or green tea and a fungus culture known as a kombucha "mushroom"—a pancake-shaped mass of bacteria and yeast. Both beverages contain lactic acid and supply beneficial probiotics, enzymes, and minerals to the digestive system.[†]

Kvass is hard to find, and in this country, must usually be purchased online. (Whole Foods, for instance, sells kvass only in New York City because of the large Russian immigrant population.) They say that opening a bottle of kvass releases a fragrant bouquet reminiscent of freshly baked bread cooling on a windowsill.

Kombucha, on the other hand, is widely available in health food stores after gaining popularity around ten years ago. You could say that kombucha has almost a cult-like following, especially among the celebrity set. Hollywood actress Lindsay Lohan has been pictured often clutching a bottle of kombucha, which, in liquid form, contains a small trace of alcohol. Some brands, however, may have *too much* alcohol. Recently, several kombucha brands have been recalled because they were found to have as much as 3 percent alcohol, which is close to the amount of alcohol in beer. Be careful with store-bought kombucha, as many contain significant levels of sugar as well.

When fermented correctly, though, kombucha is as tart as a Granny Smith apple and delivers a cidery flavor and a kick of fizziness. I was introduced to kombucha around 2003 and have come to enjoy its sweet-and-sour effervescent taste. I soon figured out that kombucha wasn't a drink you guzzle down on a hot summer's day, however. You want to sip kombucha slowly, not taking more than four ounces at a time. Kombucha can be purchased or made at home utilizing a fairly simple process.

Water kefir is kefir grains that have been placed in water and some type of sugar and allowed to grow for a day or more at room temperature. I'm going to be honest: water kefir tastes sour and is not easy to drink, but it has been reported to support healthy digestion.[†] You usually have to make your own water kefir, which means purchasing a water kefir kit online.

"New wine," also known as grape cooler, is a lacto-fermented beverage made from fresh grape juice that is mildly effervescent but not alcoholic. Other fruits can be used as well. I know in Europe that the Germans and Swiss will make a variant of apple cider known as Apfelmost. New wine and other lacto-fermented fruit juice beverages can be made at home by adding probiotic whey or a kefir or cultured veggie starter to raw fruit juice. This enjoyable raw drink is fizzy and refreshing, can double as punch at your dinner party, and is great for your digestive health.

Check Out Coconut Water and Coconut Kefir

The final two raw beverages I want to discuss are ones I'd really like you to make an effort to try: **coconut water and coconut kefir**.

Coconut water is nature's sports drink and has been a staple for tropical regions around the world for centuries. Coconut water is much, much healthier for you than sports drinks or fitness waters. Popular sports drinks contain a

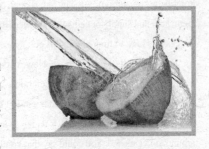

combination of tap water, sucrose, glucose, and fructose (in other words, sugars), and artificial colors with some potassium and sodium (the electrolytes) in their chemical form. I shake my head every time that a bottle of "water" can still be called water when sugar has been added.

Give coconut water a try instead. Drinking raw coconut water right from the coconut or purchased frozen from better health food stores can replenish electrolytes without the ill effects of added sugar, caffeine, or chemicals. Eight ounces of coconut water give you a low-calorie, fat-free, pure form of liquid nourishment that is also an excellent source of potassium—more potassium than what's found in a banana and around fifteen times more than most sports drinks.

Remember, coconut water should not be confused with the thick, white coconut milk that comes from mature coconuts and is made into coconut cream, as I described in the last chapter. Coconut water is the clear juice of young coconuts and is refreshing and naturally sweet.

You can readily find fresh mature or young coconuts in your local health food store. To get to the water, you will need to puncture the coconut with a knife or screwdriver and drain the coconut water. Health stores and natural groceries sell coconut water, but they are sterilized, pasteurized, and sold in aseptic packaging. There is one brand of frozen raw coconut water available in select health food stores in the freezer section that I recommend, however. (See the RAW Truth Resource Guide for more information.)

Perhaps my favorite raw beverage of all is **raw coconut kefir,** first recommended by Donna Gates, author of *The Body Ecology Diet*. Raw coconut kefir is made from raw coconut water that has been cultured with probiotics in a way similar to kefir, but is dairy-free, suitable for vegans, and promotes a healthy intestinal environment supporting your body's immune and digestive systems.

My friend Renee Ainlay, whose company makes my favorite raw fat on the planet— raw coconut cream—also produces a powerful raw coconut kefir probiotic beverage. You can certainly juice your own raw coconuts and add a kefir starter culture at home (see the RAW Truth Resource Guide for more information on a starter culture), but if you choose to purchase raw coconut kefir probiotic from Renee, you'll be sipping one of the most hydrating, digestive-supporting beverages on the planet. This naturally fermented drink made from organic coconuts contains a blend of probiotics that can aid in both hydration and digestive health support. (See the RAW Truth Resource Guide to purchase this amazing product.)

Proper hydration is critical to experiencing extraordinary health. The best sources of hydration are raw beverages that contain the most highly organized and ionized source of water that is bound to key essential elements that promote the proper function of all the body's organs and systems

CHAPTER 14

The Raw Truth

Nutrition Plan

The following chapter outlines the RAW Truth Nutrition Plan. You will see that I have listed two versions:

1. **A vegan-friendly program with all plant-based foods**
2. **An omnivorous program that adds animal foods**

Each program places an emphasis on the consumption of nutrient-dense, "living," enzyme- and probiotic-rich foods and healthy fats, while avoiding the overconsumption of foods high in carbohydrates, especially grains.

It should be noted that while people who follow a raw diet may feel immediate positive results, a portion of first-time raw food dieters might experience a "detox," or cleansing. During this period, they may temporarily feel lethargic, have an increase in food cravings, experience mild headaches, or even undergo changes in bowel habits. This is the body's normal reaction to the increase of nutrients and the elimination of unhealthy and even addictive foods.

I highly recommend that you keep a daily chart or journal of your progress so that you can understand how you're progressing each day and how certain foods or combination of foods affect your physical and emotional health.

Whether you're going on a raw food diet for a defined period of time as a "cleanse," or you've decided to begin a raw diet as a way of life, I believe your health is about to undergo a major positive transformation.

Congratulations for taking your next step on the road to Extraordinary Health.

The RAW Truth Vegan Food List

Fats and oils (organic, extra virgin, raw)
- flaxseed oil
- hempseed oil
- coconut cream (raw, not canned)
- extra-virgin olive oil
- avocado
- sunflower oil
- poppyseed oil
- evening primrose oil
- raw cacao butter

Vegetables (organic and fresh)
- squash (winter or summer)
- broccoli
- asparagus
- beets
- cauliflower
- Brussels sprouts
- cabbage
- carrots
- celery
- cucumber
- eggplant
- pumpkin
- garlic
- onion
- okra
- mushrooms

- peas
- peppers (red, yellow, orange, green)
- string/green beans
- tomatoes
- lettuce (all varieties)
- spinach
- artichokes (French, not Jerusalem)
- leafy greens (kale, collard, broccoli rabe, mustard greens, etc.)
- wheat grass (juice)
- sprouts (broccoli, sunflower, pea shoots, radish, etc.)

- sea vegetables (kelp, dulse, nori, kombu, hijiki, etc.)
- raw, fermented vegetables (lacto-fermented only, no vinegar)
- corn
- sweet potatoes
- white potatoes

Nuts, seeds and their butters (e.g. almond butter)
- organic, raw, soaked; chew well
- almonds

- coconut meat
- pumpkin seeds
- hempseed
- flaxseed
- sunflower seeds
- almond butter
- hempseed butter
- sunflower butter
- tahini (sesame butter)
- pumpkin seed butter
- macadamia nuts
- hazelnuts
- pecans
- walnuts
- Brazil nuts
- chia seeds
- cashews

Condiments, spices, seasonings, cooking ingredients, and salad dressings (organic are best)

- salsa (raw, organic)
- guacamole (fresh)
- apple cider vinegar
- coconut sap vinegar
- soy sauce (wheat-free, raw), tamari
- Herbamare seasoning
- Celtic sea salt
- umeboshi paste
- balsamic vinegar
- herbs and spices (air dried, no added stabilizers)
- pickled ginger (preservative- and color-free)
- wasabi (preservative-and color-free)
- homemade salad dressings and marinades using allowable ingredients

Fruits (organic fresh or frozen are allowed)

- blueberries
- strawberries
- blackberries
- raspberries
- cherries
- grapefruit
- lemon
- lime
- pomegranate
- cranberries
- apples (with skin)
- melons
- apricots
- peaches
- grapes
- orange
- pears
- papaya
- kiwi
- nectarines
- pineapple
- plums
- figs
- durian
- jackfruit
- cherimoya
- persimmon
- mamey
- sapote
- bananas
- mangoes
- mulberries
- goji
- dried fruit (low-temperature dehydrated

Beverages

- coconut water (from young or mature coconut)
- coconut kefir
- herbal teas (sun-steeped, not boiled)—unsweetened or with a small amount of honey
- raw vegetable juice (beet or carrot juice—maximum 25 percent of total)
- lacto-fermented beverages (kombucha, kvass)
- purified, non-chlorinated water
- natural sparkling water, no carbonation added

Sweeteners

- date paste (made from raw dates)
- coconut sap nectar

Snacks/Miscellaneous

- raw cacao (nibs or powder)

Need Recipes?

You'll find raw vegan-friendly recipes involving fermented foods, sprouted grains, and dairy-rich smoothies in Chapter 16, "RAW Truth Recipes." You'll also encounter some cleansing recipes made from delicious raw foods. For additional healthy and delicious raw vegan recipes, visit www.gardenoflife.com.

Disclaimers Regarding Raw Dairy, Raw Eggs, Raw Fish, and Raw Juice

- Raw milk products may contain disease-causing microorganisms. Persons at highest risk for of disease from these organisms include newborns and infants, the elderly, pregnant women, those taking corticosteroids, antibiotics and antacids, and those having chronic illnesses and other conditions that weaken their immunity.

- Consuming raw or undercooked eggs may increase your risk of food-borne illness.

- Consuming raw or undercooked seafood may increase your risk of food-borne illness.

- Juice that has not been pasteurized may contain bacteria that can increase the risk of food-borne illness. People most at risk are children, the elderly and persons with a weakened immune system.

Note: I am the founder of Garden of Life, and, where applicable, I am am recommending my company's products.Other companies I recommend, I do so because I consume their products and find them to be of good taste and/or (nutritional) quality. Garden of Life cannot be help responsible for the quality or claims of these products. Please research them and consult with your healthcare practitioner prior to starting any new diet or supplement program.

The RAW Truth Vegan Nutrition Plan
Sample 3-Day Nutrition Plan

Day 1

Upon waking

- Perfect Food RAW: one serving mixed in 12 ounces of raw vegetable juice or water
- RAW Probiotics: three capsules

Breakfast

Six ounces of blueberries

Two ounces raw coconut cream

Raw nuts and seeds (soaked is best)

- Vitamin Code: two capsules
- RAW Calcium: three capsules
- RAW Enzymes: one capsule

Lunch

Paul's Powerful Salad
(see page 185 for recipe)

Tahini Dressing

Mushroom Pizza *(see page 185 for recipe)*

- Vitamin Code: two capsules
- RAW Calcium: two capsules
- RAW Enzymes: one capsule

Dinner

Two ounces of raw coconut kefir or kvass

Marinated Veggies *(see page 186 for recipe)*

Green salad with mixed greens, tomatoes, avocado, carrots, cucumbers, celery, red cabbage, red peppers, red onions, and sprouts

For the salad dressing, mix extra-virgin olive oil, apple cider vinegar or lemon juice, Celtic sea salt, herbs, and spices

Raw Applesauce *(see page 187 for recipe)*

- RAW Enzymes: one capsule

RAW snack

One serving of raw coconut kefir

- RAW Meal: one serving mixed in raw juice or water

Before bed

- RAW Fiber: one serving mixed in raw veggie juice or water

Day 2

Upon waking

- Perfect Food RAW: one serving mixed in 12 ounces of raw vegetable juice
- RAW Probiotics: three capsules

Breakfast

Coconut Shake *(see page 188 for recipe)*

- Vitamin Code: two capsules
- RAW Calcium: three capsules
- RAW Enzymes: one capsule

Lunch

Paul's Favorite Salad *(see page 186 for recipe)*

Chia "tapioca" pudding
(see page 186 for recipe)

- Vitamin Code: two capsules
- RAW Calcium: two capsules
- RAW Enzymes: one capsule

Dinner

Two ounces of raw coconut kefir or kvass

Green salad with mixed greens, tomatoes, avocado, carrots, cucumbers, celery, red cabbage, red peppers, red onions, and sprouts

For the salad dressing, mix extra-virgin olive oil, apple cider vinegar or lemon juice, Celtic sea salt, herbs, and spices, or you may add 1 tablespoon of extra-virgin olive oil

Paul's Coconut Fruit Pie
(see page 187 for recipe)

- RAW Enzymes: one capsule

RAW snacks

Flaxseed crackers and raw pesto
(see page 184 for recipe)

- RAW Meal: one serving mixed in raw juice or water.

Before bed

- RAW Fiber: one serving mixed in raw veggie juice or water

Day 3

Upon waking

- Perfect Food RAW: one serving mixed in 8 ounces of raw juice or water
- RAW Probiotics: three capsules

Breakfast

Coconut Avocado Drink
(see page 188 for recipe)

- Vitamin Code: two capsules
- RAW Calcium: three capsules
- RAW Enzymes: one capsule

Lunch

Blended Salad/Raw Soup
(see page 189 for recipe)

Raw coconut cream with pineapple

- Vitamin Code: two capsules
- RAW Calcium: two capsules
- RAW Enzymes: one capsule

Dinner

Two ounces of raw coconut kefir or kvass

Green salad with mixed greens, tomatoes, avocado, carrots, cucumbers, celery, red cabbage, red peppers, red onions, and sprouts

Carrot Ginger Dressing
(see page 184 for recipe)

Strawberry Cheesecake
(see page 188 for recipe)

- RAW Enzymes: one capsule

RAW snacks

Raw veggies (carrots, celery, etc.) dipped in raw almond butter or sesame tahini

Raw coconut cookies

- RAW Meal: one serving mixed in raw juice or water.

Before bed

- RAW Fiber: one serving mixed in raw veggie juice or water

The RAW Truth Omnivore Nutrition Plan

The RAW omnivore nutrition plan allows for the addition of raw animal foods. When consuming raw animal foods, please make sure that the source is organic and for fish, wild caught. When consuming dairy or eggs, make sure to purchase from a farm that allows the animals to consume their natural forage-based diets. (Be sure to see the disclaimer at the beginning of this chapter.)

Fish (wild freshwater/ocean-caught fresh or previously frozen)
- salmon
- halibut
- tuna
- cod
- grouper
- eggs (pastured, organically raised)
- chicken eggs (whole with yolk)
- duck eggs (whole with yolk)

Dairy (raw, grass-fed, organically produced)
- whole milk yogurt (plain)
- sheep's milk yogurt (plain)
- goat's milk yogurt (plain)
- soft goat's, cow's, or sheep's milk cheese
- cow's milk hard cheese (must be really raw, not heated above 100 degrees)
- sheep's milk hard cheese (must be really raw, not heated above 100 degrees)
- goat's milk hard cheese (must be really raw, not heated above 100 degrees)
- feta cheese (sheep's milk or goat's milk)
- full-fat plain kefir
- full-fat cottage cheese
- ricotta cheese
- cultured buttermilk
- probiotic whey

Fats and oils (organic, raw, local, and extra virgin)
- cow's milk butter
- goat's milk butter
- cow's milk cream
- cow's milk cultured cream (crème fraîche)
- flaxseed oil
- hempseed oil
- coconut cream (raw, not canned)
- extra-virgin coconut oil
- extra-virgin olive oil
- avocado
- sunflower oil
- poppyseed oil
- evening primrose oil
- raw cacao butter

Vegetables (organic and fresh)
- squash (winter or summer)
- broccoli
- asparagus
- beets
- cauliflower
- Brussels sprouts
- cabbage
- carrots
- celery
- cucumber
- eggplant
- pumpkin
- garlic
- onion
- okra
- mushrooms
- peas
- peppers (red, yellow, orange, green)
- string/green beans
- tomatoes
- lettuce (all varieties)
- spinach
- artichokes (French, not Jerusalem)
- leafy greens (kale, collard, broccoli rabe, mustard greens, etc.)
- wheat grass (juice)
- sprouts (broccoli, sunflower, pea shoots, radish, etc.)
- sea vegetables (kelp, dulse, nori, kombu, hijiki, etc.)
- raw, fermented vegetables (lacto-fermented only, no vinegar)
- corn
- sweet potatoes
- white potatoes

Nuts, seeds, and their butters (e.g. almond butter)
- organic, raw, and soaked; be sure to

chew well
- almonds
- coconut meat
- pumpkin seeds
- hempseed
- flaxseed
- sunflower seeds
- almond butter
- hempseed butter
- sunflower butter
- tahini (sesame butter)
- pumpkin seed butter
- macadamia nuts
- hazelnuts
- pecans
- walnuts
- Brazil nuts
- chia seeds
- cashews

Condiments, spices, seasonings, cooking ingredients, and salad dressings (organic are best)

- salsa (raw, organic)
- guacamole (fresh)
- apple cider vinegar
- coconut sap vinegar
- soy sauce (wheat-free, raw), tamari
- Herbamare seasoning
- Celtic sea salt
- umeboshi paste
- balsamic vinegar
- herbs and spices (air dried, no added stabilizers)
- pickled ginger (preservative and color free)
- wasabi (preservative and color free)
- homemade salad dressings and marinades using-allowable ingredients

Fruits (organic fresh or frozen are allowed)

- blueberries
- strawberries
- blackberries
- raspberries
- cherries
- grapefruit
- lemon
- lime
- pomegranate
- cranberries
- apples (with skin)
- melons
- apricots
- peaches
- grapes
- orange
- pears
- papaya
- kiwi
- nectarines
- pineapple
- plums
- figs
- durian
- jackfruit
- cherimoya
- persimmon
- mamey
- sapote
- bananas
- mangoes
- mulberries
- goji
- dried fruit (low temperature dehydrated)

Beverages

- coconut water (from young or mature coconut)
- coconut kefir
- probiotic whey beverage
- herbal teas (sun-steeped, not boiled)—unsweetened or with a small amount of honey
- raw vegetable juice (beet or carrot juice—maximum 25 percent of total)
- lacto-fermented beverages (kombucha, kvass)
- purified, non-chlorinated water
- natural sparkling water, no carbonation added

Sweeteners

- raw, unheated honey
- date paste (made from raw dates)
- coconut sap nectar

Snacks/Miscellaneous

- raw cacao (nibs or powder)

RAW Truth Omnivore Nutrition Plan
Sample 3-Day Nutrition Plan

Day 1

Upon waking

- Perfect Food RAW: one serving mixed in 12 ounces of raw veggie juice
- RAW Probiotics: three capsules

Breakfast

Jordan's Raw Smoothie
(see page 193 for recipe)

- Vitamin Code: two capsules
- RAW Calcium: three capsules
- RAW Enzymes: one capsule

Lunch

Two ounces raw coconut kefir, kombucha or kvass

Orange Salmon Ceviche
(see page 192 for recipe)

Green salad with mixed greens, tomatoes, avocado, carrots, cucumbers, celery, red cabbage, red peppers, red onions, sprouts, and two ounces of really raw cheese

For the salad dressing, mix extra-virgin olive oil, apple cider vinegar or lemon juice, Celtic sea salt, herbs, and spices, or you may add 1 tablespoon of extra-virgin olive oil

- Vitamin Code: two capsules
- RAW Calcium: two capsules
- RAW Enzymes: one capsule

Dinner

Two ounces raw coconut kefir or kvass

Toss a green salad with mixed greens, tomatoes, avocado, carrots, cucumbers, celery, red cabbage, red peppers, red onions, sprouts, and two ounces of really raw cheese

Tahini dressing
(see page 190 for recipe)

Turtle Cheesecake
(see page 190 for recipe)

- RAW Enzymes: one capsule

RAW snacks

JR's Carb Juice *(see page 192 for recipe)*

Raw coconut cream, raw honey, pineapple

- RAW Meal: one serving mixed in raw juice or water.

Before bed

- RAW Fiber: one serving mixed in raw veggie juice or water.

Day 2

Upon waking

- Perfect Food RAW: one serving mixed in 12 ounces of raw veggie juice
- RAW Probiotics: three capsules

Breakfast

Jordan's Raw Smoothie
(see page 193 for recipe)

- Vitamin Code: two capsules
- RAW Calcium: three capsules
- RAW Enzymes: one capsule

Lunch

Two ounces raw coconut kefir, kombucha or kvass

Spicy Salmon Ceviche
(see page 193 for recipe)

Green salad with mixed greens, tomatoes, avocado, carrots, cucumbers, celery, red cabbage, red peppers, red onions, sprouts, and two ounces really raw cheese

For the salad dressing, mix extra-virgin olive oil, apple cider vinegar or lemon juice, Celtic sea salt, herbs, and spices

Three ounces raw coconut cream and honey

- Vitamin Code: two capsules
- RAW Calcium: two capsules
- RAW Enzymes: one capsule

Dinner

Two ounces raw coconut kefir or kvass

Toss a green salad with mixed greens, tomatoes, avocado, carrots, cucumbers, celery, red cabbage, red peppers, red onions, sprouts, and two ounces really raw cheese

Carrot ginger dressing
(see page 184 for recipe)

Raw Apple Pie *(see page 184 for recipe)*

- RAW Enzymes: one capsule

RAW snacks

Really raw cheese, raw almonds, and one apple

Three ounces raw coconut cream, honey, pineapple

- RAW Meal: one serving mixed in raw juice or water.

Before bed

- RAW Fiber: one serving mixed in raw veggie juice or water.

Day 3

Upon waking

- Perfect Food RAW: one serving mixed in 12 ounces of raw veggie juice
- RAW Probiotics: three capsules

Breakfast

Jordan's Raw Smoothie
(see page 193 for recipe)

- Vitamin Code: two capsules
- RAW Calcium: three capsules
- RAW Enzymes: one capsule

Lunch

Two ounces raw coconut kefir, kombucha or kvass

Orange Salmon Ceviche
(see page 192 for recipe)

Green salad with mixed greens, tomatoes, avocado, carrots, cucumbers, celery, red cabbage, red peppers, red onions, and sprouts

For the salad dressing, mix extra-virgin olive oil, apple cider vinegar or lemon juice, Celtic sea salt, herbs, and spices

- Vitamin Code: two capsules
- RAW Calcium: two capsules
- RAW Enzymes: one capsule

Dinner

Two ounces raw coconut kefir or kvass

Toss a green salad with mixed greens, tomatoes, avocado, carrots, cucumbers, celery, red cabbage, red peppers, red onions, and sprouts.

Tahini dressing *(see page 185 for recipe)*

Vanilla Ice Cream *(see page 193 for recipe)*

Raw Chocolate Sauce

- RAW Enzymes: one capsule

RAW snacks

Raw yogurt, kefir or cottage cheese and blueberries

Raw coconut cookies

- RAW Meal: one serving mixed in raw juice or water.

Before bed

- RAW Fiber: one serving mixed in raw veggie juice or water.

Need Recipes?

You'll find raw omnivore-friendly recipes in Chapter 16, "RAW Truth Recipes." For additional healthy and delicious raw omnivore-friendly recipes, visit www.gardenoflife.com.

Shopping Tips for the RAW Truth Nutrition Plan

When it comes to following the RAW Truth Nutrition Plan, changing the way you shop for foods will change the way you eat. In addition to shopping at your local health food grocery, I recommend you look into local farmer's markets, small farms, and even CSAs (Consumer-Supported Agriculture co-ops). If you're interested in acquiring raw dairy products, only a handful of states offer these products for sale on the store shelf, with California being the most prominent, but you can still buy direct from the farmer. A great way to find raw dairy is to visit www.realmilk.com, which gives a list of local farms offering raw dairy in every state.

It's critical to purchase organically grown or raised foods. Many local farms, ranches, and producers are not certified organic, but they still follow the principles of organic by using no chemicals, synthetic fertilizers, antibiotics, and hormones. When purchasing and consuming raw eggs, it's very important to purchase organically produced eggs from pastured chickens as the risk of salmonella is drastically reduced. You should also wash the outside of the eggshell with warm water or even a diluted solution of hydrogen peroxide. (Please see the U.S. government warning regarding the consumption of raw eggs on page 141.)

If you can't afford or find organic produce, however, the next best thing to organic is to apply a veggie wash to your conventionally grown vegetables and fruits. Keep in mind that it's much better to consume fruits and vegetables than not to—even if they're not organic. That said, many regular grocery stores are now carrying certified organic produce.

Fruits and Vegetables

Certified organic fruits and vegetables have an incredible amount of nutrients—vitamins, minerals, live enzymes, antioxidants, and many other healthy compounds. Depending on what season it is, there are different fruits and vegetables available, but every fruit and vegetable has something unique to offer. Let's take a closer look at them:

- **Berries.** These are some of the most important fruits you can consume. Strawberries, blueberries, blackberries, and raspberries are all high in antioxidants. Antioxidants are nutrients found naturally in the body and in plants such as fruits and vegetables—especially berries.

As cells function normally in the body, they produce oxidized molecules: these are called free radicals. Free radicals are highly unstable and steal components from other cells. This continues in a chain reaction, and some cells die off.

This process can be beneficial because it helps the body destroy cells that have outlived their usefulness, and it kills germs and parasites. When left unchecked, though, this process can create havoc with healthy cells. Eating high-antioxidant foods can help the proliferation of healthy cells.

Of course, buying your berries fresh is best. That way, the most amounts of nutrients are preserved. Be aware that:

- **Blueberries** are prized as a high source of antioxidants.

- **Cranberries**, usually consumed seasonally, are another great source of antioxidants. They are excellent for supporting urinary tract health and come to a harvest peak in November; thus their association with Thanksgiving.

- **Raspberries** contain ellagic acid, which is an antioxidant and possesses excellent benefits for female health. They are also high in pectin, which makes them an excellent thickener in homemade jellies and jams.

- **Pineapple** has something called bromelain, an enzyme that aids digestion and causes fruit salads to get soggy after only a short period of time. Eat pineapple fresh, not canned.

So for your fruits, focus on strawberries, raspberries, blueberries and blackberries, cherries, lemons, limes, and grapefruit.

If you eat dried fruits, avoid the kind with sulfate or sulfite preservatives. Sulfites, or sulfur-based preservatives, are artificial chemicals added to hundreds of foods to stop spoilage, but these chemicals can be toxic to the human body.

- **Avocado.** This much-maligned food is a fruit, not a vegetable. Avocados contain high-quality fats as well as vitamin E and are a great source of fiber and other minerals. Avocados are 75 percent water and contain good fats, similar to olive oil.

- **Coconut.** As previously mentioned, coconut is not a nut but a one-seeded drupe. And what a drupe it is. When shopping for coconuts, purchase either young coconuts (off-white in color with an outer husk that resembles a hat) or mature brown coconuts. Consume both the meat and water for some of the best nutrition available. Run the meat of the mature coconut through a high power juicer to create raw coconut cream, which may be the healthiest fat on the planet.

- **Lettuce.** There are several varieties of lettuce, which is high in fiber. It is difficult to know which ones to choose. We are used to consuming iceberg lettuce, but today there are many great brands of mixed salad blends. These mixed blends contain

organic baby lettuces, green oak leaf, organic baby spinach, red and green chard, and arugula. They're popular, they're pre-washed, and they're easy for people who don't have a lot of time on their hands. These greens contain virtually every mineral and trace element and large amounts of beta-carotene, which fits into the nutritional category of carotenoids, a

class of very important antioxidants that give fruit and vegetables their bright colors. Cabbage is also excellent for the digestive tract, particularly when cooked or juiced because it contains something called vitamin U.

This would also be a good time to add raw fermented vegetables like cultured veggies, kimchi, natto, and sauerkraut to your shopping list. Very few Americans eat any fermented vegetables, which is a shame since they are one of the healthiest types of food available for those concerned with maintaining digestive health. Other examples of raw fermented vegetables include pickled carrots and fermented beets. These probiotic-rich cultured foods possess a phenomenal source of vitamins, minerals, and live enzymes as well as beneficial microorganisms.

- **Mushrooms.** These are high in nutrients, particularly the mineral selenium, which works with vitamin E as an antioxidant and binds with toxins in the body. Mushrooms are over 90 percent water and are high in biotin, one of the B-complex vitamins. Mushrooms are one of those foods that should be eaten organically because of where they are grown. If they are grown in a non-organic environment, many times mushrooms are high in heavy metals, so you want to be careful about eating non-organic mushrooms. Despite what you hear, eating mushrooms does not contribute to yeast overgrowth in the body. Some people who are yeast sensitive, however, have cross-sensitivities to mushrooms.

- **Peppers.** Rich in antioxidants, green peppers may be more difficult to digest than other colored peppers, so if you have difficulty digesting green peppers, you should eat yellow, orange, or red peppers. The different colors are rich in different nutrients as well. Red peppers are substantially higher in vitamins C and A than green peppers.

- **Sweet potatoes.** These vegetables are one of the highest sources of beta-carotene. Studies have linked the high intake of foods rich in beta-carotene to a healthy immune system. Sweet potatoes also contain vitamin C, calcium, potassium, carbohydrates, and fiber.

- **Green drinks.** In addition to your daily supply of fruits and vegetables, green drinks are another way to supplement your diet with whole food nutritional supplements. The best are made with nutrient-rich cereal grasses, which are a "super food." Cereal grasses are the only foods in the vegetable kingdom that, even if consumed alone, enable animals to continually maintain weight, strength, and optimal health. Wheat, barley and oat grass juices are richer in nutrients than spinach, broccoli, eggs, and chicken in virtually all categories, including protein.

When you consume a green drink, you're consuming the recommended amount of vegetables for that day—and more! In today's hectic lifestyle, it's nearly impossible to eat enough vegetables, especially greens, to satisfy our body's needs. Because of this, we are depriving ourselves of nature's ultimate insurance policy. Green drinks can meet the demands of our fast-paced lives by supplying every nutrient our body requires to sustain optimal levels of health.

Dairy Products

Here are my recommendations:

Dairy. When purchasing raw dairy products, I recommend sheep's milk and goat's milk because they contain proteins that are less allergenic than those contained in most cow's milk. Raw, grass-fed cow's milk is beneficial for most individuals, but consuming cow's milk from heritage breeds such as Guernsey, Jersey, and Brown Swiss may be more digestible for certain individuals. Ask your local dairy farmer what breed of cattle they are milking before making a decision.

Be aware of the difference between dairy from grass-fed cows vs. grain-fed cows. Grass-fed is extremely important as cows are designed to live on grass, not grain. Grass-fed animals produce healthier milk and higher nutrients such as vitamins A, D, and E, and conjugated linoleic acid, more commonly known as CLA, which is a naturally occurring fatty acid found mainly in milk fat and meat. CLA is a nutrient the body cannot produce.

A few years ago, CLA received media attention when it was identified as a component of red meat and dairy from grass fed animals that supports a healthy immune system. CLA, which is actually a form of *healthy* trans fat, is a potent immune-balancing agent, as well as a fat-burning agent. CLA is found in meat and milk, but it's most highly concentrated in milk fat. So forget about skim or low fat—you need that full fat found in dairy. Furthermore, full fat or whole milk products from grass-fed cows contain as much as five times more CLA than milk from standard grain-fed cows.

Remember, raw—meaning not pasteurized or processed—cow's, sheep's, and goat's milk, hard cheeses (with milk not heated higher than cow body temperature), butter, and cream are best. Make sure you buy cheese made only from grass-fed cows that are fed no grain.

† These statements have not been evaluated by the Food and Drug Administration. This product is not intended to diagnose, treat, cure or prevent any disease.

Always buy whole fat, organic dairy products instead of skim or 2 percent dairy products, which have undergone processing that removes beneficial enzymes.

Cheese. There are many different varieties of cheese to choose from, but if you can find cheeses made from raw milk, you'll be far better off. Besides raw cow's milk cheese, goat's milk and sheep's milk cheese is widely available. Look for the really raw designation on the label, or purchase imported raw milk cheese produced from raw milk that has not been heated above 100 degrees.

Yogurt and kefir. During the fermentation process that takes place in a cultured dairy product like yogurt or kefir, many digestive enzymes are created that aid in the assimilation of food nutrients. This makes yogurt and kefir some of the highest quality protein available. When purchasing any dairy product—milk, cheese, yogurt, or kefir—choose the full-fat version because the fat in dairy is crucial for calcium absorption.

Eggs. Eggs contain all the known nutrients except for vitamin C. They are good sources of the fat-soluble vitamins A and D as well as certain carotenoids that help fight free radicals in the body. They also contain lutein, which has been shown to promote healthy eyes. But note, when it comes to healthy kinds of eggs, not just any old egg will do.

What kind of eggs should you look for in your health food store? Answer: organic, free-range, high omega-3 eggs. When possible, try to buy eggs from farms where the chickens are allowed to roam free and eat their natural diet. Eggs produced from chickens in their natural environment contain a healthy balance of omega-3 to omega-6 fatty acids and DHA, which is good for the maintenance of brain and eye function. High omega-3/DHA or organic eggs have six times the vitamin E and nine times the omega-3 fatty acids as regular store-purchased eggs.

Fish

Here are some recommendations:

Fish. For seafood, eat only fish with fins and scales caught in the ocean or freshwater, not farm-raised fish. Salmon, halibut, tuna, cod, snapper and sea bass are highly recommended, but don't eat shellfish and crustaceans because they may contain abundant toxins from their water-bound scavenging habits. In fact, scientists gauge the contaminant levels of our oceans, bays, and rivers by measuring the biological toxin levels in the flesh of crabs, oysters, clams, and lobsters.

Wild-caught tuna is wonderful. Research shows that fattier cuts of tuna contains less mercury than other types because the natural oils contained in fish are detoxifiers of heavy metals. So, when consuming tuna, try to eat the fattier variety, which is often called toro at Japanese restaurants.

Omega-3 fatty acids—the fats we lack the most in our diet—are critical in negating the effects of the overabundance of omega-6 acids and hydrogenated fats found in the standard American diet. The ratio of omega-3 to omega-6 fatty acids can be balanced by consuming more omega-3 foods such as ocean-caught fish with fins and scales (salmon and tuna) and pastured eggs.

Oils, Spices, Condiments, and Salt

Here are my recommendations:

Fats and oils. When it comes to oils, I highly recommend consuming saturated fats. Some of the best raw saturated fats come from the coconut and palm kernel as well as raw cacao butter. If consuming an omnivore diet, organic butter from grass-fed animals is wonderful. These fats can withstand room temperature and even heat without oxidizing.

Olive oil is extremely healthy, but olive oil should be used only on food and never heated. Look for certified organic extra-virgin olive oil in a dark bottle since light coming into clear bottles can decrease some of the important health properties of the oil as well as its freshness. Extra-virgin olive oil is produced from the first cold pressing of the olives, and that's where you'll get the most antioxidants and other nutrients. Choose a colorful oil with a rich aroma.

Spices. The best spices are organic, air-dried spices because they don't contain caking agents and other preservatives that you may find in non-organic spices. Flavored spices are combination seasonings with a variety of organic herbs and spices. Some other favorite seasonings include unrefined sea salt. You can use them in cooking and add them to your favorite foods.

Condiments. Cultured veggies and spicy kimchi are condiments *par excellence*. Be brave and give them a try.

This would also be a good time to clear your refrigerator and pantry of any commercial ketchup, mustard, mayonnaise, pickled relish, or other common condiments. Organic versions of these popular condiments are readily available these days, even in supermarkets. They come without refined sugar and preservatives.

Salt. Regular table salt is highly refined with chemical and high temperature processes. These processes remove many of the valuable minerals, use harmful and potentially

toxic additives, and employ bleaching agents to make the salt pristine white. Unrefined sea salt, however, still has all the important minerals, and is actually slightly gray in color. Celtic Sea Salt and RealSalt are recommended brands.

Sweeteners

We've all seen the pink, blue, and yellow packets on restaurant tables. Stay away from those artificial sweeteners! Aspartame, saccharin, sucralose, and their sweet cousins are made from chemicals that have sparked debate for decades. Though the Food and Drug Administration has approved the use of artificial sweeteners in drinks and food, these chemical additives may prove to be detrimental to your health in the long term.

Many people have switched to raw agave as a sweetener. I am not in favor of using agave as a sweetener for many reasons, including the fact that it contains fructose as well as oligosaccharides that can lead to excess weight, gas, and bloating in some individuals. I also believe many agave products are mislabeled as raw when in fact they require significant heat during processing. There have been many rumors over the last few years that certain brands of agave have been "spiked" with high-fructose corn syrup.

The best sweetener you should be using is raw, unheated honey. Raw honey should always be labeled as unheated, preserving its rich storehouse of naturally occurring enzymes and bee pollen. If you are a vegan, make date paste from raw dates or try raw coconut sap nectar, which has a great taste and low glycemic index.

Snacks from Nuts and Seeds

Here are my recommendations:

Snacks. Some of the most convenient and healthiest snacks are nuts and seeds, which are great sources of fiber, healthy fats, and nutrients. If properly prepared, they are extremely nutritious. "Properly prepared" means raw or better yet soaked and then air-dried or low temperature dehydrated. Just make sure they are organic. Try almonds, walnuts, pecans, pumpkin seeds, and sunflower seeds, or make your own healthy trail mix.

Raw coconut cookies made from coconut, dates and seeds are great for the entire family. High in fiber and loaded with good fats, these cookies truly are a guiltless indulgence.

Raw nut butters, made from almonds, cashews, and sunflower seeds, are something worth checking out. They're special because when they're raw, not roasted or heated, they're easy to digest and still have their vitamins, minerals, and enzymes. Nut butters can be used as a veggie dip or spread on fresh fruit such as apple slices.

It is worthy to note that the phytates found on the covering of grains and seeds "grab" minerals in the intestinal tract and block their absorption. The sprouting process effectively removes these phytates from the outer covering of the natural grain. Germination initiates a chemical transformation in the seed grains that neutralizes the phytates, causing them to come alive, making all of the nutrition within the seed available for digestion.

Beverages. If you're used to drinking sports drinks, sodas, sweet teas, and fruit juices, you may be in for a rude awakening because I'm asking you to drink a lot of raw fluids during the RAW Truth Nutrition Plan. The water I want you to hydrate with should be purified or naturally carbonated.

You can purchase purified water at the store or have a filtering system hooked up to your kitchen sink and shower. Why the shower? Because chlorine is absorbed through the skin when you take a shower. As for drinking household water, chlorine found in tap water kills both friendly and unfriendly bacteria.

It is risky enough to drink chlorinated tap water, but the mass exposure created by swimming in a chlorinated pool or taking extended hot showers in heavily chlorinated water isn't very healthy at all. That's because the heat opens skin pores and increases the already high absorption rate of chlorine through the skin.

As for fruit and veggie juices, they must be consumed raw and fresh as bottled or boxed juices are full of concentrated sugars with a loss of nutrients from pasteurization and concentration, often times making it as nutritionally void as refined white flour.

This is the time to be brave and try some of those lacto-fermented beverages that I've been telling you about like coconut kefir, probiotic whey, kombucha, and kvass. If kombucha is too fizzy for you, you can always sip on sun-steeped herbal teas. Studies are revealing many beneficial effects of tea—particularly green tea—on the heart and cardiovascular system. Many of these teas have been studied for their antioxidant effects. Make sure to drink only organic herbal teas that are unsweetened, but you can add a small amount of raw honey or coconut sap nectar.

CHAPTER 15

The Raw Truth
Nutrition Plan

I believe that the RAW Truth Nutrition Plan can transform your health, and there are ways to "fine tune" the RAW Truth Nutrition Plan that can better target the results you're looking to achieve.

Please know that anyone with a medical condition should consult a licensed physician prior to starting any aspect of the RAW Truth Nutritional Plan. Before taking any dietary supplement, you should consult with your healthcare practitioner before using the product, especially if you are pregnant, nursing, taking medications, or are otherwise under medical supervision.

THE RAW TRUTH

Women's Health

Description: The RAW Truth Nutritional Plan supports women's health on multiple levels, providing support for the digestive system, female reproductive system, healthy hormones, breast health, bone health, cardiovascular support, and brain health.[†]

Dietary instructions: Follow the basic principles of the RAW Truth Nutrition Plan. Focus on consuming the following foods and supplements as often as possible.

Living foods:

- fresh veggie juice, high in greens such as celery, parsley, cucumber, and cilantro, is a terrific daily detoxification tonic

- avocados are an excellent source of vitamin E and potassium as well as healthy fats and fiber

- flaxseed and chia seed products, including fresh ground seed and oil, can boost energy levels and promote healthy hormones

- wild salmon ceviche (not suitable for vegetarians or vegans) is a superb source of omega-3 fatty acids, the antioxidant astaxanthin, and vitamin D

- raw cultured dairy (not suitable for vegans), especially yogurt and kefir (sheep and goat's milk may be more tolerable, but as long as the dairy is raw and comes from grass-fed animals, cow's milk should be fine)

- raw coconut cream contains medium-chain fatty acids, vitamins, and minerals to support overall health and detoxification

- raw coconut kefir, which is loaded with probiotics and minerals and supports digestive health and immune system function while delivering active probiotic cultures, provides electrolytes for proper hydration

- really raw cheese from grass-fed cows contains probiotics, protein, minerals, fat-soluble vitamins, and healthy fats, including CLA and omega-3s, to support healthy digestion and immune system function (not suitable for vegans)

Living nutrients:

- **Perfect Food RAW: one serving of powder or caps upon waking, mixed in or swallowed with water or raw vegetable juice**
- **Vitamin Code for Women: 4 capsules per day, with or without food**
- **RAW Probiotics for Women: 3 capsules per day, with or without food**
- **RAW Enzymes for Women: 1-3 capsules per meal**
- **RAW Calcium: 5 capsules per day with meals**
- **RAW D3: 1-5 capsules (2,000-10,000IU) per day, with meals based on average sun exposure and vitamin D levels**
- **RAW Protein: 1-2 servings daily mixed in water, raw juice, or raw dairy after exercise or as a between-meal protein boost**

[†] These statements have not been evaluated by the Food and Drug Administration. This product is not intended to diagnose, treat, cure or prevent any disease.

THE RAW TRUTH

Men's Health

Description: The RAW Truth Nutritional Plan supports men's health on multiple levels, providing support for the digestive system, prostate health, cardiovascular health, brain health, and support for stress.[†]

Dietary instructions: Follow the basic principles of the RAW Truth Nutrition Plan. Focus on consuming the following foods and supplements as often as possible.

Living foods:

- fresh veggie juice, high in greens such as celery, parsley, cucumber, and cilantro, is a terrific daily detoxification tonic

- avocados are an excellent source of vitamin E and potassium as well as healthy fats and fiber

- pumpkin seeds are high in zinc, phytosterols, and healthy fats to support prostate health

- tomatoes are high in lycopene to support cardiovascular and prostate health

- berries of the dark variety, including blueberries, raspberries and blackberries, are an excellent source of antioxidants and fiber

- wild salmon ceviche (not suitable for vegetarians or vegans) is a superb source of high-quality protein, omega-3 fatty acids, the antioxidant astaxanthin, and vitamin D

- if available, consume raw cultured dairy (not suitable for vegans), especially yogurt and kefir as well as soft and hard cheeses (sheep and goat's milk may be more tolerable, but as long as the dairy is raw and comes from grass-fed animals, cow's milk should be fine)

- raw coconut cream contains medium-chain fatty acids, vitamins, and minerals to support overall health and detoxification

- raw coconut kefir, which is loaded with probiotics and minerals and supports digestive health and immune system function while delivering active probiotic cultures, provides electrolytes for proper hydration

- really raw cheese from grass-fed cows contains probiotics, protein, minerals, fat-soluble vitamins, and healthy fats, including CLA and omega-3s, to support healthy digestion and immune system function (not suitable for vegans)

Living nutrients:

- **Vitamin Code for Men: 4 capsules per day, with or without food**

- **RAW Probiotics for Men: 3 capsules per day, with or without food**

- **RAW Enzymes for Men: 1-3 capsules per meal**

- **RAW Protein: 1-2 servings daily, mixed in water, raw juice, or raw dairy after exercise or as a between-meal protein boost**

[†] These statements have not been evaluated by the Food and Drug Administration. This product is not intended to diagnose, treat, cure or prevent any disease.

Disclaimers Regarding Raw Dairy, Raw Eggs, Raw Fish, and Raw Juice

Raw milk products may contain disease-causing microorganisms. Persons at highest risk for of disease from these organisms include newborns and infants, the elderly, pregnant women, those taking corticosteroids, antibiotics and antacids, and those having chronic illnesses and other conditions that weaken their immunity.

- Consuming raw or undercooked eggs may increase your risk of food-borne illness.
- Consuming raw or undercooked seafood may increase your risk of food-borne illness.
- Juice that has not been pasteurized may contain bacteria that can increase the risk of food-borne illness. People most at risk are children, the elderly and persons with a weakened immune system.

Women's Health 50+

Description: The RAW Truth Nutritional Plan supports the health of women age 50 and up on multiple levels, providing support for the digestive system, female reproductive system, eye health, healthy hormones, breast health, bone health, cardiovascular health, and brain health.[†]

Dietary instructions: Follow the basic principles of the RAW Truth Nutrition Plan. Focus on consuming the following foods and supplements as often as possible.

Living foods:

- apple cider vinegar (unpasteurized) provides an appreciable amount of potassium and malic acid
- fresh veggie juice, high in greens such as celery, parsley, cucumber, and cilantro, is a terrific daily detoxification tonic
- avocados are an excellent source of vitamin E and potassium as well as healthy fats and fiber
- flaxseed and chia seed products, including fresh ground seed and oil, can boost energy levels and promote healthy hormones
- wild salmon ceviche (not suitable for vegetarians or vegans) is a superb source of omega-3 fatty acids, the antioxidant astaxanthin, and vitamin D
- raw cultured dairy (not suitable for vegans), especially yogurt and kefir
- raw coconut cream contains medium-chain fatty acids, vitamins, and minerals to support overall health and detoxification
- raw coconut kefir, which is loaded with probiotics and minerals and supports digestive health and immune system function while delivering active probiotic cultures, provides electrolytes for proper hydration
- really raw cheese from grass-fed cows contains probiotics, protein, minerals, fat-soluble vitamins, and healthy fats, including CLA and omega-3s, to support healthy digestion and immune system function (not suitable for vegans)

Living nutrients:

- **Perfect Food RAW: one serving of powder or caps upon waking, mixed in or swallowed with water or raw vegetable juice**
- **Vitamin Code for Women 50 and Wiser: 4 capsules per day, with or without food**
- **RAW Probiotics for Women 50 and Wiser: 3 capsules per day, with or without food**
- **RAW Enzymes for Women 50 and Wiser: 1-3 capsules per meal**
- **RAW Calcium: 5 capsules per day with meals**
- **RAW D3: 1-5 capsules (2,000-10,000IU) per day with meals, based on average sun exposure and vitamin D levels**
- **RAW Protein: 1-2 servings daily, mixed in water, raw juice, or raw dairy after exercise or as a between-meal protein boost**

[†] These statements have not been evaluated by the Food and Drug Administration. This product is not intended to diagnose, treat, cure or prevent any disease.

Men's Health 50+

Description: The RAW Truth Nutritional Plan supports the health of men age 50 and up on multiple levels, providing support for the digestive system, prostate health, eye health, cardiovascular health, brain health, and support for stress and energy.[†]

Dietary instructions: Follow the basic principles of the RAW Truth Nutrition Plan. Focus on consuming the following foods and supplements as often as possible.

Living foods:

- fresh veggie juice, high in greens such as celery, parsley, cucumber, and cilantro, is a terrific daily detoxification tonic

- avocados are an excellent source of vitamin E and potassium as well as healthy fats and fiber

- pumpkin seeds are high in zinc, phytosterols, and healthy fats to support prostate health

- tomatoes are high in lycopene to support cardiovascular and prostate health

- berries of the dark variety, including blueberries, raspberries, and blackberries, are an excellent source of antioxidants and fiber

- wild salmon ceviche (not suitable for vegetarians or vegans) is a superb source of high-quality protein, omega-3 fatty acids, the antioxidant astaxanthin, and vitamin D

- raw cultured dairy (not suitable for vegans), especially yogurt and kefir, contains healthy fats and calcium

- raw coconut cream contains medium-chain fatty acids, vitamins, and minerals to support overall health and detoxification

- raw coconut kefir, which is loaded with probiotics and minerals and supports digestive health and immune system function while delivering active probiotic cultures, provides electrolytes for proper hydration

- really raw cheese from grass-fed cows contains probiotics, protein, minerals, fat-soluble vitamins, and healthy fats, including CLA and omega-3s, to support healthy digestion and immune system function (not suitable for vegans)

Living nutrients:

- **Vitamin Code for Men 50 and Wiser: 4 capsules per day, with or without food**

- **RAW Probiotics for Men and Wiser: 3 capsules per day, with or without food**

- **RAW Enzymes for Men 50 and Wiser: 1-3 capsules per meal**

- **RAW Protein: 1-2 servings daily, mixed in water, raw juice, or raw dairy after exercise or as a between-meal protein boost**

Healthy Blood Sugar

Description: To support healthy blood sugar levels already in the normal range, it's imperative to consume the highest-quality foods and nutritional supplements containing healthy fats and fiber. Balanced blood sugar levels are critical to supporting healthy weight, cardiovascular health, and a healthy immune system.†

Dietary instructions: Follow the basic principles of the RAW Truth Nutrition Plan. Focus on consuming the following foods and supplements as often as possible.

Living foods:

- fresh veggie juice, high in greens such as celery, parsley, cucumber, and cilantro, provides daily detoxification, and blending a peeled cucumber into the juice adds fiber, which is important for healthy blood sugar levels
- berries such as blueberries and raspberries are high in fiber and low in sugar, making them ideal for maintaining balanced blood sugar
- avocados, an excellent source of vitamin E and potassium as well as healthy fats and fiber, can be combined with raw fruits such as berries to support already normal blood sugar levels
- flaxseeds and chia seeds (ground) are loaded with healthy fats and fiber
- wild salmon ceviche (not suitable for vegetarians or vegans) is a superb source of omega-3 fatty acids, the antioxidant astaxanthin, and vitamin D
- if available, consume raw cultured dairy (not suitable for vegans), especially yogurt and kefir (sheep and goat's milk may be more tolerable, but as long as the dairy is raw and comes from grass-fed animals, cow's milk should be fine), and the high protein and healthy fat content are great for maintaining balanced blood sugar levels
- raw coconut cream contains medium-chain fatty acids, vitamins, and minerals to support overall health and detoxification
- raw coconut kefir, which is loaded with probiotics and minerals and supports digestive health and immune system function while delivering active probiotic cultures, provides electrolytes for proper hydration
- really raw cheese from grass-fed cows contains probiotics, protein, minerals, fat-soluble vitamins, and healthy fats, including CLA and omega-3s, to support healthy digestion and immune system function (not suitable for vegans)

Living nutrients:

- **Perfect Food RAW: one serving of powder or caps upon waking, mixed in or swallowed with water or raw vegetable juice**
- **RAW Fiber: 1-2 servings per day (morning and afternoon is ideal), and may be combined with Perfect Food RAW as the ultimate morning cleansing and detoxification tonic†**
- **Vitamin Code Perfect Weight: 4 capsules per day, with or without food**
- **RAW Probiotics: 3 capsules per day, with or without food**
- **RAW Enzymes: 1-3 capsules per meal**
- **RAW Protein: 1-2 servings per day, mixed in water or raw juice**
- **RAW Meal: 1 serving per day, mixed in water or raw juice to replace a meal, or a half-serving as a between-meal snack**

† These statements have not been evaluated by the Food and Drug Administration. This product is not intended to diagnose, treat, cure or prevent any disease.

Energy

Description: The consumption of raw foods and raw nutrients can go a long way toward providing consistent and balanced energy.[†]

Dietary instructions: Follow the basic principles of the RAW Truth Nutrition Plan. Focus on consuming the following foods and supplements as often as possible.

Living foods:

- fresh veggie juice, high in greens such as celery, parsley, cucumber, cilantro, provides a wonderful energy boost

- avocados are an excellent source of vitamin E and potassium as well as healthy fats and fiber

- flaxseed and chia seed products, including fresh ground seed and oil, can provide balanced energy levels

- wild salmon ceviche (not suitable for vegetarians or vegans) is a superb source of omega-3 fatty acids, the antioxidant astaxanthin, and vitamin D

- bananas are an outstanding source of quick energy and minerals such as potassium

- unheated honey (not suitable for vegans) provides an excellent source of glucose for quick energy and contains dozens of nutrients, bioactive compounds, and enzymes

- raw cultured dairy (not suitable for vegans), especially yogurt and kefir, provides powerful nutrients and compounds to promote healthy energy levels

- raw coconut cream contains medium-chain fatty acids, vitamins, and minerals to support overall health and detoxification

- raw coconut kefir, which is loaded with probiotics and minerals and supports digestive health and immune system function while delivering active probiotic cultures, provides electrolytes for proper hydration

- really raw cheese from grass-fed cows contains probiotics, protein, minerals, fat-soluble vitamins, and healthy fats, including CLA and omega-3s, to support healthy digestion and immune system function (not suitable for vegans)

Living nutrients:

- **RAW Cleanse: a seven-day raw cleanse unlocks latent energy in the body by removing unwanted toxins[†]**
- **Perfect Food RAW: one serving of powder or caps upon waking, mixed in or swallowed with water or raw vegetable juice**
- **Vitamin Code Perfect Weight: 4 capsules per day, with or without food**
- **RAW Probiotics: 3 capsules per day, with or without food**
- **RAW Enzymes: 1-3 capsules per meal**
- **RAW Calcium: 5 capsules per day, with meals**
- **RAW B complex: 2 capsules per day, with or without meals**

Healthy Hormones (Women's Health)

Description: Supporting the health of key organs that positively influence hormone balance is critical for the overall health and wellness of every woman.[†] The following protocol is for adult women of all ages, from young women who want to support reproductive health and vitality, to older women desiring to maintain balanced hormones during pre-menopause through post-menopause and beyond.[†]

Dietary instructions: Follow the basic principles of the RAW Truth Nutrition Plan. Focus on consuming the following foods and supplements as often as possible.

Living foods:

- fresh green veggie juice, using celery, parsley, cucumber, and cilantro, is a terrific daily detoxification tonic
- avocados are an excellent source of vitamin E and potassium as well as healthy fats and fiber
- flaxseed-ground oil, as well as cold-pressed oil, can support healthy hormonal balance
- wild salmon ceviche (not suitable for vegetarians or vegans) is a superb source of omega-3 fatty acids, the antioxidant astaxanthin, and vitamin D
- if available, consume raw cultured dairy (not suitable for vegans), especially yogurt and kefir (sheep and goat's milk may be more tolerable, but as long as the dairy is raw and comes from grass-fed animals, cow's milk should be fine)
- raw coconut cream contains medium-chain fatty acids, vitamins, and minerals to support overall health and detoxification
- raw coconut kefir, which is loaded with probiotics and minerals and supports digestive health and immune system function while delivering active probiotic cultures, provides electrolytes for proper hydration
- really raw cheese from grass-fed cows contains probiotics, protein, minerals, fat-soluble vitamins, and healthy fats, including CLA and omega-3s, to support healthy digestion and immune system function (not suitable for vegans)

Living nutrients:

- **Perfect Food RAW: one serving of powder or caps upon waking, mixed in or swallowed with water or raw vegetable juice**
- **Vitamin Code Perfect Weight: 4 capsules per day, with or without food**
- **RAW Probiotics for Women or Women 50+: 3 capsules per day, with or without food, to promote digestive health and normal immune system function†**
- **RAW Enzymes for Women or Women 50+: 1-3 capsules per meal**
- **RAW D3: 1-5 capsules (2,000-10,000IU) per day with meals, based on average sun exposure and vitamin D levels**
- **RAW Fiber: 1-2 servings daily mixed in water or raw juice to support digestion, detoxification, and healthy hormone balance†**

[†] These statements have not been evaluated by the Food and Drug Administration. This product is not intended to diagnose, treat, cure or prevent any disease.

Brain Health

Dietary instructions: Follow the basic principles of the RAW Truth Nutrition Plan. Focus on consuming the following foods and supplements as often as possible.

Living foods:

- raw green juice, including celery, cucumber, parsley and cilantro, is an important source of nutrients, including powerful antioxidant enzymes

- avocados are an excellent source of vitamin E and potassium as well as healthy fats, which support brain function

- flaxseed and chia seed products, including fresh ground seed and oil, can support overall health and wellness

- wild salmon ceviche (not suitable for vegetarians or vegans) is a superb source of omega-3 fatty acids, the antioxidant astaxanthin, and vitamin D—wonderful nutrients to support a healthy brain

- raw cultured dairy (not suitable for vegans), especially yogurt and kefir, contains high-quality proteins and fats to support healthy digestion and elimination

- raw coconut cream contains medium-chain fatty acids, vitamins, and minerals to support overall health and detoxification

- raw coconut kefir, which is loaded with probiotics and minerals and supports digestive health and immune system function while delivering active probiotic cultures, provides electrolytes for proper hydration

- really raw cheese from grass-fed cows contains probiotics, protein, minerals, fat-soluble vitamins, and healthy fats, including CLA and omega-3s, to support healthy digestion and immune system function (not suitable for vegans)

Living nutrients:

- **Perfect Food RAW: one serving of powder or caps upon waking, mixed in or swallowed with water or raw vegetable juice**

- **Vitamin Code Perfect Weight: 4 capsules per day, with or without food**

- **RAW Probiotics: 3 capsules per day, with or without food**

- **RAW Enzymes: 1-3 capsules per meal**

- **RAW Calcium: 5 capsules per day with meals**

- **RAW D3: 1-5 capsules (2,000-10,000IU) per day with meals, based on average sun exposure and vitamin D levels**

- **RAW B-12: 1-2 capsules daily**

Digestive Health

Description: I believe a healthy, functioning digestive tract is the key to the health and wellness of the entire body. Extraordinary digestive health supports the health of the brain, normal immune system function, detoxification, and elimination.[†] The following living foods and nutrients support colon health and reduce occasional constipation, gas, and bloating and help maintain healthy bowel movements.[†]

Dietary instructions: Follow the basic principles of the RAW Truth Nutrition Plan. Focus on consuming the following foods and supplements as often as possible.

Living foods:

- blueberries are an important source of fiber and powerful antioxidants that support normal bowel function
- fresh veggie juice, high in greens such as celery, parsley, cucumber, and cilantro, is a terrific daily digestive tonic
- avocados are an excellent source of vitamin E and potassium as well as healthy fats and fiber
- flaxseed and chia seed products, including fresh ground seed and oil, can support healthy digestive function
- wild salmon ceviche (not suitable for vegetarians or vegans) is a superb source of omega-3 fatty acids, the antioxidant astaxanthin, and vitamin D
- raw cultured dairy (not suitable for vegans), especially yogurt and kefir, is wonderful to support healthy digestive function (sheep and goat's milk may be more tolerable, but as long as the dairy is raw and comes from grass-fed animals, cow's milk should be fine)
- raw coconut cream contains medium-chain fatty acids, vitamins, and minerals to support overall health, detoxification, and a healthy intestinal flora balance
- raw coconut kefir, which is loaded with probiotics and minerals and supports digestive health and maintains normal immune system function while delivering active probiotic cultures, provides electrolytes for proper hydration
- really raw cheese from grass-fed cows contains probiotics, protein, minerals, fat-soluble vitamins, and healthy fats, including CLA and omega-3s, to support healthy digestion and immune system function (not suitable for vegans)

Living nutrients:

- **RAW Cleanse: the seven-day raw cleanse system is an ideal jump-start to extraordinary digestive health[†]**
- **Perfect Food RAW: one serving of powder or caps upon waking, mixed in or swallowed with water or raw vegetable juice**
- **Vitamin Code Multivitamins: 4 capsules per day, with or without food**
- **RAW Probiotics: 3-9 capsules per day, with or without food**
- **RAW Enzymes: 1-3 capsules per meal**
- **RAW Fiber: take 1-2 servings per day, mixed in water or raw juice**
- **RAW D3: 1-5 capsules (2,000-10,000IU) per day with meals, based on average sun exposure and vitamin D levels**

[†] These statements have not been evaluated by the Food and Drug Administration. This product is not intended to diagnose, treat, cure or prevent any disease.

Yeast Balance

Description: Hundreds of different microbial species normally reside in the digestive tract. Yeast species that are neutral or beneficial in small amounts can overgrow, creating an imbalance in the gut and even toxins that can make their way into other parts of our body. The key is to maintain the ideal microbial balance of beneficial microorganisms in the gut, which promotes extraordinary digestive health.[†]

Dietary instructions: Follow the basic principles of the RAW Truth Nutrition Plan. Focus on consuming the following foods and supplements as often as possible.

Living foods:

- blueberries are an important source of fiber and powerful antioxidants that support healthy bowel function and healthy intestinal flora
- fresh veggie juice, high in greens such as celery, parsley, cucumber, and cilantro, is a terrific daily digestive tonic
- avocados are an excellent source of vitamin E and potassium as well as healthy fats and fiber
- flaxseed and chia seed products, including fresh ground seed and oil, can support healthy digestive function
- wild salmon ceviche (not suitable for vegetarians or vegans) is a superb source of omega-3 fatty acids, the antioxidant astaxanthin, and vitamin D
- raw cultured veggies such as sauerkraut and kimchi are a first-rate source of probiotics and organic acids, which help create a healthy intestinal environmental balance
- raw cultured dairy (not suitable for vegans), especially yogurt and kefir, supports digestive function and intestinal balance
- raw coconut cream contains medium-chain fatty acids, vitamins, and minerals to support overall health, detoxification, and a healthy intestinal flora balance
- raw coconut kefir, which is loaded with probiotics and minerals and supports digestive health and helps maintain immune system function while delivering active probiotic cultures, provides electrolytes for proper hydration

Living nutrients:

- **RAW Cleanse: the seven-day raw cleanse system is an ideal jump-start to extraordinary digestive health and intestinal flora balance[†]**
- **Yeast FREEze: 2-4 capsules daily on an empty stomach to support a balanced, healthy digestive tract (while not a raw supplement, this formula can be beneficial for those looking to support an optimal environment for the growth and colonization of a wide variety of probiotic bacteria necessary for healthy digestion and immune system function)[†]**
- **Vitamin Code Multivitamins: 4 capsules per day, with or without food**
- **RAW Probiotics: 9 capsules per day, with or without food**
- **RAW Enzymes: 3 capsules per meal**
- **RAW Fiber: take 1-2 servings per day, mixed in water or raw juice**
- **RAW D3: 1-5 capsules (2,000-10,000IU) per day with meals, based on average sun exposure and vitamin D levels**

THE RAW TRUTH

Fitness/Muscle Building

Description: Building muscle and burning fat is a goal for virtually everyone, especially those engaged in fitness and exercise programs. When combined with resistance training, consuming live foods with high-quality proteins, fats, vitamins, minerals, and enzymes support the building of lean body mass as well as the metabolism of fat.[†]

Dietary instructions: Follow the basic principles of the RAW Truth Nutrition Plan. Focus on consuming the following foods and supplements as often as possible.

Living foods:

- fresh veggie juice, high in greens such as celery, parsley, cucumber, and cilantro, provides daily detoxification, and blending a peeled cucumber into the juice adds fiber, which is important for the maintenance of healthy blood sugar levels already in the normal range

- berries such as blueberries and raspberries are high in fiber and low in sugar, making them an ideal source of carbohydrates for balanced energy

- avocados, an excellent source of vitamin E and potassium as well as healthy fats and fiber, can be combined with raw fruits such as berries to support healthy blood sugar levels that are already in the normal range, which can limit the storage of excess fat in the body

- ground chia seeds, loaded with healthy fats and fiber, provide balanced energy, which is perfect for exercise

- wild salmon ceviche (not suitable for vegetarians or vegans) is one of the best sources of raw protein on the planet and also provides omega-3 fatty acids, the antioxidant astaxanthin, and vitamin D

- eggs (not suitable for vegans or vegetarians) are loaded with high-quality proteins, fats, vitamins, and minerals, and consuming organic, raw eggs from pastured chickens in smoothies or raw recipes is a marvelous way to get high-quality proteins into your diet

- raw cultured dairy (not suitable for vegans), such as yogurt and kefir, contains pre-digested, high-quality, muscle-building protein and is loaded with vitamins and minerals for energy

- raw coconut cream contains medium-chain fatty acids, vitamins, and minerals to support overall health and detoxification while providing healthy raw fats for energy and muscle support

[†] These statements have not been evaluated by the Food and Drug Administration. This product is not intended to diagnose, treat, cure or prevent any disease.

- raw coconut kefir, which is loaded with probiotics and minerals and supports digestive health and immune system function while delivering active probiotic cultures, provides electrolytes for proper hydration

- really raw cheese from grass-fed cows contains probiotics, protein, minerals, fat-soluble vitamins, and healthy fats, including CLA and omega-3s, to support healthy digestion and immune system function (not suitable for vegans)

Living nutrients:

- **Perfect Food RAW: one serving of powder or caps upon waking, mixed in or swallowed with water or raw vegetable juice, cleanses and detoxifies while providing important minerals to the body[†]**

- **Vitamin Code Perfect Weight: 4 capsules per day, with or without food**

- **RAW Calcium: 5 capsules with meals per day provide minerals and fat-soluble vitamins important for muscle health[†]**

- **RAW Probiotics: 3-9 capsules per day, with or without food, help with digestion of foods, including proteins and support for a normal immune system[†]**

- **RAW Enzymes: 1-3 capsules per meal to support protein digestion and utilization[†]**

- **RAW Protein: 1-3 servings per day, mixed in water or raw juice within one hour of exercise and between meals**

- **RAW Meal: 1 serving per day, mixed in water or raw juice to replace a meal, or a half-serving as a between-meal snack provides 33 grams of protein per serving**

Upper GI Health

Description: According to the latest government statistics, at least 85 million American have reported experiencing the occasional occurrence of heartburn. To help digest food, the stomach produces about a quart of hydrochloric acid each day to aid in the digestion process. The acid doesn't usually present a problem because the gastrointestinal tract is coated with a protective mucous lining, but when hydrochloric acid moves up the esophagus, watch out. The delicate tissue of the esophagus doesn't have a protective lining like the stomach, which means that the corrosive nature of the hydrochloric acid produces an unpleasant burning sensation.

Dietary instructions: Follow the basic principles of the RAW Truth Nutrition Plan. Focus on consuming the following foods and supplements as often as possible.

Living foods:

- blueberries are an important source of fiber and powerful antioxidants that support healthy bowel function
- fresh veggie juice, high in greens such as celery, parsley, cucumber, and cilantro—combined with a generous amount of cabbage juice—provides vitamin U, which supports upper GI health
- avocados are an excellent source of vitamin E and potassium as well as healthy fats and fiber
- flaxseed and chia seed products, including fresh ground seed and oil, can support healthy digestive function
- wild salmon ceviche (not suitable for vegetarians or vegans) is a superb source of omega-3 fatty acids, the antioxidant astaxanthin, and vitamin D
- raw cultured veggies such as sauerkraut and kimchi are a first-rate source of probiotics and organic acids, which help create a balanced intestinal environment
- raw cultured dairy (not suitable for vegans), especially yogurt and kefir, supports healthy digestive function (sheep and goat's milk may be more tolerable, but as long as the dairy is raw and comes from grass-fed animals, cow's milk should be fine)
- raw coconut cream contains medium-chain fatty acids, vitamins, and minerals to support overall health and detoxification while providing healthy raw fats for energy and muscle support
- raw coconut kefir, which is loaded with probiotics and minerals and supports digestive health and immune system function while delivering active probiotic cultures, provides electrolytes for proper hydration
- really raw cheese from grass-fed cows contains probiotics, protein, minerals, fat-soluble vitamins, and healthy fats, including CLA and omega-3s, to support healthy digestion and immune system function (not suitable for vegans)

Living nutrients:

- **RAW Cleanse: the seven-day raw cleanse system is an ideal jump-start to extraordinary digestive health**[†]
- **Perfect Food RAW: one serving of powder or caps upon waking, mixed in or swallowed with water or raw vegetable juice**
- **Vitamin Code Multivitamins: 4 capsules per day, with or without food**
- **RAW Probiotics: 3-9 capsules per day, with or without food**
- **RAW Enzymes: 1-3 capsules per meal**
- **RAW Fiber: take 1-2 servings per day, mixed in water or raw juice**
- **RAW D3: 1-5 capsules (2,000-10,000IU) per day with meals, based on average sun exposure and vitamin D levels**

[†] These statements have not been evaluated by the Food and Drug Administration. This product is not intended to diagnose, treat, cure or prevent any disease.

Skin Health

Description: Our skin, which forms a protective barrier from the outside world, is also an important eliminative organ. To promote healthy skin, it's important to consume a wide range of antioxidants in your diet since optimal digestive and balanced immune function go hand-in-hand with healthy skin.† The first step in any skin health regimen is starting with a raw food diet, and a seven-day cleanse is highly recommended.†

Dietary instructions: Follow the basic principles of the RAW Truth Nutrition Plan. Focus on consuming the following foods and supplements as often as possible.

Living foods:

- blueberries are an important source of fiber and powerful antioxidants that support healthy skin
- tomatoes, mixed with a healthy fat such as avocado, are great for skin health
- fresh veggie juice, high in greens such as celery, parsley, cucumber, and cilantro, is a terrific daily digestive tonic
- avocados, an excellent source of vitamin E and potassium as well as healthy fats, are essential for healthy skin
- flaxseed and chia seed products, including fresh ground seed or oil, can promote healthy skin
- wild salmon ceviche (not suitable for vegetarians or vegans) is a superb source of omega-3 fatty acids, vitamin D, and the antioxidant astaxanthin, which has been shown to act as an internal sunscreen to protect skin from overexposure to the sun's UV rays
- raw cultured dairy (not suitable for vegans), especially yogurt and kefir, supports healthy digestive function and promote healthy skin
- raw coconut cream contains medium-chain fatty acids, vitamins, and minerals to support overall health and detoxification while providing health fats to promote vibrant-looking skin
- raw coconut kefir, which is loaded with probiotics and minerals and supports digestive health and normal immune system function while delivering active probiotic cultures, provides electrolytes for proper hydration
- really raw cheese from grass-fed cows contains probiotics, protein, minerals, fat-soluble vitamins, and healthy fats, including CLA and omega-3s, to support healthy digestion and immune system function (not suitable for vegans)

Living nutrients:

- **RAW Cleanse: the seven-day raw cleanse system is an ideal jump-start to extraordinary skin health†**
- **Perfect Food RAW: one serving of powder or caps upon waking, mixed in or swallowed with water or raw vegetable juice**
- **Vitamin Code Perfect Weight: 4 capsules per day, with or without food**
- **RAW Probiotics: 3-9 capsules per day, with or without food**
- **RAW Enzymes: 1-3 capsules per meal**
- **RAW Fiber: take 1-2 servings per day, mixed in water or raw juice**
- **RAW D3: 1-5 capsules (2,000-10,000IU) per day with meals, based on daily sun exposure and vitamin D levels**

THE RAW TRUTH

Weight Management

Description: As a culture, we are a little taller but a lot heavier than we were a generation ago; today we weigh twenty-five pounds more than our grandparents or parents did in the 1960s, with the biggest weight gains attached to men forty and older. Believe it or not, many overweight people are deficient in nutrients, but a raw diet and nutrition plan promotes healthy weight and metabolism better than any other diet plan I know of.[†]

Dietary instructions: Follow the basic principles of the RAW Truth Nutrition Plan. Focus on consuming the following foods and supplements as often as possible.

Living foods:

- fresh veggie juice, high in greens such as celery, parsley, cucumber, and cilantro, provides daily detoxification, and blending a peeled cucumber into the juice adds fiber, which is important for cleansing and maintaining healthy blood sugar levels already in the normal range
- berries are loaded with antioxidants low in sugar and high in fiber, making makes them ideal fruits for any weight-loss program
- avocados, an excellent source of vitamin E and potassium as well as healthy fats and fiber, can be combined with raw fruits such as berries to help support weight management
- flaxseed and chia seeds (ground) are loaded with healthy fats and fiber that help nourish the body at the cellular level and promote a feeling of fullness
- wild salmon ceviche (not suitable for vegetarians or vegans) is a superb source of omega-3 fatty acids, the antioxidant astaxanthin, and vitamin D
- raw cultured dairy (not suitable for vegans), especially yogurt and kefir, is a great source of high-quality protein and balanced nutrition
- raw coconut cream contains medium-chain fatty acids, vitamins, and minerals to support overall health and detoxification while supporting healthy weight management
- raw coconut kefir, which is loaded with probiotics and minerals and supports digestive health and immune system function while delivering active probiotic cultures, provides electrolytes for proper hydration
- really raw cheese from grass-fed cows contains probiotics, protein, minerals, fat-soluble vitamins, and healthy fats, including CLA and omega-3s, to support healthy digestion and immune system function (not suitable for vegans)

Living nutrients:

- **Perfect Food RAW: one serving of powder or caps upon waking, mixed in or swallowed with water or raw vegetable juice**
- **RAW Fiber: 1-2 servings per day (morning and afternoon is ideal), and may be combined with Perfect Food RAW as the ultimate morning cleansing and detoxification tonic[†]**
- **Vitamin Code Perfect Weight: 4 capsules per day, with or without food**
- **RAW Probiotics: 3 capsules per day, with or without food**
- **RAW Enzymes: 1-3 capsules per meal**
- **RAW Protein: 1-2 servings per day, mixed in water or raw juice**
- **RAW Meal: one serving per day, mixed in water or raw juice to replace a meal, or a half-serving as a between-meal snack**

† These statements have not been evaluated by the Food and Drug Administration. This product is not intended to diagnose, treat, cure or prevent any disease.

Upper Respiratory and Sinus Health

Description: The health of the upper respiratory tract and sinus can be maintained by keeping the body stocked with the living nutrients it needs to keep a healthy immune system in balance.[†]

Dietary instructions: Follow the basic principles of the RAW Truth Nutrition Plan. Focus on consuming the following foods and supplements as often as possible.

Living foods:

- fresh veggie juice, including carrots as well as greens such as celery, parsley, cucumber, and cilantro, provides antioxidants and aids in detoxification
- blueberries, an important source of fiber and powerful antioxidants, support healthy bowel function
- avocados are an excellent source of vitamin E and potassium as well as healthy fats and fiber
- flaxseed and chia seed products, including fresh ground seed and oil, support healthy digestion and maintain normal immune function
- wild salmon ceviche (not suitable for vegetarians or vegans) is a superb source of omega-3 fatty acids, the antioxidant astaxanthin, and vitamin D
- citrus fruit, especially lemon juice, can reduce mucus
- small amounts apple cider vinegar, mixed with raw honey, can help also thin mucus in the body
- raw cultured dairy (not suitable for vegans), especially yogurt and kefir (sheep and goat's milk may be more tolerable and less mucus-forming, but as long as the dairy is raw and comes from grass-fed animals, cow's milk should be fine), supports healthy digestive function
- raw coconut cream contains medium-chain fatty acids, vitamins, and minerals to support overall health and detoxification while supporting healthy weight management
- raw coconut kefir, which is loaded with probiotics and minerals and supports digestive health and maintains normal immune system function while delivering active probiotic cultures, provides electrolytes for proper hydration
- really raw cheese from grass-fed cows contains probiotics, protein, minerals, fat-soluble vitamins, and healthy fats, including CLA and omega-3s, to support healthy digestion and immune system function (not suitable for vegans)

Living nutrients:

- **Immune Balance Sinus: 2 capsules per day to provide multidimensional support for seasonal sinus and respiratory health and wellness (while not a raw supplement, this formula is ideal for those looking to support a balanced immune system response for seasonal protection of sinus and respiratory health)[†]**
- **Perfect Food RAW: one serving of powder or caps upon waking, mixed in or swallowed with water or raw vegetable juice**
- **Vitamin Code Multivitamins: 4 capsules per day, with or without food**
- **RAW Probiotics: 3-9 capsules per day, with or without food**
- **RAW Enzymes: 1-3 capsules per meal**
- **RAW Antioxidants: 2 capsules per day provide powerful antioxidants that support a healthy immune system[†]**
- **RAW D3: 1-5 capsules (2,000-10,000IU) per day with meals, based on daily sun exposure and vitamin D levels**

Gluten-Free Lifestyle

Description: Gluten, the sticky protein found in wheat, rye, and barley, can interfere with the absorption of nutrients from food in sensitive individuals. Gluten is present in just about every commercially baked product on store shelves as well as virtually every packaged and processed food, which makes gluten difficult to eliminate from the diet. Many gluten-sensitive individuals pursuing a gluten-free diet experience difficulty digesting starches from grains as well as table sugar and lactose and casein from dairy. A diet consisting of raw, whole foods as well as living nutrients and digestive enzymes, however, can promote extraordinary digestive health.[†]

Dietary instructions: Follow the basic principles of the RAW Truth Nutrition Plan. Focus on consuming the following foods and supplements as often as possible.

Living foods:

- blueberries, an important source of fiber and powerful antioxidants, support healthy bowel function
- fresh veggie juice, high in greens such as celery, parsley, cucumber, and cilantro, is a terrific daily digestive tonic
- avocados are an excellent source of vitamin E and potassium as well as healthy fats and fiber
- flaxseed and chia seed products, including fresh ground seed and oil, can support healthy digestive function
- wild salmon ceviche (not suitable for vegetarians or vegans) is a superb source of omega-3 fatty acids, the antioxidant astaxanthin, and vitamin D
- raw cultured dairy (not suitable for vegans), especially yogurt and kefir (sheep and goat's milk may be more tolerable, but as long as the dairy is raw and comes from grass-fed animals, cow's milk should be fine), supports healthy digestive function—but keep in mind that dairy from grass-fed animals contains butyric acid, which supports the health of the intestinal lining
- raw coconut cream contains medium-chain fatty acids, vitamins, and minerals to support overall health, detoxification, and digestive wellness
- raw coconut kefir, which is loaded with probiotics and minerals and supports digestive health and immune system function while delivering active probiotic cultures, provides electrolytes for proper hydration
- really raw cheese from grass-fed cows contains probiotics, protein, minerals, fat-soluble vitamins, and healthy fats, including CLA and omega-3s, to support healthy digestion and maintain normal immune system function (not suitable for vegans)

Living nutrients:

- **Gluten FREEze: one capsule with each meal helps provides a broad range of highly active digestive enzymes that help break down components found in grains and dairy to ease digestion, including DPP-IV and other high activity proteases specifically targeting gluten and casein[†]**
- **Vitamin Code Multivitamins: 4 capsules per day, with or without food**
- **RAW Probiotics: 3-9 capsules per day, with or without food**
- **RAW Enzymes: 1-3 capsules per meal**
- **RAW Fiber: take 1-2 servings per day, mixed in water or raw juice**
- **RAW D3: 1-5 capsules (2,000-10,000IU) per day with meals, based on average sun exposure and vitamin D level**

[†] These statements have not been evaluated by the Food and Drug Administration. This product is not intended to diagnose, treat, cure or prevent any disease.

Liver and Gallbladder Heath

Description: The liver and gallbladder work as a team to eliminate toxins and other potentially harmful agents taken into the body. The liver does most of the work, while the gallbladder stores the bile that the liver produces and empties the bile into the small intestine, where it's further broken down for absorption. Since the liver and gallbladder are tied at the hip, so to speak, with your digestive system, eating a raw food diet may send fewer toxins to the liver and gallbladder. Following the RAW Truth Nutrition Plan can help take stress off the liver and gallbladder while promoting overall digestive and detoxification support.[†]

Dietary instructions: Follow the basic principles of the RAW Truth Nutrition Plan. Focus on consuming the following foods and supplements as often as possible.

Living foods:

- fresh veggie juice from beets, carrots, and greens such as celery, parsley, cucumber, and cilantro, is a terrific daily digestive tonic that supports liver health
- avocados, an excellent source of vitamin E and potassium as well as healthy fats and fiber, can promote liver health
- flaxseed and chia seed products, including fresh ground seed and oil, can support healthy digestive function
- wild salmon ceviche (not suitable for vegetarians or vegans) is a superb source of omega-3 fatty acids, the antioxidant astaxanthin, and vitamin D
- raw coconut cream contains medium-chain fatty acids, vitamins, and minerals to support overall health, immune system function, and the fats in raw coconut cream help support healthy intestinal flora balance and take some of the burden off the liver since many of the fatty acids are processed by the lymphatic system and bypass the liver and gallbladder
- raw coconut kefir, which is loaded with probiotics and minerals and supports digestive health and immune system function while delivering active probiotic cultures, provides electrolytes for proper hydration
- really raw cheese from grass-fed cows contains probiotics, protein, minerals, fat-soluble vitamins, and healthy fats, including CLA and omega-3s, to support healthy digestion and immune system function (not suitable for vegans)

Living nutrients:

- **RAW Cleanse: the seven-day raw cleanse system is an ideal jump-start to extraordinary digestive health and support of healthy liver function[†]**
- **Perfect Food RAW: one serving of powder or caps upon waking, mixed in or swallowed with water or raw vegetable juice**
- **Vitamin Code Multivitamins: 4 capsules per day, with or without food**
- **RAW Probiotics: 3-9 capsules per day, with or without food**
- **RAW Enzymes: 1-3 capsules per meal for potent levels of lipase, the fat-digesting enzymes critical to supporting healthy liver and gallbladder function[†]**
- **RAW Fiber: take 1-2 servings per day, mixed in water or raw juice, to help remove excess fats from the digestive tract[†]**

Immune Health

Description: Following a diet rich in raw foods and living nutrients can support a healthy immune system all year-round, while specific raw foods and nutrients can support your body's immune system through the cold weather season or any time you feel less than your extraordinary self.[†]

Dietary instructions: Follow the basic principles of the RAW Truth Nutrition Plan. Focus on consuming the following foods and supplements to support your body's immune system through the cold weather season or any time you feel less than your extraordinary self.

Living foods:

- fresh veggie juice, containing carrot and greens such as celery, parsley, cucumber, and cilantro in the amount of 32-48 ounces per day, should be consumed to support your body's immune system through the cold weather season or any time you feel less than your extraordinary self

- raw garlic (1-3 cloves per day, peeled and blended into veggie juice) is a potent botanical to promote immune system balance

- ginger juice, as an addition to veggie juice, supports healthy inflammation

- apple cider vinegar, mixed with water and raw honey and consumed 1-3 times per day, can help thin mucus

- citrus juice, especially lemon juice, is wonderful for immune system health

- raw coconut cream contains medium-chain fatty acids, vitamins, and minerals to support overall health, immune system function, and detoxification

- raw coconut kefir, which is loaded with probiotics and minerals and supports digestive health and immune system function while delivering active probiotic cultures, provides electrolytes for proper hydration

Living nutrients:

- **Immune Balance Rapid Extra Strength: 4 lozenges per day to provide multi-dimensional to support your body's immune system through the cold weather season or any time you feel less than your extraordinary self (while not a raw supplement, this formula is ideal for those looking to support their immune system)[†]**
- **Vitamin Code Multivitamins: 4 capsules per day, with or without food**
- **RAW Vitamin C: 6-12 capsules per day for five days**
- **RAW Probiotics: 9 capsules per day, with or without food**
- **RAW Enzymes: 3 capsules per meal**
- **RAW Antioxidants: 2-6 capsules per day**
- **RAW D3: 1-5 capsules (2,000-10,000IU) per day with or without meals**

Urinary Tract Health

Description: Your urinary system is composed of the kidneys, ureters, bladder, and urethra—the structures that urine passes through before being eliminated from the body. A healthy microbial balance in the digestive tract is essential for healthy urinary tract function.[†]

Dietary instructions: Follow the basic principles of the RAW Truth Nutrition Plan. Focus on consuming the following foods and supplements as often as possible to experience extraordinary health.

Living foods:

- blueberries, an important source of fiber and powerful antioxidants, support a healthy urinary tract

- cranberries, regarded as a top food to promote healthy urinary tract function, can be mixed with blueberries and raw honey in a purée to powerfully promote urinary tract health

- fresh veggie juice, high in greens such as celery, parsley, cucumber, and cilantro, is a terrific daily digestive tonic that also supports healthy urinary tract function

- avocados are an excellent source of vitamin E and potassium as well as healthy fats and fiber

- flaxseed and chia seed products, including fresh ground seed and oil, can support healthy digestive function

- wild salmon ceviche (not suitable for vegetarians or vegans) is a superb source of omega-3 fatty acids, the antioxidant astaxanthin, and vitamin D

- raw cultured dairy (not suitable for vegans), especially yogurt and kefir, supports healthy digestive function and intestinal microbial balance

- raw coconut cream contains medium-chain fatty acids, vitamins, and minerals to support overall health, immune system function, and detoxification

- raw coconut kefir, which is loaded with probiotics and minerals and supports digestive health and normal immune system function while delivering active probiotic cultures, provides electrolytes for proper hydration

Living nutrients:

- **RAW Cleanse: the seven-day raw cleanse system is an ideal jump-start to extraordinary digestive health and maintaining normal immune system health**[†]
- **Perfect Food RAW: one serving of powder or caps upon waking, mixed in or swallowed with water or raw vegetable juice**
- **Vitamin Code Multivitamins: 4 capsules per day, with or without food**
- **RAW Probiotics: 3-9 capsules per day, with or without food, support a healthy microbial balance**
- **RAW Enzymes: 1-3 capsules per meal**
- **Yeast FREEze: take 2-4 capsules per day to support natural microbial balance in the digestive system**[†]
- **RAW D3: 1-5 capsules (2,000-10,000IU) per day with meals, based on daily sun exposure and vitamin D levels**

THE RAW TRUTH

Healthy Cholesterol Levels

Description: Some so-called "high fat" foods—avocados and coconuts, for instance—actually contain fats that your body needs for optimal health. We *need* these fats to do the following functions: play a vital role in bone health, support the immune system, protect the liver from alcohol and other toxins, and guard against harmful microorganisms in the digestive tract. Consuming raw, living foods and nutrients is a great way to support healthy cholesterol levels already in the normal range.[†]

Dietary instructions: Follow the basic principles of the RAW Truth Nutrition Plan. Focus on consuming the following foods and supplements as often as possible.

Living foods:

- fresh veggie juice high in greens such as celery, parsley, cucumber, and cilantro, provides daily detoxification, and blending a peeled cucumber into the juice adds fiber, which is important for maintaining healthy blood cholesterol levels that are already in the normal range
- avocados, an excellent source of vitamin E and potassium as well as healthy fats and fiber, can help in maintaining healthy blood cholesterol levels that are already in the normal range.
- flaxseed and chia seeds (ground) are loaded with healthy omega-3 fats and fiber
- wild salmon ceviche (not suitable for vegetarians or vegans) is a superb source of omega-3 fatty acids, the antioxidant astaxanthin, and vitamin D, all of which help maintain healthy blood lipid levels
- berries such as blueberries and raspberries are loaded with antioxidants, high in fiber, and low in sugar, making them ideal to maintain healthy blood cholesterol levels that are already in the normal range.
- raw coconut cream contains medium-chain fatty acids, vitamins, and minerals to support overall health, normal immune system function, and detoxification, and while coconut cream is high in saturated fat, it has not been shown to increase cholesterol levels
- raw coconut kefir, which is loaded with probiotics and minerals and supports digestive health and normal immune system function while delivering active probiotic cultures, provides electrolytes for proper hydration

Living nutrients:

- **Perfect Food RAW: one serving of powder or caps upon waking, mixed in or swallowed with water or raw vegetable juice**
- **RAW Fiber: 1-2 servings per day (morning and afternoon is ideal), and the soluble fiber in RAW Fiber supports already healthy cholesterol levels[†]**
- **Vitamin Code Perfect Weight: 4 capsules per day, with or without food**
- **RAW Probiotics: 3 capsules per day, with or without food**
- **RAW Enzymes: 1-3 capsules per meal**
- **RAW Protein: 1-2 servings per day, mixed in water or raw juice**
- **RAW Meal: 1 serving per day, mixed in water or raw juice to replace a meal, or a half-serving as a between-meal snack**

[†] These statements have not been evaluated by the Food and Drug Administration. This product is not intended to diagnose, treat, cure or prevent any disease.

Immune System Maintenance

Description: Consuming a diet based on raw living foods, probiotics, and nutrients supports the immune system through multiple pathways, including optimizing the health of the digestive tract and facilitating the removal of toxins.[†]

Dietary instructions: Follow the basic principles of the RAW Truth Nutrition Plan. Focus on consuming the following foods and supplements as often as possible.

Living foods:

- berries such as blueberries, raspberries, and strawberries are a great source of fiber and powerful antioxidants that support healthy immune system function
- fresh veggie juice, high in greens such as celery, parsley, cucumber, and cilantro, is a terrific daily tonic
- broccoli sprouts contain powerful compounds that support healthy immune system function on the cellular level
- avocados are an excellent source of vitamin E and potassium as well as healthy fats and fiber
- flaxseed and chia seed products, including fresh ground seed and oil, can support healthy immune system function
- wild salmon ceviche (not suitable for vegetarians or vegans) is a superb source of omega-3 fatty acids, the antioxidant astaxanthin, and vitamin D, perhaps the most critical nutrient to support a balanced immune system
- raw cultured veggies such as sauerkraut and kimchi are loaded with powerful immune-supportive phytochemicals
- raw cultured dairy (not suitable for vegans), especially yogurt and kefir, supports healthy digestive and immune system function
- raw coconut cream contains medium-chain fatty acids, vitamins, and minerals to support overall health, immune system function, and detoxification
- raw coconut kefir, which is loaded with probiotics and minerals and supports digestive health and immune system function while delivering active probiotic cultures, provides electrolytes for proper hydration
- really raw cheese from grass-fed cows contains probiotics, protein, minerals, fat-soluble vitamins, and healthy fats, including CLA and omega-3s, to support healthy digestion and maintain normal immune system function (not suitable for vegans)

Living nutrients:

- **RAW Cleanse: the seven-day raw cleanse system is an ideal jump-start to extraordinary digestive health and maintaining an already healthy immune system[†]**
- **Perfect Food RAW: one serving of powder or caps upon waking, mixed in or swallowed with water or raw vegetable juice**
- **Vitamin Code Multivitamins: 4 capsules per day, with or without food**
- **RAW Probiotics: 3-9 capsules per day, with or without food**
- **RAW Enzymes: 1-3 capsules per meal**
- **RAW Calcium: 5 capsules per day provide minerals and fat-soluble vitamins to support a healthy immune system[†]**
- **RAW D3: 1-5 capsules (2,000-10,000IU) per day with meals, based on daily sun exposure and vitamin D levels**
- **RAW Protein 1-2 servings per day, mixed in water, fresh juice, or raw dairy, provides the amino acid-building blocks to build the body and support a healthy immune system**

THE RAW TRUTH

Bone Health

Description: Building strong, healthy bones requires more than just calcium. A diet rich in raw, living nutrients including fat-soluble vitamins D and K and alkaline-forming foods promotes a concept known as "calcium homeostasis," which prepares the body to utilize dietary calcium.[†] Emerging research shows that you can build strong, healthy bones at any age.[†]

Dietary instructions: Follow the basic principles of the RAW Truth Nutrition Plan. Focus on consuming the following foods and supplements as often as possible.

Living foods:

- fresh veggie juice, high in greens such as celery and parsley, contains alkalizing minerals and is a terrific daily tonic
- avocados are an excellent source of vitamin E and potassium as well as healthy fats and fiber
- flaxseed and chia seed products, including fresh ground seed and oil, contains the important bone nutrient phosphorus
- wild salmon ceviche (not suitable for vegetarians or vegans) is a superb source of omega-3 fatty acids, the antioxidant astaxanthin, and vitamin D, perhaps the most critical nutrient, next to calcium, to promote healthy bones
- raw cultured dairy (not suitable for vegans), especially yogurt and kefir, provides healthy fats and calcium
- raw coconut cream contains medium-chain fatty acids, vitamins, and minerals to support overall health, immune system function, and detoxification
- raw coconut kefir is loaded with probiotics and minerals and supports digestive health and maintains immune system function while delivering active probiotic cultures
- really raw cheese from grass-fed cows contains probiotics, protein, minerals, fat-soluble vitamins, and healthy fats, including CLA and omega-3s, to support healthy digestion and maintain normal immune system function (not suitable for vegans)

Living nutrients:

- **Perfect Food RAW: one serving of powder or caps upon waking, mixed in or swallowed with water or raw vegetable juice, helps to promote calcium homeostasis[†]**
- **Vitamin Code Multivitamins: 4 capsules per day, with or without food**
- **RAW Probiotics: 3 capsules per day, with or without food**
- **RAW Enzymes: 1 capsule per meal**
- **Grow Bone System: 5 capsules per day of RAW Calcium and 3 capsules per day of Growth Factor S provides minerals and fat-soluble vitamins to reduce the risk of osteoporosis, stimulate bone growth, and strengthen bones by increasing bone mineral density[†], [††]**
- **RAW D3: 1-5 capsules (2,000-10,000IU) per day with meals, based on daily sun exposure and vitamin D levels**

[†] These statements have not been evaluated by the Food and Drug Administration. This product is not intended to diagnose, treat, cure or prevent any disease.

Healthy Inflammation

Description: Supporting healthy inflammation response in the body is critical to overall health and wellness.[†]

Dietary instructions: Follow the basic principles of the RAW Truth Nutrition Plan. Focus on consuming the following foods and supplements as often as possible.

Living foods:

- blueberries, an important source of fiber and powerful antioxidants, support a healthy inflammatory response in the body
- fresh veggie juice, high in greens such as celery, parsley, cucumber, and cilantro, is a terrific daily tonic
- avocados are an excellent source of vitamin E and potassium as well as healthy fats and fiber
- flaxseed and chia seed products, including fresh ground seed and oil, contain omega-3 fats to promote healthy inflammation
- wild salmon ceviche (not suitable for vegetarians or vegans) is a superb source of omega-3 fatty acids, the antioxidant astaxanthin, and vitamin D, and may be the most powerful single food to support a healthy inflammatory response
- pineapple (slightly unripe is best) contains the enzyme bromelain to support healthy inflammation
- papaya (slightly unripe is best) contains the enzyme papain to support healthy inflammation
- raw cultured dairy (not suitable for vegans), especially yogurt and kefir, supports healthy inflammation response (sheep and goat's milk may be more tolerable, but as long as the dairy is raw and comes from grass-fed animals, cow's milk should be fine)
- raw coconut cream contains medium-chain fatty acids, vitamins, and minerals to support overall health, immune system function, and detoxification
- raw coconut kefir, which is loaded with probiotics and minerals and supports digestive health and immune system function while delivering active probiotic cultures, provides electrolytes for proper hydration

Living nutrients:

- **Wobenzym N: 6 capsules twice daily on an empty stomach, in the original systemic enzyme formula, supports healthy inflammation response, healthy joints, and ligaments and tendons, promotes mobility and flexibility, and provides minor relief from everyday aches and pains (while not a raw supplement, this formula is ideal for those looking to support healthy inflammation in the body)[†]**
- **Vitamin Code Multivitamins: 4 capsules per day, with or without food**
- **RAW Probiotics: 3-9 capsules per day, with or without food**
- **RAW Enzymes: 1-3 capsules per meal**
- **RAW Antioxidants: take 2-4 capsules per day to support healthy inflammatory response[†]**
- **RAW D3: 1-5 capsules (2,000-10,000IU) per day with meals, based on daily sun exposure and vitamin D levels**

[†] These statements have not been evaluated by the Food and Drug Administration. This product is not intended to diagnose, treat, cure or prevent any disease.

CHAPTER 16

The Raw Truth

Recipes

By now, you know how healthy it can be to consume a diet based on raw foods. Here are some of my favorite raw food recipes that will satisfy your taste buds.

The following recipes come from my good friend and raw food author and teacher, Paul Nison. Paul has taught thousands of people to transform their health with the power of raw nutrients. Paul's latest book, *The Daylight Diet*, is available at www.RawLife.com.

Carrot Ginger Salad Dressing

Ingredients

5 carrots
2-inch piece fresh ginger
¼ cup water or apple cider vinegar
1 date

Directions

Process all ingredients in blender or food processor until completely smooth. Makes about 2 cups.

Recipe courtesy of Paul Nison, author of Raw Food: *Formula for Health*

Raw Tomato Sauce

Ingredients

3 tomatoes
½ cup sun-dried tomatoes (not packed in oil)
1 clove garlic
½ Tablespoon chopped fresh basil
½ Tablespoon chopped fresh oregano
1 small hot pepper, such as a jalapeño or serrano

Directions

Place all ingredients into blender or food processor. Process until completely smooth. Makes about 2 cups. You can also add a chopped avocado and serve with raw pasta dishes.

Recipe courtesy of Paul Nison, author of Raw Food: *Formula for Health*

Chia Tapioca Pudding

Ingredients

¼ cup of chia seeds
1 cup almond, banana, or coconut milk or water
2 Tablespoons raisins
ground cinnamon to taste

Directions

In a medium bowl, mix chia seeds and milk. Place into refrigerator for 10 minutes. Add raisins and stir in cinnamon. Return to refrigerator overnight, stirring several times. Stir once again before serving. Makes about 1½ cups.

Recipe courtesy of Paul Nison, author of Raw Food: *Formula for Health*

Raw Pesto

Ingredients

2-4 cloves garlic
2 bunches spinach
1 bunch fresh basil
juice of ½ medium lemon
1 cup pine nuts
½ teaspoon sea salt
½ cup olive oil

Directions

Place garlic into a food processor. Process until the garlic is well minced. Add all remaining ingredients and process until completely smooth. Serve as a dip or over pasta. Makes 4 servings.

Recipe courtesy of Paul Nison, author of Raw Food: *Formula for Health*

Disclaimer Regarding Raw Dairy, Raw Eggs, Raw Fish, and Raw Juice

- Raw milk products may contain disease-causing microorganisms. Persons at highest risk for of disease from these organisms include newborns and infants, the elderly, pregnant women, those taking corticosteroids, antibiotics and antacids, and those having chronic illnesses and other conditions that weaken their immunity.

- Consuming raw or undercooked eggs may increase your risk of food-borne illness.

- Consuming raw or undercooked seafood may increase your risk of food-borne illness.

- Juice that has not been pasteurized may contain bacteria that can increase the risk of food-borne illness. People most at risk are children, the elderly and persons with a weakened immune system.

Tahini Dressing

Ingredients

½ cup raw tahini
juice of ½ medium-size lemon
1 clove garlic
pinch of cayenne
Nama Shoyu

Directions

Combine tahini, lemon juice, garlic, and cayenne in a blender and process until completely smooth. With blender running, add water, 1-2 teaspoons at a time, until dressing is the consistency you desire. Season with Nama Shoyu, a raw, unpasteurized Japanese soy sauce, to taste. This delicious, all-purpose salad dressing can be used year round. Store covered in the refrigerator. Makes 5 servings.

Paul's Powerful Salad

Ingredients

fresh spinach leaves (as much as you like)
1 ripe avocado, peeled, pitted and chopped
½ medium-size cucumber, chopped
½ red bell pepper, cored, seeded, and chopped (optional)
½ stalk celery, chopped
juice of 1 lemon
1-2 Tablespoons ground flaxseeds

Directions

Place spinach, avocado and cucumber, optional bell pepper, and celery in large bowl. Toss gently to combine. Sprinkle with lemon juice and flaxseeds. This salad is called "powerful" because every ingredient is a powerhouse of nutrients. Makes 1 serving.

Recipe courtesy of Paul Nison, author of Raw Food: *Formula for Health*

Paul's Favorite Salad

Ingredients

2 large heads romaine lettuce, chopped
2 ripe avocados, peeled, pitted, and chopped
2 ripe tomatoes, diced
¼ cup sunflower seeds or almonds
¼ cup raisins or currants
3 Tablespoons cold-pressed extra virgin olive oil
1 Tablespoon freshly squeezed lemon juice
2 teaspoons sea salt
2 teaspoons raw apple cider vinegar
1 teaspoon crushed red pepper flakes

Directions

Combine all ingredients in large bowl. Mix well. Let salad rest for 10 minutes before serving. Makes 4 servings.

Recipe courtesy of Paul Nison, author of Raw Food: *Formula for Health*

Mushroom Pizza

Ingredients

1 large Portobello mushroom
1 lemon
¼ cup raw tahini or almond butter
1 ripe tomato, thinly sliced
¼ ripe avocado, peeled, pitted and thinly sliced (optional)

Directions

Remove and discard stem of the mushroom and clean the mushroom cap. Turn cap upside down and place on a serving plate. Squeeze the lemon juice over it, then pour on the tahini. Top with the tomato and optional avocado.
Makes 1 serving.

Recipe courtesy of Paul Nison, author of Raw Food: Formula for Health

Marinated Veggies

Ingredients

1 medium-size yellow summer squash, chopped
1 medium-size zucchini, chopped
juice of 2 lemons

Directions

Place squash and zucchini in large bowl and sprinkle with the lemon juice. Marinate for 4 to 6 hours before serving.
Makes 1 serving.

Recipe courtesy of Paul Nison, author of Raw Food: *Formula for Health*

Cauliflower "Mashed Potatoes" with Mushroom Gravy

Ingredients

cauliflower florets
½ cup pine nuts
½ cup fresh thyme leaves
¼ cup freshly squeezed lemon juice
2 cloves garlic
sea salt
olive oil

Directions

Combine all ingredients in a food processor, adding salt and olive oil to taste. Process until mixture is consistency of mashed potatoes. Add a small amount of water, if necessary, to facilitate processing and achieve the desired consistency.
Makes 5 servings.

Recipe courtesy of Paul Nison, author of Raw Food: *Formula for Health*

Mushroom Gravy

Ingredients

4 Portobello mushrooms
1 jar (8 ounces) raw almond butter
1 cup water
2 ripe plum tomatoes, coarsely chopped
1 medium-size red onion, coarsely chopped
2 cloves garlic, coarsely chopped
sea salt

Directions

Remove and discard the stems of the mushroom. Clean and coarsely chop the cups. Transfer to food processor along with all of the remaining ingredients, adding salt to taste. Process until completely smooth. Serve this over the Cauliflower "Mashed Potatoes." Makes 8-12 servings.

Recipe courtesy of Paul Nison, author of Raw Food: *Formula for Health*

Raw Applesauce

Ingredients

3 apples, cored and coarsely chopped
1 ripe banana, cut into 4 or 5 large pieces
4 pitted soft dates
¼ cup water
ground nutmeg (optional)

Directions

Place apples, banana, dates, and water in blender and process until completely smooth. Sprinkle with nutmeg if desired. Makes 2 servings.

Recipe courtesy of Paul Nison, author of Raw Food: *Formula for Health*

Paul's Coconut Fruit Pie

Ingredients for the crust

2 cups chopped walnuts
2 cups chopped pecans
½ cup freshly squeezed orange juice
7 pitted Medjool dates
1 ripe banana, thinly sliced
1 ripe mango, peeled, pitted and thinly sliced

Ingredients for the filling:

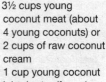

3½ cups young coconut meat (about 4 young coconuts) or 2 cups of raw coconut cream
1 cup young coconut juice/water (from 1 young coconut)
1 ripe banana (optional)
6 pitted Medjool dates
1 Tablespoon ground chia seeds
Shredded coconut and raisins or pine nuts

Directions

To prepare the crust, place walnuts, pecans, orange juice, and dates in a food processor and process until the mixture has the consistency of pastry dough. Press the mixture into an 8-inch glass pie plate to form the crust.
Makes 8 servings.

To prepare the filling, place coconut meat, coconut juice/water, optional banana, dates, and ground chia seeds in a blender and process until completely smooth. Pour into the pie crust. Garnish the edges of the pie with shredded coconut and raisins or pine nuts.

Recipe courtesy of Paul Nison, author of Raw Food: *Formula for Health*

Strawberry "Cheesecake"

Ingredients for the crust:

2 cups pecans or walnuts
1 cup pitted dates, soaked in water for 5 minutes and drained
¼ cup ground flaxseeds
½ teaspoon sea salt
½ raw vanilla powder

Ingredients for the filling:

3 cups cashews, soaked in water for at least 1 hour and drained
1 cup soaked dates
½ cup freshly squeezed lemon juice
¼ cup raw coconut cream (optional)
1 teaspoon vanilla powder
½ teaspoon sea salt

Ingredients for the topping:

2 cups frozen strawberries
1 cup pitted dates, soaked in water for 10 minutes and drained
¼ cup almond milk

Directions

To prepare the crust, place pecans in a food processor and process or pulse until finely chopped. Add the dates, flaxseeds, salt, and vanilla and process until mixture forms a ball. Turn out into an 8-inch springform pan and press the mixture into a crust.

To prepare the filling, drain the dates and mash into a paste and place the date paste, cashews, lemon juice, optional coconut oil, vanilla, and sea salt in a food processor. Process until completely smooth, adding 1 teaspoon of water at a time, if necessary, to thin the mixture and obtain the desired consistency. Pour into the crust. Tap the pan on the counter to remove air bubbles.

To prepare the topping, place the strawberries, dates, and almond milk in food processor and process until very smooth.

Recipe courtesy of Paul Nison, author of Raw Food: *Formula for Health*

Pour over the filling.

Freeze the cheesecake for several hours until firm. To serve, remove the cheesecake from the springform pan while still frozen. Makes 8 servings.

Coconut Shake

Ingredients

meat from 3 young coconuts
water from 1 young coconut
(about 1 cup)

Directions

Place coconut meat in blender or food processor. Add coconut water and process until smooth. Keep in mind that young coconuts have more meat, are more tender, and contain more water than older coconuts, so they're tastier and more nutritious. Look for them in Asian or Mexican markets or order online.
Makes 1 serving.

Coconut Avocado Drink

Ingredients

meat and water from 1 young coconut
or 4 ounces of raw coconut cream
1 ripe avocado, peeled and pitted

Place coconut meat or coconut cream, coconut water, and avocado in blender and process until smooth. Coconut and avocado make a surprisingly good combination. Makes 1 serving.

Nut Milk

Ingredients

½ cup soaked almonds or other nut of choice
1 cup water
4 pitted Medjool dates

Directions

Place almonds and water in blender. Add dates and blend until smooth. Strain through cheesecloth and discard the residue. Medjool dates, large and extraordinarily sweet, are native to Morocco, but they are also grown in the United States. Makes about 4 cups.

Blended Salad

Ingredients

1 cup spinach or lettuce leaves
1 cup sunflower sprouts (optional)
1 ripe avocado, peeled and pitted
1 ripe tomato, coarsely chopped
½ rep bell pepper, cored, seeded, and cut into 4 or 5 pieces (optional)
½ medium-size cucumber, cut into 3 or 4 pieces
1 stalk celery, cut into 3 or 4 pieces
juice of ½ lemon
1 teaspoon flaxseed oil or cold-pressed extra-virgin olive oil (optional)
1 tablespoon raw coconut cream

Directions

Combine all ingredients in a food processor or blender and process until smooth. For better digestion, try blending your salads instead of chewing them. Makes 2-3 servings.

Recipe courtesy of Paul Nison,
author of Raw Food: *Formula for Health*

Renee Ainlay created the recipes below. Renee was introduced to a raw omnivorous diet when she was suffering from a major health challenge. After two years of eating a nutrient-rich, raw food diet, Renee got on the road to extraordinary health. Today, Renee is creating healthy and creating wonderful raw food recipes that I absolutely love.

Delicious Raw Apple Pie

Ingredients

10 Medjool dates, pitted
¼ cup honey
2 cups ground almonds (raw, no salt
1 teaspoon almond extract

Directions

Put almonds in food processor. When finely ground, add remaining ingredients until mixture is sticky and can form a ball. Do not overprocess. Oil 9-inch glass pie plate with coconut oil and wipe with paper towel. Press crust mixture evenly into pie plate. Put in freezer while you make caramel sauce.

Caramel Sauce

Ingredients

15 Medjool dates, pitted
3/4 cup butter
1/4 cup honey
1 teaspoon vanilla
1 Tablespoon cinnamon

Directions

Put dates, butter, honey, and vanilla in food processor until mixture is smooth and creamy like caramel. This can take a few minutes. Put in bowl and stir in cinnamon. Set aside while you cut your apples.

Apple Filling

Ingredients

6 Honey Crisp or Pink Lady apples

Directions

Core, peel, and slice 6 Honey Crisp or Pink Lady apples. Thin slices are important. As you slice the apples, add them to the caramel mixture. Set aside.

Crumble Topping

Ingredients

3/4 cup walnuts
1/8 cup honey
2 Tablespoons cinnamon

Directions

In a food processor, rough chop the walnuts. Take out and put in bowl, add honey, and mix well so all walnut crumbs are coated with honey. Add cinnamon and mix well. Set aside. Then get crust out of freezer. Add apple caramel mixture, then top with crumble topping. Refrigerate overnight or at least 6 hours before serving. Gluten free, sugar free, and sodium free.

Recipe courtesy of Renee Ainlay of Nature's Juice Co-Op

Turtle Cheesecake

Ingredients

10 Medjool dates, pitted
¼ cup honey
2 cups ground pecans (raw, no salt)
¼ cup cacao powder (raw cacao)

Directions

Put pecans in food processor. When ground, add remaining ingredients until mixture is sticky and can form a ball. Do not overprocess. Oil 9-inch glass pie plate with coconut oil and wipe with paper towel. Press crust mixture evenly in pie plate. Put in freezer while you complete the remaining steps.

Recipe courtesy of Renee Ainlay of Nature's Juice Co-Op

Cheesecake Filling

Ingredients

11 ounces raw salted or unsalted Colby or cheddar cheese, room temperature

1 3/4 cups raw cream (preferred)
1/2 cup honey
1 teaspoon vanilla

Directions

Cut up cheese and put in food processor, add remaining ingredients. Process until cheese mixture is creamy (no lumps). Do not overprocess since overprocessing can result in separation of cheese and oils. This step can take a few minutes. When cheese mixture is complete, add to pie crust and refrigerate for 2 hours before completing final steps.

Recipe courtesy of Renee Ainlay of Nature's Juice Co-Op

Caramel Sauce

Ingredients

15 Medjool dates, pitted
3/4 cup butter
1/4 cup honey
1 teaspoon vanilla

Directions

Put dates, butter, honey, and vanilla in food processor until mixture is smooth and creamy like caramel.
This can take a few minutes. Set aside while you make chocolate sauce.

Chocolate Sauce

Ingredients

¼ cup raw cacao powder
¼ cup honey

Directions

Mix honey and cacao powder thoroughly with a spoon. If honey is thick and not

liquid, put honey in a small jar or bowl and place in hot water to thin out. The water should not be too hot to the touch. Stir constantly until thin. When thin, add to cacao powder and mix. Keep mixture warm until you take the cheesecake out of refrigerator.

Wait 2 hours, and then spread caramel sauce evenly over cheesecake. Drizzle chocolate sauce over caramel. Top with chopped pecans. Refrigerated for overnight or at least 6 hours before serving.

Recipe courtesy of Renee Ainlay of Nature's Juice Co-Op

Lemon Cheesecake with Blueberry Topping

Ingredients

10 Medjool dates, pitted
¼ cup honey
2 cups ground pecans (raw, no salt)
1 teaspoon vanilla extract

Directions

Put pecans in food processor. When ground, add remaining ingredients until mixture is sticky and can form a ball. Do not overprocess. Oil 9-inch glass pie plate with coconut oil and wipe with paper towel. Press crust mixture evenly in pie plate. Put in freezer while you complete the remaining steps.

Blueberry Topping

Ingredients

2 cups fresh blueberries
1/3 cup honey (may need a little more honey if berries are tart)

Directions

Blend blueberries and honey until well blended. Let sit in refrigerator for ½ hour while pie is finishing in refrigerator. Then take out cheesecake from refrigerator and spread blueberry topping evenly over cheesecake. Refrigerate overnight or at least 6 hours before serving.

Recipe courtesy of Renee Ainlay of Nature's Juice Co-Op

Decadent Chocolate Sauce

Ingredients

2 cups honey
2 cups cacao powder (raw cacao powder)

Directions

Mix honey and cacao powder thoroughly with a spoon. If honey is thick and not liquid, put honey in a small jar or bowl and place in hot water to thin out. The water should not be too hot to the touch. Stir constantly until thin. When thin, add to cacao powder and mix. Store in cabinet and use when making smoothies, chocolate ice cream, chocolate milk, etc. Makes 1 pint.

Recipe courtesy of Renee Ainlay of Nature's Juice Co-Op

Hydrating Sports Drink I

Ingredients

8 ounces coconut water
(from fresh, mature coconut)
4 ounces sparkling mineral water
(may substitute mineral water)
3 Tablespoons lemon juice
(fresh squeezed)
2 Tablespoons honey

Directions

Blend or stir together coconut water, lemon juice, and honey. When mixed thoroughly, add sparkling water and drink.

Recipe courtesy of Renee Ainlay of Nature's Juice Co-Op

Hydrating Sports Drink II

Ingredients

8 ounces coconut water (from fresh, mature coconut)
4 ounces sparkling mineral water (may substitute mineral water)
3 Tablespoons lime juice (fresh squeezed)
3 Tablespoons honey

Directions

Blend or stir together coconut water, lime juice, and honey. When mixed thoroughly, add sparkling water and drink.

Recipe courtesy of Renee Ainlay of Nature's Juice Co-Op

JR's Carb Juice

Ingredients

10 ounces celery stalks with leaves
1 pound carrots
1 pound, 2 ounces cucumbers (peeled)
¼ cup zucchini
1/8 bunch of parsley
2 ounces lemon juice (squeezed by hand)
2 ounces honey

Directions

Wash all veggies. Juice ingredients in Green Star or Champion juicer. Stir in lemon and honey. Makes approximately 32 ounces.

Green Juice

Ingredients

10 ounces celery stalks with leaves
½ pound carrots
1/8 bunch of parsley
1/8 bunch cilantro
2 pounds cucumber (peeled)
2 ounces honey (optional)

Directions

Wash all veggies. Juice ingredients in Green Star or Champion juicer, but not including cucumber. Then blend in honey and cucumber. Makes approximately 32 ounces.

Recipe courtesy of Renee Ainlay of Nature's Juice Co-Op

Orange Salmon Ceviche

Ingredients for orange sauce (first step)

½ cup olive oil
2/3 cup juice from orange
½ teaspoon orange zest
1 Tablespoon red bell pepper (cubed)
1 Tablespoon red onion
1/8 jalapeño pepper

1/8 habanera pepper
1/8 cup cilantro (rough chopped)
1 Tablespoon honey

Directions

Put ingredients in blender and blend lightly. Let sit overnight in refrigerator so flavors in ingredients meld together.

Salmon (second step)

Ingredients

2 pounds sockeye salmon, fresh, skinned and boned (can substitute frozen salmon for fresh)
1 cup lemon juice, strained
¼ cup water (filtered)

Directions

Juice lemons, then strain and add water. Set aside. Cut salmon into cubes. Put salmon in lemon water for 2-4 hours. Shake or stir twice. Rinse salmon, spin dry, and add sauce, using salad spinner. Add red bell pepper and chopped cilantro to salmon and sauce mixture. Garnish with chopped cilantro. Makes 4 servings.

Recipe courtesy of Renee Ainlay of Nature's Juice Co-Op

Spicy Salmon Ceviche

Ingredients for Spicy Sauce

½ cup olive oil
¼ cup juice from lemons (strained)
2 Tablespoons lime zest
1 Tablespoon red bell pepper
1 Tablespoon red onion
1/8 cup fennel (chopped)
½ jalapeño pepper
¼ habanera pepper
1/8 cup parsley (chopped)
2 Tablespoons honey

Directions

Put ingredients in blender and blend lightly. Let sit overnight in refrigerator so flavors in ingredients meld together.

Recipe courtesy of Renee Ainlay of Nature's Juice Co-Op

Salmon (second step)
Ingredients

2 pounds sockeye salmon, fresh, skinned and boned (can substitute frozen salmon for fresh)
1 cup lemon juice, strained
¼ cup water (filtered)

Directions

Juice lemons, then strain and add water. Set aside. Cut salmon into cubes. Put salmon in lemon water for 2-4 hours. Shake or stir twice. Rinse salmon, spin dry, and add sauce, using salad spinner. Add chopped fennel and peppers to salmon and sauce mixture. Garnish ceviche with chopped parsley. Makes 4 servings.

Recipe courtesy of Renee Ainlay of Nature's Juice Co-Op

Below are two of my favorite raw food desserts that are both delicious and healthy and consumed by my family several times per week.

Jordan's Raw Smoothie
Ingredients

8 ounces raw milk, yogurt, or kefir
1 cup of fresh or frozen fruit
1-2 raw eggs (optional)
1 Tablespoon raw coconut cream
1 Tablespoon flaxseed oil
1 Tablespoon raw honey
1 serving of RAW Protein

Directions

Combine all ingredients in a blender and blend. Makes 1 serving.

Raw Vanilla Ice Cream
Ingredients

4 ounces raw whole milk
4 ounces raw cream
1 ounce raw coconut cream
1 raw egg yolk (optional)
1-2 Tablespoons raw honey
½ teaspoon organic vanilla extract
dash of sea salt

Directions

Combine all ingredients in a

blender and pour into a bowl or porcelain baking dish. Cover and place in the freezer for 2-3 hours. Makes 2 servings.

Raw Piña Colada Ice Cream
Ingredients

4 ounces raw coconut cream
4 ounces raw coconut water
½-1 cup of pineapple
1 raw egg yolk (optional)
1-2 Tablespoons raw honey
½ teaspoon organic vanilla extract
dash of sea salt

Directions

Combine all ingredients in a blender and pour into a bowl or porcelain baking dish. Cover and place in the freezer for 2-3 hours. Makes 2 servings.

RAW RESOURCES
RAW EXPERTS

Angela Stokes-Monarch

Award-winning author Angela Stokes lost an amazing 160 pounds with a raw lifestyle. The 32-year-old went raw in May 2002 and her life was dramatically transformed. Her website, **www.RawReform.com** shares her amazing story of recovery, along with guidance and inspiration for others. She shares videos, before/after pictures and also blogs almost daily www.rawreform.blogspot.com.

Angela offers books, retreats, consultations and lectures internationally on raw foods. In February 2007, she completed a 92-Day Juice Feast and her juicing book inspires countless others into juicy journeys. Her most recent book '*Raw Emotions*' explores raw food transformations beyond the physical level.

Matt Monarch

Matt Monarch has been 100% raw vegan for 13 years. Matt dove head-first into this lifestyle after reading Norman Walker's classic book *Becoming Younger*. After five years raw, Matt wrote the book *Raw Spirit*, covering various topics that going raw can involve. Matt considers his second book, *Raw Success*, his "Bible" for being raw. He travels worldwide teaching about eating healthily and also has the largest raw online store in the world, TheRawFoodWorld.com, along with a daily online raw food TV show and a newsletter.
www.TheRawFoodWorld.com

Debra Garner is a chef specializing in vegan and raw vegan cuisine. She struggled with obesity for 12 years before finding success with veganism and eventually with raw veganism. After being vegan for six months, she was ready to make the transition to raw foods. She started her journey by taking courses from raw chefs Alissa Cohen and Carolyn Akens. Eventually she lost 100 pounds and realized that one of her goals in life was to help mothers like herself attain optimal health so they could live vibrant, joyful lives. The first step was her DVD, *In the Kitchen with Debra*, an introduction to a vegan and raw vegan diet including a 360 page

ebook full of resources and more than 250 vegan and raw vegan recipes. She has also worked with many companies by reviewing their supplements, food products, and healthy living items and has had the opportunity to speak at several vegan conferences where she demonstrated many raw and vegan dishes.

A wife and a mother of seven children, Debra is happiest when she's in the kitchen and teaching others how to life a healthier lifestyle.

www.veganfamilystyle.com www.veganfamilystyle.blogspot.com
www.inthekitchenwithdebra.com

Kristen Suzanne, owner of KristensRaw.com, is an accomplished raw vegan chef, author, and teacher with a passion for helping people get started and succeed with a raw food diet. As a former competitive bodybuilder, she's been studying nutrition, fitness, and food preparation for fifteen years. Kristen is the author of eleven raw vegan recipe and lifestyle books (with her newest title

Kristen Suzanne's EASY Raw Vegan Transition Recipes).

She also maintains her popular blog (http://KristensRaw.com/blog).
She's a frequent guest on television and radio shows such as *Good Morning Arizona*, *Sonoran Evening Live*, and *Culinary Confessions*, and has been featured several times in *VegNews* Magazine.

www.KristensRaw.com www.KristensRaw.com/blog

Sarma Melngailis

is the Proprietor and Co-Founder of NYC's premier raw and vegan restaurant, Pure Food and Wine. She is also the Founder and CEO of One Lucky Duck Holdings, LLC, which operates the One Lucky Duck brand.

This includes the company's online boutique, www.oneluckyduck.com, which offers carefully selected products all in support of living a raw, vegan, organic and eco-friendly lifestyle. One Lucky Duck also carries its own line of snack products all made and packaged by hand at Pure Food and Wine. These are sold at oneluckyduck.com and in the restaurant's own One Lucky Duck takeaway and retail shop, as well as its more recently opened One Lucky Duck across town in Manhattan's famous Chelsea Market.

She is the co-author of *Raw Food/Real World* (Harper Collins, 2005), a book of recipes, practical advice and the story of how she made the change to a raw and vegan diet. Her second book with Harper Collins, *Living Raw Food*, was published in June 2009. *Living Raw Food* includes even more raw vegan recipes, as well as information and advice on how to successfully maintain a raw food diet after a number of years.

Sarma is a graduate of the French Culinary Institute. She holds a B.S. in Economics and a B.A. in Economics from the Wharton School at the University of Pennsylvania. She worked in investment banking and private equity before beginning her career in the food world.

www.oneluckyduck.com
www.twitter/sarma
www.facebook.com/sarmamelngailis

Siegren Johnson is a certified Raw Vegan Chef and owner of Raw Rejuvenation in Scottsdale, Arizona. She has been educated extensively in the theory of Raw Nutrition and Raw Food Preparation, and is in high demand as a Personal Raw Food Chef.

Chef Siegren's interest in the benefits of Raw and Living Foods piqued after she experienced a personal health crisis. Motivated to help herself through food, she participated in an intense educational program based on the teachings of raw food pioneer, Dr. Gabriel Cousens. After graduation, Siegren felt compelled to share her knowledge and experience and opened Raw Rejuvenation & "Raw on the Run" delivery service.

Raw Rejuvenation offers both private and group classes in raw & living food preparation and education, as well catering, and personal consulting for specific health goals.

"Raw on the Run" provides delicious raw, organic snacks, soups, salads, sides, entrees, and desserts to busy Valley residents each week.

For more information on upcoming Raw Rejuvenation classes or "Raw on the Run" delivery service, please contact Chef Siegren Johnson (480) 406-9275 or visit www.**Raw-Rejuvenation.com**.

Penni Shelton has a powerful story embracing a diet rich in raw and living foods. Her story of life transformation first appeared in Carol Alt's book, *The Raw 50*. Penni is an award winning blogger at Real Food Tulsa, an avid health food and lifestyle writer, passionate living foods chef and is the creator and facilitator of her international virtual holistic retreat center & web community, Raw Food Rehab.

Penni lives in Tulsa, Oklahoma with her husband, 2 children and 3 dogs.

Penni's book can be found in bookstores and on Amazon while her blog and other information can be found at www.**RawRehab.com**

Ani Phyo is on a mission to show the world that eating healthy doesn't have to mean forcing down boring salads every day. The author of three popular cookbooks: *Ani's Raw Food Essentials*, *Ani's Raw Food Desserts*, and *Ani's Raw Food Kitchen* (awarded Best Vegetarian Cookbook USA 2007), Ani has quickly become the 'go to girl' on healthy living using fresh, whole and raw food ingredients. She is the recipient of four Best of Raw 2008 Awards for Best Chef, Favorite Cookbook and Favorite Educator. She has also won Sexiest Raw Vegan Woman for both 2008 and 2009.

As one of the prominent experts in the raw food community, Ani has developed raw vegan menus for Carnival Cruise Lines, ADIDAS, STOMP, and Whole Foods Markets. Ani is the host of *Ani's Raw Food Kitchen Show*, the award-winning #1 uncooking show on 'YouTube'. She has appeared on the Travel Channel's *Bizarre Foods with Andrew Zimmern*, San Francisco's *View From the Bay featuring Spencer Christian*, FOX Network, and NBC New York's LX New York. She has also been featured in numerous magazines including *Food & Wine*, *Food Network*, *Alternative Medicine*, *Oxygen*, *VegNews*, *Delicious Living*, *Vegetarian Times*, and *Get Fresh*.

In August 2010, Ani was selected one of 12 'warriors' in Sambazon Acai's 'Warrior Up' advertising campaign. In honor of her work with the Pedal Patch Community, a non-profit organization where she teaches at-risk Los Angeles youth how to garden and make food in urban areas, images of Ani wearing warrior headdress are now featured on billboards and bus stops around southern California.

Ani lives in Los Angeles with her Rhodesian Ridgeback, Kanga, whom she rescued in 2001. Fifty pounds underweight when she got her, Ani healed Kanga back to health with raw foods by applying the same principles that she uses for humans to her beloved dog.

Ani is currently working on her next book along with planning projects for TV, DVD, and the web. To keep track of Ani's latest projects, visit her at:
www.AniPhyo.com
www.facebook.com/Ani.Phyo.RawFood
www.GoSuperLife.com

Alissa Cohen is one of the world's leading authorities on raw food and healthy living and is internationally recognized author, speaker, and raw food chef and consultant. Cohen gained an international reputation for her book, *Living on Live Food*, distributed through the U.S., Canada, England, Australia, and many other parts of the world. Covering every aspect of a living foods lifestyle, the book catapulted her into the international limelight, landing her an appearance on the *Today* show, The *Tyra Banks* show, an "*Ask Alissa*" food column, a nationally aired raw food cooking show and a worldwide following that looks to her for weight loss and healthy living advice through raw foods.

Cohen's deep knowledge and enthusiasm for food as a life-promoting experience has attracted major media. Since appearing on NBC's *Today* show in August 2005 as a nutrition expert, promoting the benefits of raw food for its "10 Secrets for Staying Young" segment, Cohen has appeared on numerous television and radio shows as well as magazines and newspapers in the U.S. and abroad.

Cohen also advocates the benefits of raw foods through speaking engagements and her multimedia website, Alissacohen.com.

Aimed at a mass audience, Cohen's recipes are user friendly, cognizant of modern life's time constraints, and require only common household appliances such as a blender or a food processor. Most of all, the recipes celebrate food that gives us joy beyond the moment of consumption.

Cohen currently certifies teachers in her Living on Live Food Program. Classes are held in her Maine center as well as in California, England, Australia and other areas of the world.

Cohen opened Grezzo restaurant in January of 2008. Grezzo is located in the heart of Boston's historic North End (known as "Little Italy"). Grezzo is Boston's premiere 100% raw organic vegan restaurant.

Cohen's passion for healthy living has also led her to create her clothing line, Live Juicy Eat Raw, made of Fair Trade, Organic Cotton.

Cohen is also a Certified Fitness Trainer, Nutritional Consultant and Mind-Body Therapist.

She has been eating and teaching raw foods since 1986.

www.alissacohen.com
www.RawFoodTalk.com
www.RawTeacher.com

Vegan foodie and yoga aficionado, **Charlie Pinkston**, is the creator of *The Vegan Muse*™. Charlie admits without hesitation, she is a fearless vegan kitchen dweller. She loves trying new techniques and new ingredients. When it comes to dinner in her home, she makes dishes that she and her two children can enjoy together. Her children, Madison and Jules have learned to be fearless as well, exploring new plant-based foods. Her first project began with the recent publication of *The Vegan Muse & Friends...Recipes & Musings for a Plant-Based Lifestyle Aficionado's Mind, Body, & Soul*, recipes & musings for a plant-based lifestyle aficionados mind, body & soul. It's a cookbook created for people who have a voracious appetite for nutrient rich, vegan foods. She captured an intuitive completeness to the overall book that provides a balance of compassionate, swoon-worthy vegan recipes, thoughts and musings from other vegans, raw foodies, yoginis and yogis worldwide.

After training at The Florida College of Natural Health, Charlie received a neuromuscular massage therapy license, and worked in the Winter Park, Florida area with local Reiki and Meditation masters. This path led to a passion for yoga, earning a 200-hour teacher training as a student of Didier Razon and Ann Kiyonaga-Razon with Two Suns Rising Yoga. Living near the beaches she developed a love for long boarding which led to opportunities training local surfers to incorporate the practice of yoga to improve their surfing techniques. As her local community is important to her, Charlie's charity work developed into the founding of Mused-Works™. Mused-Works™ is a non-profit, community based charity inviting transformation, nurturing the mind, body and soul of those in need via free yoga, juicing, and meditation. She joins hands with other instructors to help bring awareness to her community about the many benefits of veganism, yoga, and meditation. Her personal mantra is "Be happy so long as breath is in you…"

"I would rather have kale on my table than fine china." ~ Charlie Pinkston aka The Vegan Muse™

www.theveganmuse.com ~ A plant-based lifestyle inspired

Juicing and yoga enthusiast, **Penny Powell**, is the creator of JuicYoga™ featured in the cookbook, *The Vegan Muse & Friends...Recipes & Musings for a Plant-Based Lifestyle Aficionado's Mind, Body, & Soul* by Charlie Pinkston. JuicYoga™ is a fun and conscious taste of health that can also be used to help balance each of the body's main chakras (energy centers) via a mixture of seven colorful juicing recipes and yoga postures. "There's nothing quite as refreshing as fresh juice with a little yoga on the side," says Penny who explains that while yoga nourishes her like food, when literally consuming food, she prefers a mostly raw-vegan diet. In June 2008, Penny attended the 10-day Healthy Lifestyle Course at the Living Foods Institute in Atlanta, GA. She has also

photo by ruth shepherd

worked as Editor-in-Chief of *Pear Magazine*, a living foods and organics lifestyle resource published by raw-food gurus, Storm and Jinjee Talifero, creators of TheGardenDiet.com. Penny has written for a variety of newspapers, magazines, and websites, and formerly served as a columnist for a raw-food related website. She holds a master's degree in humanities with a focus in journalism and a graduate certificate in professional writing, but she says her most important "degree" is raising her vibrant teenager, Caleb, with her husband, Collin.

Penny's passion for yoga led her to a 200-hour teacher training course with Two Suns Rising Yoga where she and The Vegan Muse™ (Charlie Pinkston) met and later joined their health interests and talents to create the inspiring *The Vegan Muse & Friends* cookbook. Penny teaches yoga classes in Orange Park, Florida at Life's Journey Yoga & Wellness Center where she also served as Wellness Coordinator and interim Studio Manager. Additionally, she teaches at Anytime Fitness and a mostly-chair yoga class at The Allegro, a residential facility for seniors where her regular yoga students range between 90 and 100 years old. Trained in the Radiant Child Yoga Program (RCYP), Penny has been featured on a "Yoga For Kids" segment of *"The Morning Show"* at a local television station where she was thrilled to explain some of the many benefits of yoga to parents. More recently, Penny's love of yoga landed her a traveling yoga teacher position with NRG2GO (Energy To Go), a Canadian-based company that sends yoga teachers on "working vacations" to teach yoga (and other fitness modalities) for a week or two at resorts in Jamaica, Mexico, and Cuba. Penny invites you to take a trip of your own to her "The Juice Muse" page on TheVeganMuse.com to sip a juice with her and/or relax in a yoga pose.

She can be contacted at **penny@theveganmuse.com**.

Joyce Oliveto is a Certified Naturopath, Certified Nutritional Consultant and a 1 Act Certified Colon Hydrotherapist and Instructor. She is also a Live and Raw Foods Chef and a pioneer in the field of living and raw foods since 1981 and founder of Health Horizons in 1986. Health Horizons is a natural healing center focusing on lifestyle change through education, detoxification, raw & live foods and nutrition.

Joyce is a dedicated, passionate, motivating teacher and an expert in live foods, nutrition and internal detoxification. She inspires thousands of people worldwide to make the choices and take the steps necessary to make lifestyle changes to achieve vibrant health through her books, classes, workshops and retreats. Drawing from years of education and experience, she has written hundreds of articles in natural health publications and travels worldwide speaking these life changing truths.

Joyce is the former director of the Creative Health Institute (formerly Hippocrates Midwest) in Coldwater, Michigan. A dedicated teacher committed to the living foods lifestyle, Joyce was selected by Dr. Ann Wigmore to be the President of the Midwest Living Foods Association in 1986. She was instrumental in the development of Dr. Ann's Health Practitioners Program for Hippocrates Health Institute in Boston, Massachusetts. in 1987. Mentored by studied intimately and traveled nationally with Dr. Ann and Viktoras Kulvinkas.

Joyce shares her heart's calling and her personnel journey as she teaches others how this revolutionary journey can open up a whole new way of thinking and living. Her life was impacted profoundly in 1980 while attending the Hippocrates Health Institute in Boston, Massachusetts.

Joyce has an amazing ability to create mouth-watering, delicious live and raw food recipes. As a child she always loved to cook with her mother who taught her the importance of home cooking and developing recipes from scratch. Joyce loves to be in the kitchen!

Joyce has 3 children, 7 grandchildren and 2 great grandchildren.

To learn more visit Joyce's websites: **NaturalAgelessLiving.com** and **LivingSimplyRaw.com.**

Look for her books *Living Simply Raw* and D*esserts and Dheydrated Delicacies* and DVD *The Living and Raw Food Lifestyle Made Easy*.

Look for Joyce on youtube for raw food demos and contact her at **rejoyce@comcast.net**

RESOURCE GUIDE

BARS

Go Raw -Freeland Foods
650-962-9299
650-962-9099
www.goraw.com

Love Raw Foods
540-745-5128
www.bluemountainorganics.com

GaVi's Goodness
772-418-4013
www.gavisgoodness.com
gavisgoodness@gmail.com

LoveForce
513-470-1787
www.loveforce.net

GoPals Health Foods
866.646.7257
www.gopalshealthfoods.com

BEVERAGES

Kvass
ZUKAY Live Foods LLC
(610) 286-3077
www.zukay.com
www.getyourfermenton.
blogspot.com

Kombucha
Katalyst Kombucha*
413-773-9700
info@katalystkombucha.com
www.katalystkombucha.com
*Available only in the NE &
Mid-Atlantic Regions of the US

BREADS, CRACKERS,CHIPS

Flat Breads, Breadsticks,
Crackers, Kale Chips
Raw Makery
702-644-7785
info@rawmakery.com
www.rawmakery.com

Flax Crackers
Foods Alive
260-488-4497
www.foodsalive.com
info@foodsalive.com

Kale Chips
Earth Chips
540-745-5128
www.bluemountainorganics.com

Flax Crackers & Superfood
Chips
Go Raw -Freeland Foods
650-962-9299
650-962-9099
www.goraw.com

Flax & Kale Chips
Brad's Raw Chips
215-766-3739
www.bradsrawchips.com

Pizza Crusts & Crackers
GaVi's Goodness
772-418-4013
www.gavisgoodness.com
gavisgoodness@gmail.com

BREADS

LoveForce
Cincinnati Ohio 45206
513-470-1787
www.loveforce.net

Flax Crackers
Food On Purpose
505-920-2959
info@foodonpurpose.com
www.foodonpurpose.com

SNACKS
Didi's Baking For Health
212-505-2232
snacks@bakingforhealth.com
www.bakingforhealth.com

CELTIC SEA SALT

Selina Naturally
1-800-867-7258
www.selinanaturally.com

COCONUT CREAM

Living Coconut
Phone: See website for details
www.livingcoconut.com
www.livingcoconut.com
info@livingcoconut.com

COCONUT KEFIR

Living Coconut
Phone: See website for details
www.livingcoconut.com
www.livingcoconut.com
info@livingcoconut.com

COCONUT MEAT

Frozen Young Coconut Meat
Body Ecology
130 Conway Dr. Suite D
Bogart, GA 30622
800-511-2660

COCONUT WATER

Frozen Coconut Water
Body Ecology
800-511-2660

CONDIMENTS

Probiotic-Rich Salsa & Relish
ZUKAY Live Foods LLC
(610) 286-3077
www.zukay.com
www.getyourfermenton.blogspot.com

Raw Coconut Aminos
Coconut Secret
Leslie's Organics, LLC
888) 369-3393
www.coconutsecret.com

Selina Naturally
1-800-867-7258
www.selinanaturally.com

Pickles & Fermented Veggies
Real Pickles*
413- 774-2600
www.realpickles.com
*Available only in the NE Region of
the US

Liquid Aminos
Bragg Live Foods, Inc.
1-800-446-1990
www.bragg.com

Raw Soy Sauce
Oshawa Nama Soya
1-800-475-3663
www.goldminenaturalfoods.com

Cultured Veggies
Rejuvenative Foods
1-800-805-7957
www.rejuvenative.com

CULTURE STARTERS

Kefir & Veggie Culture
Starters
Body Ecology
800-511-2660

DAIRY—RAW

Raw Cheeses
Really Raw Cheese
Phone: See website for
details
www.reallyrawcheese.com
www.reallyrawcheese.com
info@reallyrawcheese.com

DESSERT

Raw Cookies
Raw Makery
702-644-7785
info@rawmakery.com
www.rawmakery.com

Macaroons
Hail Merry Snacks
1.888.621.2229
www.hailmerry.com

Raw Cashew Ice Creams
Cashew Creamery
540-745-5128
www.bluemountainorganics.com

Cookies, Cakes, Macaroons,
Brownies
Love Raw Foods
540-745-5128
www.bluemountainorganics.com

Cookies & Chocolate
Go Raw -Freeland Foods
650-962-9299
650-962-9099
www.goraw.com

Brittle, Fudge, Cookies, Macaroons
GaVi's Goodness
772-418-4013
www.gavisgoodness.com
gavisgoodness@gmail.com

DRESSINGS

Zukay Live Foods
(610) 286-3077
www.zukay.com
www.getyourfermenton.blogspot.com

Foods Alive
260-488-4497
www.foodsalive.com
info@foodsalive.com

Bragg Live Foods, Inc.
1-800-446-1990
www.bragg.com

DRIED FRUIT

Love Raw Foods
540-745-5128
www.bluemountainorganics.com

Selina Naturally
1-800-867-7258
www.selinanaturally.com

Navitas Naturals
888.645.4282
www.navitasnaturals.com

FATS & OILS

Cold-pressed Flax & Hemp Oils
Foods Alive
260-488-4497
www.foodsalive.com
info@foodsalive.com

Selina Naturally
1-800-867-7258
www.selinanaturally.com

Olive Oil
Bragg Live Foods, Inc.
1-800-446-1990
www.bragg.com

Raw Oils
Rejuvenative Foods
1-800-805-7957
www.rawoils.com

Flax Oil
Barlean's Organic Oils
360-384-0485
www.barleans.com

FLOUR

Raw Coconut Flour
Coconut Secret
Leslie's Organics, LLC
(888) 369-3393
www.coconutsecret.com

Raw Seed & Grain Flours
Flour for Life
540-745-5128
www.bluemountainorganics.com

GRANOLA

Hail Merry Snacks
1.888.621.2229
www.hailmerry.com

Love Raw Foods
540-745-5128
www.bluemountainorganics.com

Food On Purpose
505-920-2959
info@foodonpurpose.com
www.foodonpurpose.com

Go Raw—Freeland Foods
650-962-9299
650-962-9099
www.goraw.com

Didi's Baking For Health
212-505-2232
snacks@bakingforhealth.com
www.bakingforhealth.com

NUTS & SEEDS

Wide Variety
Living Nutz
207-780-1101
www.livingnutz.com

Flavored Varieties
Hail Merry Snacks
1.888.621.2229
www.hailmerry.com

Better Than Roasted
540-745-5128
www.bluemountainorganics.com

Selina Naturally
1-800-867-7258
www.selinanaturally.com

Living Intentions
415-824-5483
www.livingintentions.com

Navitas Naturals
888.645.4282
www.navitasnaturals.com

NUT & SEED BUTTERS

Better Than Roasted
540-745-5128
www.bluemountainorganics.com

Love Raw Foods
540-745-5128
www.bluemountainorganics.com

Rejuvenative Foods
1-800-805-7957
www.rejuvenative.com

SEA VEGETABLES

Love Raw Foods
540-745-5128
www.bluemountainorganics.com

Selina Naturally
1-800-867-7258
www.selinanaturally.com

Navitas Naturals
888.645.4282
www.navitasnaturals.com

Nori Chips
Food On Purpose
505-920-2959
info@foodonpurpose.com
www.foodonpurpose.com

Nori Power Wraps
GoPals Health Foods
866.646.7257
www.gopalshealthfoods.com

SPROUTED RAW GRAINS & LEGUMES

TruRoots—Enray Inc
925-218-2205
www.truroots.com

SUPER FOODS

Lucuma, Acai, Maca powder, Mesquite powder, Chia & more
Navitas Naturals
888.645.4282
www.navitasnaturals.com

Wild Maine Blueberries, Chia & More
Living Nutz
207-780-1101
www.livingnutz.com

Chia, Hemp seeds, Black Sesame seeds, Cacao powder, Maca powder, Mesquite powder & More
Foods Alive
260-488-4497
www.foodsalive.com
info@foodsalive.com

Lucuma, Spirulina, Maca powder, Mesquite powder & more
Love Raw Foods
540-745-5128
www.bluemountainorganics.com

Selina Naturally
1-800-867-7258
www.selinanaturally.com

SWEETENERS

Raw Coconut Crystals & Raw Coconut Nectar (Low glycemic sweeteners)
Coconut Secret
Leslie's Organics, LLC
(888) 369-3393
www.coconutsecret.com

Agave Nectar
Agave Bear
540-745-5128
www.bluemountainorganics.com

Agave Nectar & Coconut Sugar
Love Raw Foods
540-745-5128
www.bluemountainorganics.com

Stevia
Navitas Naturals
888.645.4282
www.navitasnaturals.com

Raw Honey
Really Raw Honey
800-REAL-RAW (732-5729)
info@reallyrawhoney.com
www.reallyrawhoney.com

VINEGAR

Raw Coconut Vinegar
Coconut Secret
Leslie's Organics, LLC
(888) 369-3393
www.coconutsecret.com

Apple Cider Vinegar
Bragg Live Foods, Inc.
1-800-446-1990
www.bragg.com

WILD CAUGHT ALASKAN SOCKEYE SALMON

Sugpiaq
907-345-3311
info@sugpiaq.com
www.sugpiaq.com

OTHER Resources

Raw Milk and Dairy information and locator
www.realmilk.com

Raw Products, information and equipment
www.rawlife.com

Find Local Farmer's Markets & CSA's
www.localharvest.com

VIT△MIN CODE®

RAW Vitamins for REAL People

Vitamin Code® RAW vitamins—comprehensive, body-ready formulas created using premium RAW, whole food ingredients to provide living nutrients to the body—just as nature intended.

- RAW
- Uncooked
- Unadulterated
- Untreated

- Live Probiotics & Enzymes
- Gluten Free, Dairy-Free
- No Binders, No Fillers
- No Soy Allergens

Don't settle for anything less—Vitamin Code® RAW Vitamins.